WOOD & BEER
A Brewer's Guide

By Dick Cantwell
and
Peter Bouckaert

 brewers publications

Brewers Publications
A Division of the Brewers Association
PO Box 1679, Boulder, Colorado 80306-1679
www.BrewersAssociation.org
www.BrewersPublications.com

Printed in the United States of America.

10 9 8 7 6 5 4 3 2 1

ISBN-13: 978-1-938469-21-3
ISBN-10: 1-938469-21-6

Library of Congress Cataloging-in-Publication Data

Names: Cantwell, Dick, author. | Bouckaert, Peter, 1965- author.
Title: Wood & beer : a brewer's guide / by Dick Cantwell and Peter Bouckaert.
Other titles: Wood and beer
Description: Boulder, Colorado : Brewers Publications, a Division of the
  Brewers Association, [2016] | Includes bibliographical references and
  index.
Identifiers: LCCN 2015050673| ISBN 9781938469213 (pbk. : alk. paper) | ISBN
  1938469216
Subjects: LCSH: Brewing--Equipment and supplies. | Beer. | Wood--Chemistry.
Classification: LCC TP570 .C3165 2016 | DDC 663/.42--dc23 LC record available at
  http://lccn.loc.gov/2015050673

Publisher: Kristi Switzer
Technical Editor: Fal Allen
Technical Reviewers: Andrei Prida, Jean Baptiste-Comoy
Copyediting: Christina Echols
Indexing: Doug Easton
Production and Design Management: Stephanie Johnson Martin and Jason Smith
Cover and Interior Design: Kerry Fannon
Production: Justin Petersen
Cover Photo: Luke Trautwein
Interior Images: Dick Cantwell, Peter Bouckaert, and Kerry Fannon unless otherwise noted

For Kim

—Dick

To my wife Frezi and sons Wout and Jo Wolf for lovingly dealing with my time spent on research, visits, writing, and drinking. Dank je!

—Peter

Table of Contents

Acknowledgments

Many people from many breweries, cooperages, and other organizations helped in the creation of this book, whether by showing us around their facilities, contributing written material for use both in the book's narratives and the formation of its sensibilities, or simply through the conversation and interaction by which so much knowledge is transferred within the craft brewing movement. Without exception they were unhesitatingly giving, taking time out from their schedules to spend hours talking about wood and beer, sitting down to expound at length on all they have learned and want to share with the rest of us making our way with wood.

Before we get started, this book would never have appeared in its present form if Kim Jordan of New Belgium Brewing Co. had not suggested that Dick and Peter combine forces to put Peter's knowledge and experience into words mainly crafted by Dick. There was endless back-and-forth, a lot of travel and discussion, and quite a bit of fun, much of which she was a part of. Thanks to her. Thanks also to Peter's wife Frezi Van Rafelghem for her support and sacrifice while we worked on this book. Additionally, we owe thanks to Wout Bouckaert for his dedication to taking pictures and Jo Wolf Bouckaert for his continued curiosity during so many tours of cooperages.

Thanks first to Kristi Switzer of Brewers Publications, for endless patience and encouragement, immediately afterward to Fal Allen of Anderson Valley Brewing Company for providing help with technical editing, and to Frank Boon of Boon Brewery and Wayne Wambles of Cigar City Brewing for their kind introductory words. Thanks to Will Meyers of Cambridge Brewing Co., Vinnie Cilurzo of Russian River Brewing Co., Tomme Arthur of The Lost Abbey, Matt Brynildson, Jeffers Richardson and Jim Crooks of Firestone Walker Brewing Co./Barrelworks, Rob Todd and Jason Perkins of Allagash Brewing Company, Ron Jeffries of Jolly Pumpkin Artisan Ales, Lauren Salazar and Eric Salazar of New Belgium Brewing Co., Gabe Fletcher of Anchorage Brewing Company, Jason Yester of Trinity Brewing Co., Andrei Prida of Seguin-Moreau, Preston Weesner and Ron Gansberg of Cascade Barrel House, Nathan Zeender of Right Proper Brewing Company, Yves Benoit of Brouwerij de Brabandere, Jason Ebel of Two Brothers Brewing Company, Kyle Sherrer of Millstone Cellars, Scott Christoffel of Natty Greene's Brewing Co., Patrick Rue of The Bruery, Jay Goodwin of The Rare Barrel Co., Brent Cordle of Odell Brewing Co., Pete Batule and Caleb Staton of Upland Brewing Co., Jennifer Talley of Auburn Alehouse, Paulo Cavalcante of Bodebrown Brewery, Jos Ruffell of the Garage Project, Gert Christaens of Oud Beersel, Jayson Heystek of Founders Brewing Co., Eric Ponce at Goose Island Beer Co. in Chicago (as well as Brett Porter), John Mallett of Bell's Brewery, Jeffrey Stuffings of Jester King Brewery, Garrett Oliver of Brooklyn Brewery, Khristopher Johnson of Green Bench Brewing, Dirk Lindemans of Brouwerij Lindemans, Rudi Ghequire of Brouwerij Rodenbach, Sabine Weyermann of Weyermann Specialty Malts, Cameron Parry of Groth Vineyards & Winery, Matthew Crafton from Chateau Montelena Winery, Adair Paterno of Sante Adairius Rustic Ales, Tobias Hess of Cerveza Minerva, Todd Ashman of FiftyFifty Brewing Co., Fabio Mozzone of Selezione Baladin, Paul Arney of The Ale Apothecary, Walt and Luke Dickinson of Wicked Weed Brewing, Ryan Tockstein of Scratch Brewing Co., Nathalie Deroo of Belgian Brewers, Marco Moutinho at J.Dias & Ca., Maya Friederich of KWV Wine Emporium in South Africa, Michaela Knör at Versuchs- und Lehranstalt fur Brauerei in Berlin (VLB), Conor O'Driscoll of The Woodford Reserve Distillery, Ryan Ashley of Four Roses Distillery, LLC, and Noah Steingraeber of Rocky

Mountain Barrel Company for writing back to us and providing insights and experience. Thanks also to Martin Vercouter from Swedish National Maritime Museums, Jeff Albarella at Jessup Farm Barrel House for letting us take barrel repair pictures with his empty barrels, Jason Parker and Micah Nutt at Copperworks Distilling Company in Seattle, as well as old wood-and-brewing-mates, Dan-o Beyer, Kevin Watson, Ben Cox, and Steve Luke.

Many people spent hours with us in their breweries, cooperages, and cellars, sharing beer, wine, cider, spirits, and knowledge, and in many cases in numbers (and hours) greater than expected. We were able, on our Kentucky, Ohio, and Michigan trip to spend enlightening time with Paul McLaughlin and Greg Roshkowski at Kelvin Cooperage and Brown-Forman Cooperage, respectively, in Louisville, KY (thanks also to Stirling and Jim Welch for helping us get in touch), Country Boy Brewing in Lexington, KY, Against the Grain Brewery and Smokehouse in Louisville, KY, Sam Adams/Boston Beer Co. in Cincinnati, OH, Woodford Reserve Distillery in Versailles, KY, Buffalo Trace Distillery in Franklin County, KY, Jolly Pumpkin Artisan Ales in Dexter, MI, New Holland Brewing in Holland, MI, Jason Spaulding of Brewery Vivant and Founders Brewing Co. in Grand Rapids, MI. On our Scotland trip we were shown about by Andrew Russell at Speyside Cooperage and Stuart Coil at Harviestoun Brewery in Clackmannanshire, and visited Dalwhinnie Distillery in the Scottish Highlands. In France we received very kind attention and spent a great deal of time with Jean-Baptiste Comoy, David Legac, and Hubert Staquet at Seguin-Moreau, Jean and Jean-Louis Vicard and Pierre Marchais at Tonnelerie Vicard, Laurent Lacroix at Brive Tonneliers, Stéphanie Huilizen and Nicolas Tiquet at Tonnelerie Taransaud, Erick Tourbier and Gérard Linaires at Chateau Mouton-Rothschild, Christophe Conge at Chateau Lafite Rothschild, and Patrick Guidici and Joséphine Blad at Byrrh, where resides the world's largest foeder. In the UK, Dick visited John Bexon at Greene King in Bury-St. Edmunds, Suffolk, and Alan Pateman at Elgood's in Wisbech, Cambridgeshire, as well as the boys at the Kernel in London on Zwanze Day, all of which was coordinated and implemented by good friend Mark Dorber. In addition, in California, Colorado, Washington, Europe, and elsewhere, we managed to visit Schooner Exact Brewing Co., Fremont Brewing, Crooked Stave Artisan Beer Project, Marston's PLC, De Cam Geuzestekerij, Brasserie Cantillon Brouwerij, Jayce Marci at August Schell Brewing, Troy Casey of Casey Brewing and Blending and no doubt many others momentarily overlooked and later winced over due to the fact that wonderful kindnesses were extended by some of our very best friends.

Foreword

by Frank Boon

When the craft beer revival started in Belgium with Pierre Celis in 1965, wooden beer barrels were not part of it. In those days, wooden barrels were in use only by early Belgian sour beer brewers and in lambic breweries. The monks of the Westvleteren Trappist Monastery were among the last to replace their small foeders, or oak barrels, with stainless steel tanks in 1974. Here and there, relics of cask collections with small floating barrels and cisterns could still be found in closed breweries, but the system of allowing beer to ferment in pitched shipping barrels had completely disappeared in Belgium some 50 years ago. In Great Britain, a few wooden fermentation vats remained in use in some locations and, of course, also at the Burton Unions, including the Bass Brewery. In Pilsen, small round vats of 40 hL were still in use for fermentation until 1990, as well as about 3000 pitched foeders for aging. Most brewers considered wood in the brewery as a relic from the past, with a museum as its sole possible destination. When I started the Boon Brewery in 1975, I bought lambic casks from closed breweries at $2.50 each. Other brewers thought of me then as a "retro brewer." They asked me when I would install a steam engine and a coal-fired steam kettle, and maybe get a horse and cart to maintain the proper atmosphere.

In the wine industry, wooden barrels were also viewed with pity in many regions in the 1970s. In France, the production of barriques dropped by more than half over a period of 10 years.

Still, the wooden beer or wine barrel is more than just a container.

Because the market of second-hand barrels had been completely depleted in Belgium by 1980, the only alternative in those days was to restore the existing barrels. When the last cooper in Lembeek folded, I bought his equipment and started restoring my lambic casks under his guidance. Soon I noticed that the barrels whose bottoms I had replaced with new oak yielded a different kind of lambic. I also noticed that foeders whose staves I had planed on the inside imparted very distinct flavors to the beer. This went counter to the old beer literature, which claimed that a new barrel was unusable for beer and had to be neutralized with quicklime and repeated fillings with young beer. The necessity to restore numerous barrels and foeders led the Boon Brewery to set up its own cooper shop, which today ensures the maintenance and repair of many small barrels and a collection of 130 foeders. It taught us that different kinds of oak are used according to origin and location, that there is sessile and pedunculate oak, and, of course, small grain and large grain oak. Most of our old foeders are made from Nordic oak. The oldest of these (no. 79), dating back to 1883, is still in very good condition and delivers an unmistakable lambic. Nordic oak is not from Norway, but rather from the former Memel region of what used to be East Prussia, now North Poland and Kaliningrad. The oak from this region is exceptionally hard due to its slow growth in a cold region, which causes the yearly tree rings to be very tight. These ancient foeders can have a special effect on the microflora of lambic.

Those who used second-hand barrels from the wine industry starting in the 1920s were the lambic brewers. These barrels were exclusively "pipes" or "demi-muids" (wooden barrels of 660 liters), and originated in the transport of wine or port. Port was imported in these barrels via the port of Antwerp, and the barrels were subsequently sold second-hand to brewers of lambic. The lambic from these barrels had a wine flavor and was used by brewers as young beer for the production of Kriek (cherry lambic). After two barrel fillings the lambic was suitable for the regular geuze production.

Today we are aware of the role that oak species can play in the final beer flavor, and some of the old brewers probably discreetly applied this knowledge.

My wife's grandfather was a brewer at De Greef (Rodea) Brewery in Sint-Genesius Rode, Belgium. This brewery originated in a cooperage. When there was too little cooperage work, cooper De Greef started making casks for his own use. Thanks to the special quality of the casks, his geuze-blending plant grew quickly, and in short order a brewery and a malt house were added. About 30 years after its creation, this brewery had grown to become the largest in the region. Mr. De Greef always told customers and competitors that the quality of his geuze was derived from the special characteristics of his self-made malt, and kept wisely silent about the effect of his home-made barrels. Geuze blender Petit from Vorst, Brussels, was another cooper who started in 1929. Two years later, no fewer than 2,300 hectoliters of geuze were produced—a large volume for a geuze blender.

The wooden barrel is experiencing a spectacular resurgence in beer circles. We have to go back at least 60 years to encounter similarly large numbers of barrels in breweries. But even so, the comparison doesn't work because 95% of those barrels used to be pitched transportation barrels. Today, wooden barrels serve exclusively as flavor and aroma enhancers. Whiskey distillers and blenders have been using all kinds of barrels for a very long time, and beer brewers are now doing the same thing. When they were new these barrels were filled with red or white wine, port, sherry, and, of course, also whiskey or bourbon.

Every year new brewing books are published. However, one searches usually to no avail for a chapter discussing the use of wooden barrels. Books on the cooper's craft are extremely rare, let alone books dealing with the production of foeders. Accordingly, a professional book for brewers wanting to use wooden barrels was sorely lacking. Now that gap is finally filled by this book, which you are holding in your hand, written by Dick Cantwell and Peter Bouckaert.

The chapter on the history of the cooper's trade teaches us a lot about the techniques of manufacturing wooden barrels and its many applications. Contemporary cooperies are highly mechanized plants that possess scientific knowledge about the composition and properties of oak. This allows them to meet the flavor and aroma wishes of their customers. The authors visited several cooperies and describe their various specialties. Everything is described in detail—if you're somewhat handy, you can even start your own cooper's shop!

The flavors and aromas of various species of oak and other kinds of wood, the effect of the toasting, the interesting use of barrels that contained other spirits at an earlier stage—you will find everything described clearly and in detail in this book. Many brewers who are not familiar with wooden barrels will learn a lot about cleaning, drying, and preserving barrels. With the aid of examples from practical applications, you will learn about the many ways they can be used and what kind of beer you can expect to produce. The book also discusses yeasts and bacteria, the effect of wooden barrels on the growth of these microorganisms, and the risks of fermentation and maturing at the right or wrong temperatures.

Peter Bouckaert also provides many examples from practical experience from the time he worked in a Belgian brewery and from the period in which he built up the entire oak barrel cellar of the New Belgium Brewing Company. I read with great interest the stories about the purchase of second-hand oak barrels, about the importance of proper inspection, and about poorly maintained barrels that can form a source of contamination due to mold growth. There are gripping descriptions of the disassembly and reassembly of foeders, where I learned that duct tape (!) is handy for keeping loose staves together. I myself am convinced that a large opening or hatch in a wall or roof of the storage house may be handy for moving foeders in and out, but the story of the six foeders at Anchorage Brewing proves that in some cases it is necessary to disassemble and reassemble oak barrels. That is certainly the case for foeders holding more than 200 hectoliters, which cannot be moved in one piece.

Today, the wooden barrel has once more become an indispensable tool and an ingredient that lends new dimensions to wine and beer. For us brewers, the wooden barrel provides endless opportunities to use our imagination.

It will be a challenge to apply the recommendations in this book into practice, because great care and insight are required to come up with an outstanding beer. In the worst case, one may wind up with beer vinegar, occasionally useful for imparting some additional character to young beer; but beer is not salad dressing. Similarly, one should not overdo the hops. New barrels add a lot of tannins to beer. If the beer has too many bitter hops, it may taste more like tar or paint than toasted oak. Luckily, most barrels are small and lend themselves easily to experimentation. But keep in mind that a stave is not a magic wand that can solve all of a brewer's problems with one swipe! I also wish the brewers a lot of patience. Whoever has gained experience with new barrels knows that it usually takes a year before the flavors and aromas blend harmoniously together, and the hard flavors disappear. I am convinced that in the coming years many more wonderful beers will hit the market thanks to the use of wooden barrels, both in the United States and Europe, as well as in other beer-loving regions. And I am also convinced that this book will play an important role in this development!

Frank Boon
Boon Brewery, Lembeek, Belgium

Foreword

by Wayne Wambles

> *Trees in particular were mysterious, and seemed to me direct embodiments of the incomprehensible meaning of life. For that reason, the woods were the place that I felt closest to its deepest meaning and to its awe-inspiring workings.*
>
> —C. G. Jung, *Memories, Dreams, Reflections*

I found myself standing in a large Belgian brewery's barrel room surrounded by immense Hungarian oak barrels, stacked high. My host explained that a single cooper had constructed those barrels, taking two weeks to build each one. I began counting and was awed, realizing it had taken the cooper many years to accomplish the task.

The barrels were in the size range of puncheons, but the ends of the barrels weren't slender. A similar diameter was maintained through the center of the barrel. I wondered if this was intentional or if it was simply the way that the cooper had always constructed the barrels, learning an all but lost trade over the course of many years' time.

I regained my composure and wandered into another massive barrel room. The adjoining room housed large French oak barrels. A commissioned cooper constructed barrels with French oak from different regions of France, in order to see if there was a difference in barrel character across the regions. It was essentially an experiment in wood *terroir*.

I listened intently as the conversation migrated to the topic of specific parts of the tree that might be best used in barrel construction. I was told that the trunk of the tree provided more wood sugars, introducing more vanilla and macaroon components, whereas the top of the tree produced more tannins. I pondered what the roots might do.

I recall the start of my own experimentation with wood- and barrel-aged beers. I began brewing commercially in 1996, but it wasn't until 2008 that I began to dabble with wood- or barrel-aged beers, brewing pilot batches for Cigar City Brewing Company. Implementing wood and barrels into our program was the onset of a ceaseless learning process that I am still actively pursuing today.

With Florida's history of cigar-making dating back to the 1800s, I tipped my hat to our local heritage by starting my wood experimentation with Spanish cedar, rather than traditional oak. Spanish cedar is the same wood that is used to fabricate humidors for storing cigars. The wood's unique aromatic and flavor qualities include forward white grapefruit notes, with white pepper and hints of sandalwood. Thus began my fascination with wood and barrel aging. I wanted to find other non-traditional woods and rare barrels that I could add to our program, in order to create more unique concepts and flavors. I spent hours researching and contacting distilleries.

In the meantime, wood-aging beer was going well. I established a beneficial relationship with an American company that would tolerate my requests for what I considered to be esoteric woods. This allowed for much more experimentation. Within a couple of years we began a project with The Bruery that would use the same base saison recipe and age it on three unique woods: lemon, grapefruit, and Spanish cedar. It was refreshing to notice that our efforts were not in vain.

I decided to apply this spirit of experimentation to other cultural approaches. Challenged to create a beer that best exemplified a piece of artwork for an event for the Museum of Fine Arts in Petersburg, I began trying to find a wood to represent an African mask worn by the chief of the Pende tribe that would best suit a rustic brown ale base beer. I searched through a wood supply company's website that listed the aromatic character of the wood. It was really the only thing that I had as a guideline for a project like this, so I selected a couple of samples that I considered promising and finally chose African Padauk wood. A very beautiful hardwood, it was a shame to cut it up for wood aging, but it smelled divine in the rough and it added cocoa and waffle cone notes to the beer.

Cigar City continued producing limited volumes of one-off beers and barrel-aged variants of our seasonal beers. We tried to determine the length of contact time for each beer and found that there is no single answer or length of time. Sensory is the only determination for finished barrel-aged beers.

When using second-use spirit barrels, we assessed the original resident spirit character and then designed the beer so that the flavor components allowed it to marry the barrel and spirit character. At times this was similar to making a cocktail, but I was using malt, counting on yeast byproducts at times, and sometimes making use of culinary ingredients as well.

Blending becomes an integral part of most barrel-aging programs. Sure, you can take only the best barrels and put them in the blend, but do you really have the best product in the end? We determined that all the components of the blend added complexity that we weren't getting by blending only the best barrels. A complete blend filled in the gaps and created a more complex and round beer.

Our barrel-aging program was challenging and we learned that it is imperative to have a good lab program. In the beginning we were blending beer back into a single blending tank without plating, but quickly started plating every single barrel. If the barrel passed lab but not sensory, it wasn't included in the final blend. If the barrel grew on the plate and didn't pass sensory, we would dispose of the barrel. Sometimes we had some unexpected mistakes that were quite beautiful. We would hold onto these barrels to blend back for draft only in the future, not wanting to risk the chance that we infect our packaging equipment. I also recall beers that we left in the barrel a bit too long, resulting in them being really hot or, in some cases, a bit more oxidized than we intended. Thus, we began to focus on blending. At times, we had enough foresight to store a percentage of the flat base beer in kegs, assuming that we might need to tame some of the heat from the barrel by blending back.

Static contact for wood-aged beers was our standard operating procedure, but it was much slower and more difficult to determine the results without moving the beer. We found that the wood character was stratified. Our answer was developing a recirculating infusion by creating a device that we called Spinbot 5000. The Spinbot 5000 is a converted 7-bbl grundy that resembles Sierra Nevada's torpedoes but also incorporates multi-directional inlets for more even and efficient extraction of the raw material(s). It took between 7 and 11 days on average to pick up American oak using static contact, and we were in the dark until we moved the beer. Recirculating infusions with the Spinbot 5000 achieved the same goal in 24–48 hours, and with better results.

Wood aging and barrel aging are similar but separate arts, each beautiful in its own way. Determining preference based on the intent or utilizing a combination of both is up to the creativity of the brewer. I'm barely scratching the surface of the inner stave of the barrel by sharing my experiences with you. Dick Cantwell and Peter Bouckaert have documented a vast wealth of knowledge in this book about the intricacies and history of wood- and barrel-aged beers. This book will inspire all brewers interested in the discovery and development of using wood in the artful crafting of beer. And they are thoroughly entertaining in the process, so sit back, sip a beer, and enjoy!

Wayne Wambles
Brewmaster, Cigar City Brewing

Introduction

The first wood-aged beers most of us recall having tried were invariably boozy, the massive stouts and porters and barley wines of an earlier age in craft brewing, say 15 or 20 years ago, when such a thing was synonymous with the whiskey-sodden barrels in which they'd spent some time. There was some confusion, in fact, between the flavors of wood and of alcohol, both as it was borne by the big beers that most commonly were put into barrels and of the spirits that came along with the barrels themselves. What we didn't realize then, of course—at least not articulately—was that a lot of that whiskey flavor also came from the wood. Many of us didn't even know that the brown color associated with whiskey was also wood-derived, or that by aging our beers in wood we were opening ourselves up to worlds of complexity and nuance. Many of us had been to Europe and experienced beers also aged in wooden barrels, but as these were notable more for their sourness, we concentrated almost exclusively on the effects of microbiological influence and interaction in their flavors, and chalked the use of wood up to archaism and tradition. Such was our essential misunderstanding—even mistrust—where the use of wood for aging beers was concerned, that the first barrel-aged beers submitted to the competition of the Great American Beer Festival® (GABF) were classified (as the novelties they were considered) in the catch-all category of Experimental, amid lurid flavored malt beverages (FMB) and utterly transparent iterations of light beer. Either that or they were rejected out of hand as inappropriate to style.

Well look how far we've come. Today the GABF admits several categories in which the component of wood is appropriate, even integral, including not just beers bearing the flavors of whiskey and wine, tequila, rum, and cachaça, but once-obscure Euro-regional footnotes of beers, as well as smoked beers bearing the whiff of the particular woods used to flavor the malt. Brewers Association statistician Bart Watson has determined that around 85% of all American breweries in 2015 are using wood in some form to flavor, age, and otherwise influence some of their beers. And yet the use of wood for aging beer is still experimental, still being discovered in endless variety of application and effect. Far more may be understood, appreciated, and embraced than in that earlier age, but as with many other aspects of modern craft brewing, we are also making it up as we go along.

I first heard of Peter Bouckaert a couple of years before I met him. He was still brewing at Rodenbach, and was about to make the leap across continents to take the helm at New Belgium. A woman who ran a tour company I was working with recounted having visited Rodenbach and being led on a two-hour tour of the brewery, up ladders, inside of and behind things, by the most pleasant guy who also happened to be the brewmaster—Peter. Many years later, when my company, Elysian Brewing, started working with New Belgium and I had known Peter for some time, he showed me around the brewery in Fort Collins with the same kind of gusto and enthusiasm. The first beer we brewed at New Belgium was a pumpkin beer, and in the course of adding pumpkin to the mash mixer I dropped a plastic bucket into the vessel. As I recall it took about a minute and a half to hit bottom, and once it did Peter fired me. Of course, he was laughing.

It was my girlfriend (and Peter's boss), Kim Jordan, who suggested that Peter and I write this book together. A number of worthy people, Peter among them, had been approached by Kristi Switzer at Brewers Publications to take on the task of writing a book on wood and barrel aging of beer, and all of them, including Peter, had turned her down. It was a daunting potential project, given the scarcity of scholarship where beer and wood was concerned, and the fact that everyone had jobs. Also, despite the fact that many people were doing interesting specific things with wood, no one felt sufficiently masterful about all aspects of wood and beer to presume themselves an authority on the subject. Well, that's where I came in, as I knew with no uncertainty that I was not an authority, but perhaps yoked to someone who probably had more varied and comprehensive experience with wood and beer than practically anyone else in the world today, I might be able to help sort through the stories and notes, the information and experience of such a person to help put together a narrative that at least might prove helpful to others. With some of that aspect of the project taken from his shoulders, Peter agreed, and we set about our research.

And so we walked the earth, so to speak, in the pursuit of knowledge and observation of barrels and beer. We went to Scotland, driving up to the whiskey territories and to Craigallachie, where we visited the Speyside cooperage. We went to Kentucky, Ohio, and Michigan to check out the cooperages of Brown-Forman and Kelvin, and to see our friends at Sam Adams, Founders, Jolly Pumpkin, and Brewery Vivant. On our own and together we stopped in at breweries all over the place, in this country and abroad, where people were doing interesting things with wood.

Definitely the hallmark trip we made was to France, to visit cooperages around Cognac—Vicard, Taransaud, and Seguin-Moreau—and to stop in at some of the first-growth chateaux in Bordeaux—Chateau Lafite-Rothschild and Mouton-Rothschild, in particular. Peter's whole family was along for that trip, and the five of us—Peter, me, Peter's wife, Frezi, and their two boys, Jo and Wout, jammed into a Volvo for some pretty extensive driving. It was the cooper's trail version of National Lampoon's European Vacation, but with Belgians—the van Griswolds, I inwardly dubbed them. And we had a great time, stopping in terrific hotels that Frezi picked out, and having Wout act as our photographer. It was World Cup time, too, and we watched games in cafés and hotel rooms, including the Belgians' drubbing of the US squad. Our primary objective was the seat of the apertif manufacturer Byrrh in Thuir, way over on the other side of the country, just in from the Mediterranean. It was there that we saw the million-liter foeder, standing proud in its own room within the gorgeous factory designed by Gustav Eiffel, whose better-known Parisian tower bears his name.

Mention of Peter's kids puts me back in the mind of the parentage of this project. It's our book, to be sure, but it is also the child of many other mothers and fathers, people from all over the world who shared their experiences, knowledge, and insights with the aim of spreading the word among all of us about what we've individually done with barrels, foeders, and other wood treatments, and providing inspiration for what we all might accomplish in the future. Without all of them this book would have lacked a great deal of dimension. We hope you find it interesting, inspiring, and useful.

Dick Cantwell
Co-author

1

The History of the Barrel, or There and Back Again

I t's said that necessity is the mother of invention, but that puts so much pressure on the situation. More likely, just coming upon something useful-looking is the mother of invention. Witness the ape in "*2001: A Space Odyssey*," artificially inspired though he may have been, finding a use for that bone; or imagine the gadgeteer, covered in hair, who "invented" the wheel. It seems therefore likely—and it's definitely legendary—that the first wooden vessels were not so much invented as discovered, as hollow logs variously full of rainwater. Take things a handyman's step further and both technique and materials are improved—healthy wood replacing the rotting or lightning-blasted, tools doing the work of time and happenstance, perhaps at first with a bit of hide stretched across the openings—and culture suddenly steps forward along a couple of courses, the musical and the utilitarian. We'll leave the former alone, but the latter is why we're here.

Nor is a vessel necessarily a barrel. There are bowls, there are pots, and there are jars. There are the skins of animals, stitched together and closeable, perhaps lined with something impermeable, portable for a journey. There are also buckets and tubs, pieced together from wood and somehow bound together, and this is where barrels begin to be born. An Egyptian drum in the Metropolitan Museum dated a handful of centuries BCE may not be a barrel, or even an actual vessel, but its stave construction shows an awareness of the type of handiwork later to become so familiar to innumerable generations of coopers.

Romans and (Celtic) Countrymen—Wood Replaces Clay

Before there were barrels there were amphorae. Made of hardened clay and large enough to hold a mercantile amount of contents, they were constructed for both strength and movability, and were in common use in Asia and throughout the Mediterranean region for several thousand years. A roughly egg-shaped vessel, surmounted by a relatively narrow opening and a couple of handles to facilitate rolling on a narrow reinforced foot, not unlike the way a barrel or a cylinder of compressed gas is spun along on its edge today, amphorae could be moved relatively easily for their weight, and were nestled into wagons or the holds of boats for further transport. Standard volume was about 70 liters (18.5 gallons), and their filled weight could have been in excess of 100 kg (220 pounds), given that the contents alone would comprise nearly three quarters of that. Slight differentiation of shape or construction helped a likely illiterate workforce keep the products of one merchant separate from another, but as containers of transport they were invariably switched one to another as they were reused. Pliny the Elder outlined instructions for their use as containers for wine, including a cleaning regimen involving salt water and ashes.

Huge dumps of these broken remains have been found throughout Europe, which points to their ubiquity of use. (It also points to an advantage of barrels made of wood.) Amphorae continued to be commonly used into the third century CE, but the concept that would eventually become the barrel was developed in the various Celtic territories of northern Europe between 1000 and 500 BCE. This amounted to simple bucket construction, beginning, no doubt, with a single piece of wood and the repair demanded by thrift. Over time, and by the use of tools advancing from stone to bronze to iron, multiple pieces could be dressed and joined, to the point at which it made sense to enclose the top as well as the bottom for ease of enclosure and shipment, as well as security against contamination by air and vermin. The first barrels were made of readily available and relatively malleable woods such as pine, poplar, and palm, but the bending of hardwoods with the aid of heat, as well as the advanced joinery made possible by superior tools, brought about vessels more reliably watertight and sturdy. The exchange of ideas and techniques between tribes moved development incrementally along, and as an invading presence the Romans appropriated the technology, eventually seeing fit to favor the barrel over heavier and more fragile earthenware.

A couple of key points of construction made all this possible. Some kind of bottom would need to be devised and connected to whatever wooden pieces constituted the walls. A groove running around the inner surface of the vessel would become be the best way to do this, in order to secure the bottom into each piece, or stave, and taking advantage of the fact that wood swells when wet, thereby tightening the connection. In addition, the whole thing would need to be bound together. Initially this would probably have been accomplished with hide or vines, but at some point soft and pliable wood would come to do the trick, tightening about the vessel as it dried. Finally, whether by steam or direct fire, heat applied to the wood would make it more workable, less prone to breakage when bent, and able to be brought together to hold a second head, or bottom, in place. Henry H. Work in his book *Wood, Whiskey, and Wine* (2014) suggests an inspirational waystation in the development of the barrel as the urge to stick two buckets together to form a single vessel. This seems a bit literal and cumbersome, but could possibly have provided Celtic inspiration.

Not all wood is equally suitable for the making of barrels. As time and construction advanced, different woods came to be used for different purposes as barrels, dictated by innate properties such as porosity, pliability, durability, weight, and possible flavors imparted to consumable contents. Makers of barrels were likely woodworkers of other types—boat and wagon builders, furniture makers, and the like—and oak came to be the dominant wood used. It is estimated that 45% of all fabricated oak was used during the second century CE for the production of barrels, and that figure nearly doubled in the century that followed as barrels came into more general use and the demand for them increased drastically (Work 2014).

Barrels may have gained dominance over earthenware in the early centuries CE, but their mention and appearance in classical literature and art appears far earlier. Herodotus of Halicarnassus wrote in the fifth century BCE of wine barrels made of palmwood transported along the Euphrates. The geographer Strabo (64/63 BC–24 CE) mentions barrels as big as houses, and Trajan's column, named for the Roman emperor and completed in CE 113, depicts barrels loaded aboard ships to provision the campaign against the Dacians.

Even more directly were barrels employed as tools of war, with flaming barrels filled with pitch and tallow rolled downhill by Gallic defenders against the Romans at the battle of Uxellodunum in 51 BCE, and empty barrels employed as a sort of pontoon bridge at the siege of Aquileja in 238 CE. It is from the Latin word *cupa,* meaning "tub," that words denoting cooperage derive. Also of etymological interest is the edict of Ine, a seventh century king of Wessex, prescribing rent payments in "ambers" of ale—the word certainly designating casks but deriving from the more classical *amphora.*

Figure 1.1—Trajan's column, named for the Roman emperor and completed in CE 113, depicts barrels loaded aboard ships to provision the campaign against the Dacians. Photo credit © Roger B. Ulrich by permission

Vessels of Wood—Barrels, Boats, and Brewing

Literary and historical mention of barrels, as with so many other things, mainly clams up for around a thousand years after the Classical Age, but the knowledge that brewing and winemaking continued throughout those so-called Dark Ages keeps us on the path regarding what was happening with barrels and other wooden vessels. Nordic brewing traditions extending into our own time offer perhaps a dim view of the progress and presence of carved and coopered brewing vats, including the storied hollowed log used for the making of Finnish Sahti. Its use is well described in one of the many treatises of Odd Nordland on Nordic and Scandinavian culture, *Brewing and Beer*

Traditions in Norway: the Social Anthropological Background of the Brewing Industry (1969). Hollowed lengthwise and tipped slightly to allow for gentle runoff, the log was layered with lattices of juniper, spruce, birch or alder twigs, and straw, prefiguring the slotted false bottom of later mash and lautering vessels. A typically variegated grain mash, sparged with brewing liquor often steeped with juniper, provided wort, and whether boiled or not, fermentation inevitably ensued, no doubt in wood. As with the African calabas, or fermenting gourd, the mother of invention stands by.

Other northern European brewing vessels more closely resembled barrels, and many of their descendants are still with us today. One can see broad, barrel-like brewhouse vessels of wood in the guild house of the brewers in The Grand Place in Brussels—as well as steel-lined or jacketed versions throughout Belgium and the Netherlands. These are primarily tuns used for mashing and lautering, but before copper and steel could be worked into large vessels, boiling kettles were often made of wood, fired in ancient times by the introduction of hot matter such as the super-heated stones of the atavistic German *steinbier*. In many cases the wort was simply not boiled, but mashed, lautered, fermented, racked, and packaged, all in wood.

But if our study is to stay more closely to barrels themselves we must acknowledge that the vessels we've come to consider mainly in connection with the shipment and storage of liquids were, through most of their history, ubiquitous as shipping containers for nearly anything one can think of. Barrels for volume products such as beer and wine no doubt dominated the manufacture of medieval coopers, but myriad other products, including meat and fish, sugars and syrups, soap, butter, glue, tobacco, cabbages, turpentine, and vegetable, whale, and petroleum oils, were throughout recorded history shipped in barrels requiring both sturdiness and tightness of construction. Dry products such as nails and other hardware were consigned to barrels of less exacting manufacture, but prior to the mid-twentieth century introduction of cardboard boxes, steel drums, and the standardized, box-like shipping containers that today fill barges and huge, seagoing ships, the barrel was the preeminent unit of shipping.

The warship *Vasa* was perhaps the biggest embarrassment in Swedish naval history. Constructed between 1626 and 1628, it was intended to be Sweden's flagship during its war with Poland-Lithuania. But the *Vasa* was top-heavy, and within minutes of its maiden voyage foundered and sank only 1300 meters from where it set sail. There it lay in calm, fresh-to-brackish water until rediscovered in the 1950s, and it was raised in 1961 with much of its contents well preserved, including a wealth of barrels containing butter, beer, and brandy, and smaller, one-foot-tall barrels holding the personal effects of the crew, which included knives, gloves, coins, and tools.

The *Vasa* and its contents embody two of the artisanal elements of barrel making. First there are the barrels themselves, showing by their presence and the variety of contents within them just how dominant the barrel had come to be for storage and shipping of practically anything. The other is shipbuilding, which requires the same skills of bending and joinery to craft watertight ships for war and commerce as those for making barrels and *foeders*. Barrels and ships are inextricably linked, in fact, not only through kinship of craft but in a symbiosis of purpose. Variously filled, barrels settled securely in the holds of ships, and as advancement in tools and technique allowed for the building of bigger ships, more barrels were made to fill them. Naval stores, as well, were packed in barrels, safe from spoilage and infestation. Without barrels, ships could not have sailed round the world. One might even say that barrels made long distance sailing and exploration possible.

Messages in Barrels—Regulation, the Hanseatic League, and Other Alliances of Trade

Barrels were manufactured and filled at the shipping sources of Europe, dominant beer and winemaking centers preeminent among them. Records of shipment and regulation in England and among the mercantile confederation of the Hanseatic League trace the prominence of barrels as containers for the shipping of countless products and as a commodity in themselves, influencing economies and diplomacy. Historian Richard Unger's book *Beer in the Middle Ages and the Renaissance* (2004) is peppered with references to the use, manufacture, regulation, and gradual standardization of barrels in northern Europe. The Hanseatic League bound together shipping cities along the North and Baltic Seas, providing mutual protection from marauders and regulating trade. At first, each brewing town would have its own standard-sized barrel, supposedly to eventually be returned. Marks were devised to differentiate them by brewery, town, and beer type—one such system in Ghent decreed by no less than The Holy Roman Emperor Charles V. With time, however, the wisdom of broader standardization asserted itself, and in 1375 the barrel of Rostock was adopted as the common size by Lübeck, Wismar, and other northern German towns. Hamburg kept its own-sized barrel until it, too, acceded to standardization in 1480. As today, concerns were strong that barrels would be used by brewers other than those to whom they belonged, or that they would simply disappear.

Through its increasing enabling of shipping and commerce, the cooper's trade came to be differentiated from other woodworkers and was among the first to band together as a labor union. Guild rolls in Leicester included coopers as early as 1196. Officially chartered in 1501, but thought to have existed for at least a couple of hundred years before that, the London cooper union was sufficiently esteemed to be designated several yards along the parade route of the coronation of Henry VIII. Much was decreed and legislated during Henry's reign that affected the cooperage and brewing industries. Like his European counterparts, he implemented standardization of barrel sizing, and he prohibited the shipping of beer abroad in any container larger than a barrel. In an early conservation measure expressing concern at the deforestation of Britain for the construction of barrels, legislation was also adopted requiring the importation of an amount of wood equal to that represented by the export of barrels. In France, forests that are still protected—farmed, in fact—for the ongoing production of barrels for the wine and spirits industries first came under government supervision for shipbuilding in 1669, a commitment later renewed by Napoleon II. Timber harvest in France was also prohibited within 47.2 miles (76 km) of the sea and 18 miles (29 km) from any inland waterway in order to curtail illicit cutting. Back in Britain, not many years later, the guild and its standards were further protected by the outlawing of the activities of itinerant, disenfranchised coopers. Even brewers were prohibited from making barrels themselves, generally necessitating the employment of in-house coopers. Even as recently as the turn of the nineteenth and twentieth centuries, the Bass brewery in Burton-on-Trent employed 400 coopers, and 1500 were still building barrels for the herring industry in 1913.

It may seem strange from our distance to have kings and emperors making it their business to form policies where such ordinary-seeming things as barrels are concerned. In fact, it's a kind of who's who of a couple of centuries' worth of royalty and celebrity to track some of this regulation and activity. History may have given Richard III a bit of a bum rap—being dug up from beneath a parking lot has certainly given his legacy a pathetic touch—but he, too, got into the act, setting the standard size for wine barrels at 33.5 Imperial gallons, purportedly reactive to the smaller size of Dutch barrels used for the shipping of hopped beer (Unger 2004). In 1482, toward the end of his reign, complaints from Flemish quarters caused barrels of sherry shipped northward from Spain to be standardized at 30 arrobas, or around 486 liters, and prohibitions put in place against prior use of fish or oil in barrels later used for holding beverages. Other intra-regional political drama arose concerning barrels, with supplies of beer from Bremen and Hamburg sent to Bavaria interrupted by the sectarian and geographical divisions of The Reformation. Looking at the importance of barrel-related matters below the line of royalty, a 1376 census of some 1050 citizens of Hamburg found that 457 of them declared themselves as brewers, and an additional 104 as master coopers.

Intermezzo: Everything Related

Phil Benstein had found some books on the subject earlier, but when we got together at the Coors library in Golden, Colorado, I could not get around it—there it was. The book from 1903, One Hundred Years of Brewing, *mentioned a black beer being popular in the previous century in Brussels! I found this interesting: It was not a beer I had ever encountered in Belgium, and it was hard for me to believe it actually existed. At the house of a Belgian brewer, Willem Van Herreweghe, we found two books from the 1700s, both mentioning another book from 1554. We had an excuse, we thought, to create a historical Brussels black beer, which became New Belgium's 1554.*

That book referred to a bound parchment book from September 27, 1447, 't Boeck mette Rooskens, or "book with the little roses." We found this binder of parchment in the city archives of Brussels a year later. The book was about the guild legislation for the city covering tapestry, wine, beer, mead, wool, bread, skins, fish (with herring mentioned separately), meat, vinegar, fur, and feathers. Of course, the beer section was what we were after.

Four different beers were mentioned: Waeghebaert, Hoppe, Cuyte, *and* zwert bier. *The recipes used setiers as grain units, which should have been around 116 liters, and* aimes *for water units. Aimes were quite common at that time, but were slightly different from town to town. We found it revealing that one aime was equal to three* tregelvaten (vaten *means barrels in Flemish). But we never really found what the volume for the Brussels* tregelvat *or* aime *was. As you can see, throughout history barrels were units of measure, but this was not really what we were looking for. We were wondering about the use of hops or a gruit spice blend. One of the beers would have been clearly made with hops, since* Hoppe *had it in the name. We dug around in some history and found that Emperor Charles V (1500–1556) imposed the use of hops in most of Belgium. This book was clearly earlier than that, so I assumed* zwert *(old Flemish for black)* bier *was made without hops. But though Leuven and some other cities in Brabant started earlier with hops, I did not know when.*

I grew up closer to Brugge and was more familiar with the history of that town. There the family Van der Aa was a rich family that held the gruit recht, *or the right to sell or tax gruit for use in beer. You still can visit the family house in Brugge, het Gruuthuse. They held on very long to the use of gruit since they could tax it. But something strange happened in the thirteenth century: The Hanseatic League established places of trade in Brugge, London, Bergen, and Novgorod, and they brought in hopped beer from breweries in Rostock and Hamburg that were dedicated to brewing for specific cities abroad. Of course, the family Van der Aa saw in this a potential erosion of income and supported the Hansa house levying a higher tax than the tax on locally brewed gruit ale.*

Ok, what does this have to do with the history of wood in brewing? To me, everything. *Barrels were used for any trade. The Hansa had to make barrels to be shipped through the inner waters of the low countries, since seaworthy vessels were not so much in evidence and the threat of pirates kept boats inland and close to the coast where they navigated according to depth measurement (Meier 2006), a journey that must have taken weeks. The small boats were taxed at different stations or in cities that they passed through in what is now the Netherlands. And it was still worthwhile to ship a hopped beer to Brugge! It's incredible what a trade there was going on so early in history, with everything in barrels.*

From Peter's journals, ruminating on the origins of New Belgium's 1554 Black Beer

Barrels Across the World—Exploration and Industry

Like the great mercantile era mentioned above, the age of exploration and colonization would not have been possible without the barrel. Long voyages required extensive provisioning, with barrels holding pitch for repairs, turpentine for cleaning, beer, spirits, food, and water. In his journal, Columbus noted the loading of the last barrel of beef in August of 1492 as he prepared to sail from Seville, and later replenished water barrels on the island of San

Salvador in what is now the Bahamas. In provisioning naval ships, barrels were effectively supplies of war. In an attack on Cadiz, Spain, prior to the 1588 invasion of England by the Spanish Armada, Sir Francis Drake had thousands of captured barrels destroyed. Leaky, perhaps hastily-constructed replacements laid one more straw across the back of the ill-fated attack.

Soon barrels began traversing the Atlantic, first as containers for provisions for colonizing voyages, then subsequently back in the other direction once staves and barrels came to be manufactured from native American oak (so much for the managed forests of Britain). Still, barrels in the New World—and coopers—were often scarce. In time, however, a robust coopers trade arose in the American colonies, drawing English craftsmen for its relatively high rate of pay, and exporting barrels—both assembled and in staves—as well as products such as salted cod and tobacco, which were shipped, of course, in barrels. The first American trade union is thought to have been convened by coopers and allied tradesmen in 1645; a few years later consolidating groups in Boston and Charlestown, Massachusetts, and other parts of New England. Barrels were shipped from the New World to the wine regions of Europe, eventually spurring subsequent reuse in the developing seventeenth century Scotch whiskey industry. As things soured between the American colonies and their home country, local production of both beer and barrels was deemed desirable not only for consistent supply and result, but also as lessening reliance on the economy and caprice of those across the Atlantic. Once war broke out, it was aboard a submersible barrel, the *Turtle*, that David Bushnell attempted to attach a time bomb to the British flagship *Eagle* in New York Harbor on September 7, 1776—the first submarine attack in history.

The fishing industry has been mentioned as a large consumer of barrels. Whaling, as well, demanded their use, sending coopers along on ships to manufacture heads, staves, and bungs on the outward journey, and to assemble and maintain barrels for filling with oil. And speaking of oil, once crude petroleum oil was discovered during 1859 in Pennsylvania and Ohio, so many barrels were required for shipping to refineries that supplies elsewhere were difficult to secure. The quality of barrels required for the petroleum industry was high, and they were lined with flake glue to enhance impermeability. The simultaneous, mid-nineteenth century development of the railroads did nothing to lessen demand, especially as they were large oil consumers themselves.

By this time barrels were increasingly made by machines, many types of which were devised to speed and automate the processes previously enacted by hand coopers. Stave knives and special planes and saws were manufactured beginning in the late 1830s and '40s by such firms as Baxter D. Whitney in Winchendon, Massachusetts, and Hunter Brothers Saw Manufacturing Company in Rochester, New York. The Allied Barrel Corporation in Oil City, Pennsylvania, started as a hand cooper's shop but grew into a large machine cooperage, even developing its own rail cars designed to hold over 500 50-gallon barrels. Many oil barrels saw second use as water barrels for protection against fire along the rail lines. By 1871, however, the first steel tanks began to appear for rail shipment, and in 1865 the first pipeline was laid near Oil City, five miles long and prefiguring the dramatic lessening of reliance on the cooperage industry to come.

Still, the heyday of the cooperage industry had a few more decades left, incidentally marked by the 1901 descent over Niagara Falls by Annie Edson Taylor in a barrel. Some data is relatively easy to track, as there was a duty imposed on both stave and head production. In 1906 some 721 US mills reported production of 65 million slack barrels for containment of dry goods, made from such diverse woods as elm, pine, red gum, maple, beech, red oak, chestnut, birch, ash, spruce, cottonwood, hemlock, basswood, and sycamore. That same year, 18 million tight barrels were produced, with 1.6 million for beer among them, down from 1.9 million the previous year. Pressures from two sides are cited for this decline: the rise of packaged beer in bottles, and the demand exerted by the petroleum industry, whose barrel usage rose dramatically over the decades from 5 million barrels in 1865 to 140 million in 1906, an increase of 17 million alone since 1905. A look at the inventory of barrels at the Bass brewery in Burton-upon-Trent in1889 shows 40,499 butts, 133,464 hogsheads, 127,592 barrels, 147,969 kilderkins and 68,587 firkins—over half a million, all told, and all of wood. The repeal of prohibition saw a slight and expectable rise in barrel production, but only relative to the supposedly dry years that preceded it—10 million tight barrels in 1935, with 4 million of those going to alcoholic beverages, and only 665,000 for beer. Some 10 million staves were fashioned in the interior southern states, mainly by Austrian and Yugoslav immigrants. As to the sustainability of the industry, it was estimated by Dewers (1948) that in 1947, 2,751 million board feet (6.5 million cubic meters) of oak were cut in the United States, 98% of which went to the construction of barrels, and an additional 23,200 million board feet (54.8 million cubic meters) were left standing in the forest.

The Sun Also Rises—the Shifting Nature and Use of the Barrel

But just like that the wooden barrel was relegated to retro status, something esoterically useful but generally evocative of an earlier, simpler time. As the twentieth century marched forward, tankers carried the world's oil, and steel drums contained all manner of products previously consigned to barrels. Within the beverage industries packaging methods improved to dominance as a way of getting beer, wine, and spirits to consumers in bottles and cans. Steel kegs proved more durable and reliable than wood for draft products; they did not require the services of a specialized artisan for their maintenance. A modern demand for cleanliness, consistency, and stability cast aspersions on the potential vagaries of beer poured from actual barrels, and an expanded, truer world economy sent beer across continents and oceans. The very word *barrel* came more to mean a unit of measure than to describe an object, and most people needed to be told what a cooper was. Barrels continued to be made, of course, but their use was specialized within the wine and spirits industries. In Kentucky, where bourbon reigned and barrels were still needed, legislation was adopted to protect what coopers remained by mandating the single use of a new oak barrel for production of anything carrying the name. This action alone would loom large in the next phase of life for the barrel as we now know it.

Today, as always, barrels are manufactured near the seats of production of what they will come to contain. No longer used for oil or fish or tobacco or cabbages—or hats—their use is dominated by the wine and spirits industries. In France, modern cooperages are located in Burgundy and Bordeaux, near wine and cognac producers; in Kentucky and Scotland, in connection with the Bourbon and Scotch whiskey industries; in California, Spain, and other wine growing regions. Some 2.5 million new barrels are manufactured each year. Wine and bourbon are the main industry users of new oak, with bourbon limiting use to a single turn, after which the barrels are passed on primarily to whiskey producers in Scotland and Ireland. Port, sherry, and cognac barrels also make their way into the whiskey trade.

This is where we as brewers enter the picture once more. Use of barrels in our history was primarily as a means of shipping and serving, with barrels lined with pitch or another material to enhance tightness and retain carbonation. Among the many discoveries—and rediscoveries—within the modern craft brewing movement is the second- and third-use wine and spirits barrels to age, flavor, and otherwise influence beer.

As varied and interesting as the history of the barrel itself is, it is this last use with which we are primarily concerned in this book. Other consumables industries are relevant both as engines for barrel production and as background for the uses to which barrels have been put, as well as the flavor influence that some of these other products can impart to finished beer. Wine from grapes and spirits from grains have been mentioned, but barrels used for the aging of beer have in some cases held such things as tequila, brandy, rum, sake and other non-grape wines, maple syrup—even soy, fish, and chili sauces, in many cases after first having held something else either vinous or spirituous. No less varied are the beers that have been aged in barrels. The modern use of barrels for beer may have begun with full-flavored dark beers receiving augmented flavors from bourbon barrels, but today the variety of style and treatment enacted by mainly small brewers has brought to the brewing world a whole new realm of beers dark, pale, red, woody, tart, and sour in endlessly varied combination. The emergent micro-distilling movement has made for some interesting symbioses with brewing, and brewers, too.

In the following chapters we will examine the properties and characteristics of wood—primarily oak—that make it particularly suitable and intriguing for the aging of beer. Barrels and foeders are the containers to which we will refer, with analysis and advice as to their selection, use, and maintenance. Having developed in their history from vessels to hold and store liquids to the dominant shipping container of many an age, we will bring them back to their conceptual point of origin, specifically in connection with beer.

Like any historical current, this one proceeds in fits and starts. There are precedents as well as exceptions, gradual discoveries in one quarter long in use in another. Brewing traditions in Belgium, for example, have incorporated wood for centuries, making opportunistic use in some cases of its suitability as a harbor for yeast and other microflora. Brewers in winemaking regions such as California, Spain, and Italy have borrowed from those traditions and practices to produce new beers and hybrid beverages using grapes, herbs, and spices. Sometimes there are secrets. This is not to say that the primary use of barrels as shipping containers for beer did not also contribute to its culture. As a commodity beer shaped itself as well as the world around it. There's no end of documentation to provide this picture, and while taking a quick look at it might seem tangential to those eager to put beer into barrels and see what it does there, it, too, is a part of how we all got here.

2

Cooperage

Walking through a cooperage, it's easy amid the sounds of saws, sanders, fans, and flames to imagine the small hand-cooper's workshop of days past. Any shop—wood, metal, or automotive—breathes the particularities of the job, and a cooperage has its own smells, and an awful lot of dust that settles everywhere. Smoke and the smell of toasting—and where appropriate, charring—wood dominate; in fact, the smells of wood in all its phases. Out in the drying yards it can range from the sap-laden smell of newly sawn or split staves to the tang of rain-rinsed tannins and the fungal overlay that comes with weathering and exposure. Inside it's the smells of woodworking and woodsmoke, and of course the delectable spiciness of toasting oak. Then and now there's the unceasing ring of hammers, on wood and on metal, the patient thump and insistent chock of the mallet, and the sharper, metal-on-metal impact of hammer on hoop setter. And the satisfying thunder of new-made barrels being rolled to rest.

It's easy to relate to a barrel. Its pleasing curve and solidity of construction seem to awaken an atavistic attachment to handicraft, even when one sees them turned out by the thousands at such places as Brown-Forman in Kentucky. The fundament of wood, its bending, shaping, and firing, is something that can be almost felt without touching. Mechanization came in stages, of course. Brasserie Vapeur in Pipaix, Belgium, offers a window on a bygone intermediate age of steam power, with belts driven by an old engine to turn rakes and mill grain, but such things were in use as well in coopers' shops to both speed and aid the processes of making barrels. A whole industry was once devoted to stave- and head-making machinery, successful coopers outdoing each other in their efforts to turn out more and more barrels for the industries that in turn demanded them. The processes once enacted by the saws, knives, and hammers of the hand cooper were taken over by power planers, joiners, drills, and other cutting machinery. Companies still exist today that were founded on inventions of cooperage machinery. And while the demand for barrels is less and more rarified, the tools are bigger, faster, and more exacting, employing technologies not known even to the coopers of the barrel's golden age.

Wood scrap, shavings, and wood dust still provide the fuel for the fires, even today providing heat in some of the big shops. Temporary hoops of varying sizes are stacked here and there. In the old days the tools were both simpler in function and more arcane in variety—heading and hollowing knives, bent to all angles convex and concave in order to accommodate the different diameters of the varying types of barrels to be made, floggers, flagging irons, croze cutters, side axes, bunghole reamers, dowelling drills, trammels, the cooper's adze, and graded diagonals to measure the interior capacity of the barrels. In the center of the workshop might have sat the bottom of an old tree trunk, older than the cooperage itself, on which unnumbered hammer blows would fall. A large kettle is likely on to boil, to aid in the steaming and bending of staves. Outside stands the heavy, rotating sharpening stone, next to a stack of staves or perhaps a tree cut into straight planks. Today the machinery is larger, and electrical, but no less mystifyingly specific. Lasers that mark out stave cuts or offer suggestions for cleaving bolts, and others that burn logos onto heads, huge saws that whirl to shape staves, massive turntables that provide an endless array of wood for selection and shaping, windlasses that whine as they gather the collection of raised staves into form, charring tunnels that ignite and then douse to specification, belts kicking the still-smoking barrels on to the next station along the line, and sanders that automatically remove hoops and then spin the barrels around as the belt grinds them smooth.

Traditionally, there are three types of cooperage. The one we think of most readily is the most exacting: wet cooperage for making barrels intended to store liquids without leaking. Atop this pyramid of craftsmanship is the construction of foeders, large wooden tanks made to hold wine, beer, and other beverages. Dry cooperage is—or was—for barrels that must be tight for shipping and protecting such things as fish, flour, nails, and tobacco, products that must be kept dry and safe from pests. Household or "white" cooperage provides buckets, churns, and tubs. Not all cooperages make barrels, and not all barrels are made from oak. Other woods will be considered in the section pertaining more directly to the physiology of wood, but our reckoning will run most strongly to oak, and to barrels used for wine, spirits, and beer.

The process begins in the forest. French forests are designated by region (Limousin, Vosges, etc.), and have been nationally owned, planted, managed, and sold by government agencies since the 13th century, once mainly to ensure wood supply for the manufacture of warships and more formally since the time of the Napoleons, when the Office National de Forêts (ONF) was founded. The most famous region for barrel-making is the Forest of Tronçais, located in Auvergne in the center of France. It was planted during the reign of Louis XIV. Its trees are sold at auction, and priced by the cubic meter, with as much as 70% of the tree going to waste or reused for toasting and heating. The American region in which suitable oak for barrel-making is found is much larger and, hence, more naturally administered agriculturally, extending from the East Coast westward beyond the Mississippi, as far north as parts of Minnesota and south to eastern Texas, but concentrated in Kentucky, Tennessee, Arkansas, Missouri, Ohio, and Illinois. These lands are typically private. Other world regions for the harvesting of oak for barrel-making exist in the central Balkan and Slavic countries, Spain, Portugal, and Italy—even in China and Japan. Some of these lands have been less exactingly administered, particularly during the Soviet era in respective areas, and trees are often harvested at less-than-optimal growth ages. At the time of harvest, trees are generally at least 80 years old, and are often 150 to 200 years old. A tree of 300 years can achieve a meter (3.3 feet) in width.

In France, trees are typically harvested from December to March, during winter dormancy, when the upward flow of nutrients throughout the tree is slowest. In the United States, cutting is done throughout the year, depending on region, but can be slowed by long or wet winters. The ideal tree for use in barrel making is around 30 meters tall, plus or minus 60 cm thick, straight, and with as few branches as possible between its base and crown. Selection is even done by taste, drilling a small hole at the base of the trunk to test the wood, which can have a bitter flavor, or even, perhaps fancifully, the flavor of cocoa. The central cut is taken from above where the base thickens and flares for structural stability and below where it spreads, once again, to accommodate and support the thickest crown of branches. Closeness of planting, even sometimes with the interplanting of other species, will keep the trees growing relatively straight and with fewer branches, a quality desirable because of the lower incidence of resultant knots, and the leaks that can come with them.

Once felled, trimmed, and transported to the stave mill or cooperage, the useful trunk is sawn into stave lengths, or bolts (sections of stave-length logs), typically several centimeters longer than the eventual finished stave in order to allow for degradation in shipping, storage, and processing, as well as flexibility in selection. Moisture content at cutting can be as high as 65%. The bolts are split into quarters, and then either split or sawn into planks. Lasers are used to mark out a pattern of potential splits or cuts, taking into account both maximal use and the incidence of impermeable medullary rays, the radial structural element that makes oak the prime wood for making barrels. Like a pineapple, the pithy center of the tree is trimmed away, as is the outer bark and spongy newer sapwood (see more on the physiology of oak in the wood section of the book). The resultant planks are transported to the cooperage and stacked on ricks or heaped in towers for drying in the open air. In some cases the logs or bolts are shipped whole to the cooperage to be trimmed and split on-site.

Drying times and procedures vary both by region and from cooperage to cooperage, as well as what liquid the barrel will eventually hold. Staves are stacked closely, but separated enough to allow the passage of air between them. Tonnelerie Vicard, which makes wine and spirits barrels in France's Cognac region, ages staves for two to three years in full exposure to the weather, watering the wood to aid in the washing free of tannins and other potentially harshly flavored impurities, as well as to keep pests at bay. In addition to the effects of watering, both natural and artificial, the wood invariably takes on a fungal influence, providing benign protection from other degradation and infestation and releasing some flavor precursors. At Seguin-Moreau's Cognac operation, wood is watered for 45 minutes every four hours for its first month in the yard. At nearby Taransaud Tonnelerie, some staves are aged for as long as five years. At cooperages where wooden tanks, or foeders, are manufactured from longer and thicker staves, three to five years' aging is typical.

Zemplén cooperage in Hungary dries its staves in less dense upright wind tower stacks instead of the perpendicular stacks generally seen in France and the United States. Brown-Forman cooperage in Kentucky ages its staves, which are mainly destined for whiskey production, outdoors for only four to six months. This relatively brief initial aging takes moisture levels from 65% down to about 20%, after which the wood is moved under cover and dried a further four weeks to around 15% moisture. Then it is mildly kilned for another 10 to 14 days. Climate and purposing, no doubt, come to bear on both aging and technique. Drying yards can be extensive. Vicard's measures some 14 hectares and Seguin-Moreau's 24,000 stacks on the day of a recent visit representing two years' inventory. See chapter 3 for a more complete presentation of the seasoning processes enacted by drying.

It is at this point that the handcraft of actual cooperage begins, whether these days executed by hand or aided by machinery. The staves must first be shaped to consistent size and dimension, recognizing that a collection of straight planks is to be fashioned into a rounded vessel capable of holding liquid. First the ends are trimmed to standard length. This cutting provides another opportunity for inspection, ensuring the appropriateness of grain and other structural organization, such as the vital orientation of medullary rays across the individual stave. Then begins the true transformation from plank to stave. Knives or planes are used to remove wood from the span of what will be the inside of the stave and from the ends of the outside surface. Loosely put, more wood is removed toward the center of the inside of the stave and from the ends of the outside. Already the curve of the stave is prefigured. Once this process was enacted with the handheld tools of the cooper, hollowing and rounding by eye. One can still see this technique practiced in historical demonstration at Colonial Williamsburg. Now it is done by circular machine planes, but still with the invaluable aid of the cooper's experience. It is also the cooper's eye that informs the choice of individual staves for eventual collective consistency—too wide and uniformity of curve could be compromised; too narrow and the number of staves might exceed the optimal. Each of the barrels produced by Brown-Forman, for example, consists of 33 staves. Wood pieces that are judged ultimately to have no use are called "cants," and are destined for burning, whether in toasting or charring or for heating. Next, the long edges are jointed—in the old days by hand plane and today by power jointer—smoothing the surfaces and angling them to accommodate the dual curvatures of the barrel, above all to provide a tight joint where the staves are to meet.

Figure 2.1—The Cooper's house at the Colonial Williamsburg's Revolutionary City, a living history museum in Williamsburg, Virginia. Photo used by permission of The Colonial Williamsburg Foundation.

Coopers themselves were once generally trained through apprenticeship. In some places this is still the case, such as at the Speyside Cooperage in Craigallachie, Scotland. There, the apprentices—primarily local lads—occupy one side of the shop, until they are individually graduated to the general assembly line. Legend has it that in the old days the end of the fledgling cooper's apprenticeship was marked by being rolled by his future guildmates inside a barrel. Try as we might, we failed to find modern corroboration of this practice. Today, coopers are usually simply trained on the job and differentiated by task, whether raising, planing, toasting, charring, or setting heads. A lot of cooperage consists of the repair rather than the manufacture of barrels. This is entirely the case at Speyside, through the premises of which hundreds of thousands of barrels pass each year. The international spirits giant, Diageo, operates a large cooperage in Scotland as well. Kelvin Cooperage, neighbor to Brown-Forman in Louisville, not only repairs barrels, but also manufactures new barrels and converts locally-used bourbon barrels to the dimensions and volumes specified by the Scotch and Irish whiskey industries. This involves shortening staves and adding more of them to increase diameter, and then adding new heads and hoops, resulting in a more squat, slightly larger barrel. The Independent Stave Company of Lebanon, Missouri, in addition to providing written scholarship on the use of barrels and other wood products primarily in the wine and spirits industries, also operates cooperages throughout the world, in the Napa Valley, Bordeaux, Chile, South Africa, and Australia. The stalwart brewer and spirits producer Rogue, in Oregon, has within the last few years established its own cooperage, Rolling Thunder Barrelworks, where a single cooper named Nate Lindquist turns out a few barrels a week fashioned from Oregon white oak, sourced in the nearby Coast Range. French barrel producers such as Seguin-Moreau and Taransaud also operate multiple cooperages in different regions of France and other European locations.

Once the staves are selected, the barrel is then raised. This is also the point at which toasting was first devised, in order to aid in bending; these days it is more often a process in itself, conducted after the barrel has taken on its essential shape. Staves are placed end-wise on the floor before the barrel raising cooper, in an exploded radial pattern of the eventual barrel. In the days of pure handcrafting this was done by a sort of entropic juggling act, bringing the staves together closely enough that a temporary hoop could be placed over the top end and hammered tight for later work. This practice by a skilled raiser defies description—to say nothing of emulation. One comparison that comes to mind is that of a tiny child watching its elders tying their shoes, and trying by simply waving his or her fingers to accomplish the task. These days the effect is the same, but the staves are placed within the cabled loop of a windlass; once they are properly assembled, the cable is mechanically tightened and the staves are drawn into order before receiving the temporary hoop (or hoops) from the attendant worker. In some French cooperages, rounded rings are used. At Tonnellerie Vicard in Cognac, steaming and raising is done simultaneously, in a unique enclosed box incorporating an automatic windlass. Chalk is also sometimes employed to ease the hoop onto the barrel, and this is especially true for the larger foeders. Either way, the ringing of hammers on hoop drivers seals the deal, for the moment. The splayed barrel is then inverted and the process concluded with another temporary hoop. The barrel is then ready for toasting.

As with the fleeting description above of the basic physiology of oak for barrel making, the subject of barrel toasting will be more fully explained in another chapter, having more to do with flavors from wood than its physical treatment in manufacture. Yet toasting is also a part of the physical construction of the barrel, as it aids in the greater integration of its parts, and ultimately of its character. While toasting was originally employed solely to assist in the bending of the staves into formation, its contribution to flavor, now institutionalized, came as an afterthought. In some cooperages the staves are steamed before assembly in order to more easily facilitate bending. This would more likely have been the case in the hand cooperage of yore, where there was no mechanical substitute for sheer muscle. Steaming is part of the process today at Vicard, however, and possibly pursuant to unique processes employed there later once the toasting process begins (more on this later as well). In any case, water is always on hand once heat is administered to wood, both in order to control and mitigate its effects on the barrel and for safety from fire. It's easy to see, even walking through the modern cooperage, the potential dangers posed by smoke and fire. Cooperage fires were once frequent, and newsworthy. Dust and shavings are collected and removed practically as soon as they are generated, and smoke is evacuated through huge hoods, but one feels the whole place on the edge of combustion. Always there is the smell of smoke, and of toasting wood.

Figure 2.2—Inspection of the toasting level of a wine barrel at Seguin-Moreau in Cognac, France. © Wout Bouckaert

The timing and processes of toasting are practically as numerous as there are cooperages. The classic and most common method involves lighting a fire of wood chips in a small brazier called a cresset, and then setting the open barrel atop it, with the barrel's edge resting on an iron ring set in the floor. Sparks fly and the smell of toasting wood fills the air. A worker stands by as the fire does its work, ready with water in case the interior of the barrel should ignite. At this stage, charring can create blisters in the wood, which can later cause difficulties in cleaning or compromise structural integrity. At Vicard a special radiant heating vessel is used, shaped roughly like a barrel in miniature and set within the barrel itself, keeping the wood from direct contact with the flame. Depending on the eventual use for the barrel, the toasting time can vary from 35 to 120 minutes, sometimes with a differing regimen of temperature. Cognac barrels, for example, will receive a heavier level of toast than wine barrels. A gentler, more deliberate fire can take 80 or 90 minutes for a deep, heavy toast; less time over a stronger fire will result in a heavy but shallower toast, with less penetration into the wood. Internal temperature can be monitored during toasting with an infrared heat sensor, but typically the process is done by eye and time. Vicard also scores the inside surface of the staves with regular, vertical perforations that aid in toasting, help resist blistering due to the moisture in the wood vaporizing, and eventually allow for greater penetration into the wood of the liquid to be aged in the barrel. For larger vessels such as foeders, the toasting time can be as long as several hours. This is not surprising given their size, and the care with which the fire must be managed. At Taransaud a 90-hectoliter (hL) foeder is typically toasted for four hours. In American cooperages making barrels for bourbon, the toasting time is typically shorter—15 minutes or so—as the next stage in processing is a couple of minutes of active charring, designed to have its greatest effect in the single use prescribed by bourbon protocol. At Brown-Forman this process is mechanized and automated, with lines of barrels moved into place, allowed to actively burn on their insides, and then doused with water spray before being moved out to make way for the next group. The insides of bourbon barrels, and the inner surfaces of their heads, are blistered with char, providing additional flavor to the whiskey, as well as some clarification, and the removal of undesirable flavors and aromas from the raw distillate. As bourbon barrels are used only once before passing into other hands, the niceties of later cleaning are disregarded.

More will be said later on differing levels of toast and their eventual contribution to flavor and chemical makeup. While we are still in the cooperage, however, something should be said about the almost mouth-watering effect of the aromas of toasting oak. Gingerbread, cinnamon, nutmeg, and almond all are suggested in the smells emanating from newly toasted barrels, each dependent on the degree of treatment. In fact, after a day of visiting cooperages it is possible to feel physically full, almost as though well-fed, simply from the cumulative effect of all these ordinarily food-associated smells.

In his book *The Cooper and His Trade*, Kenneth Kilby describes this richness of aroma in baking terms: "Ask any cooper to tell you what constitutes the most agreeable, the most captivating smell, and he'll tell you it is the smell of a cask immediately after it has been fired. The piping-hot oak gives off an aroma like that of a richly spiced cake being baked."

It's interesting from our modern perspective of considering the effects of toasting on flavors imparted to spirits, wine, and beer to recall that through most of their history of manufacture this toasting effect was only incidental to the eventual function of most barrels. As with more neutral steaming, the primary purpose of toasting was to aid in the bending of staves and the eventual fashioning of the barrel. Many barrels, such as those used for oil, were lined with pitch or glue, purposely neutralizing any chemical or aromatic effect on the products to be stored and transported. This stands as another dichotomy in the historically variant purpose and even consciousness of the barrel.

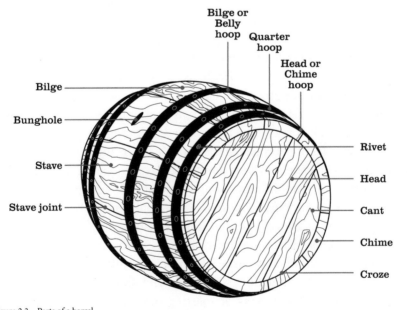

Figure 2.3—Parts of a barrel.

Once their treatments by fire are completed, the barrels are ready to receive their heads. Head production is a process in itself, of course. Relatively short planks are joined together by pegs or joints, and sometimes with glue. Vicard employs a dovetail configuration involving interlocking teeth. Plotting of planks is these days often aided by lasers, and the heads are cut round and then planed, with bevels cut top and bottom to aid in fitting into the groove, or croze, cut within the barrel. Traditional handsaws and knives would of course have been used in bygone days. The croze is cut within the ends of the barrels a few centimeters from the chime. Before being placed within the barrel, the heads as well might be toasted—and in the case of bourbon barrelheads, charred. These days this is effected by a tunnel pass-through with flame on the bottom side. In preparation for introducing the heads, the temporary hoops must be loosened, and once the heads are inserted, they are raised, traditionally using a head puller, but in the modern cooperage, done by machine. Once the heads are in place the hoops can be replaced and tightened. The head puller is a band of thin metal hooked on one end that holds the head as it is pulled into place. Having once forgotten his, Peter improvised one from a length of hoop.

Figure 2.4—A collection of cooper's tools at Seguin-Moreau. © Wout Bouckaert

Aside from being empty and therefore without practical function, an assembled and sealed barrel is a perfect thing before its bung has been drilled. It's certainly more structurally sound than afterward, yet it must be done. Care must be taken to select a bung stave of sufficient breadth to accommodate the violation inherent in placing a roughly 5 cm hole along a tensile span of oak, minimizing the risk of breakage or chipping, especially as the barrel will no doubt be rolled countless times across the compromising aperture in question. If damage does occur the bung stave must be replaced, and a new bunghole drilled in order to reclaim the barrel. In the days of hand cooperage bungholes were bored (or reamed) with a bung borer, a conically oriented knife mounted on a transverse handle similar to an old-fashioned corkscrew; indeed, some had corkscrew-like piloting aids affixed to the tip. Today the job is done with a powered drill press equipped with a super-heated bit of appropriate size, which smoothes and hardens the inner surface of the bunghole by cauterization. The barrel is then ready for pressure testing. This is done by introducing a small amount of water (no more than a liter or two), rolling the barrel around to cover the interior, and applying a few pounds of air pressure to ensure that in the course of normal, relatively low-pressure use the barrel will not leak. It is here that a barrel's first maintenance may occur, by the use of sliver-thin wedges of shaved oak or matchstick-like bits of wood that can be introduced into gaps or holes that become evident in the case of interior pressure forcing water through any hitherto undetected apertures. These plugs are gently hammered into place and then shaved level to the barrel with a light chisel. Sometimes faulty or cracked staves must be replaced, in which case the barrel is rolled aside for treatment. Once the barrel passes its pressure test it is fitted with a silicone temporary shipping bung to keep the interior inviolate until use. Before this occurs, however, the exterior of the barrel is sanded, these days on a machine that removes the hoops and steadies and rotates the barrel as a belt sander smoothes it. Then the hoops are replaced, sometimes augmented with outer hoops made from willow, as we saw at Seguin-Moreau, with the pointed ends twisted together. In the old days these willow hoops helped distract insects from more damaging infestation, but today they are referentially decorative. It's several centuries removed from the heyday of the Hanseatic League and the early marking and standardization of barrels, but modern cooperages are equipped with lasers to individualize barrels being shipped to contracted clients—primarily wineries and distilleries—by burning their logos onto the heads, ordinarily alongside the cooper's own logo and point of origin. These days more brand-oriented than protective, this burning of mark and origin harks back to a time when barrels were marked, and often burned, to ensure their eventual return.

The size at which a barrel begins to be called a foeder is somewhat unclear, especially when they are laid and used horizontally. Six hundred liters seems to be the approximate break point of designation, also determined by method of manufacture, since foeders are generally made one at a time and not in assembly lines. In Belgium, tanks both horizontal and upright are referred to as foeders, while in France "foudres" are horizontal and *cuves* are upright. For simplicity's sake, we will consider them all foeders. A separate shop is typically devoted to the production of foeders, which can take weeks for the completion of a single tank. Those coopers who construct foeders are regarded as the aristocrats of their trade.

The processes by which foeders are made are naturally governed by scale, differentiated from those of more ordinary barrels by extensions of time and much greater size, and the use of tools designed to work substantially larger pieces of wood. Due to the sheer size of foeders the wood cannot be split for staves, and must be sawn. Where barrels pass through the sequences of their construction in a sort of assembly line resulting in a constant flow of initiation, execution, and completion, the heads and assembled staves of foeders take up extended time and space on shop floors as their constituent parts are more patiently worked and married to yield tanks of often substantial size. The process is more akin to artisanal construction than manufacture, with a relationship sustained between each vessel and its crew, perhaps more like the once well-advertised group assembly of a single Saab at a time than the collectively specialized system devised by Henry Ford. A scaffolding is erected that encircles the work in progress and allows access by the foudriers, as those who work these beautiful tanks are called. Foeder construction involves contemplation and patience in a kind of communion with the wood and the task at hand. In various foeder works around France we saw artisans with tools and chins in hand, variously smoothing the channels for a manway, monitoring interior toasting, or disassembling a 13,208 gallon (500 hL) foeder bound for an Italian customer, each foudriere pondering exactly the right way to do it all. A typical foederie will turn out perhaps 200 tanks a year, compared with the spawn of tens of thousands—even hundreds of thousands, in some cases—of smaller barrels produced by their accompanying cooperages. Cranes and forklifts of course are needed to move them along the phases of their construction, as well as out the door once completed, a far cry from the benedectively dismissive roll along the way of the individual barrel.

Figure 2.5—The authors, Dick Cantwell (L) and Peter Bouckaert (R), in front of the world's largest foeder, located in Thuir, France. The foeder took 18 years and 200 trees for construction. © Wout Bouckaert

The largest foeder we are aware of, and which we saw at the lovely Eiffel-designed factory for the production of the apertif Byrrh in Thuir, in the Pyrénées-Orientales in France, once held over a million liters. It now sits empty in its own museum-like room, looking like a spacecraft in its gantry. It was built over the course of some 18 years, admittedly with the interruption of World War II. Three years alone were required to find 200 suitable trees for its construction. Foeders of several dozen to a couple of hundred hectoliters are most common, with those here and there in the thousands. Those filling row upon row in the cellars at Rodenbach in Roeselare, Belgium, stand in awesome testimony not only to wooden tank construction but the wonderful sour beers produced there. The brewery also keeps a whole tree on hand for stave replacement. The wineries of California and the chateaux of Bordeaux, as well as the spirits producers of Cognac and, more recently, the North American breweries committed to aging in wood, show an array of foeders in a range of sizes from 25 hL up to 500 or so. Built to withstand the weight and pressures of liquid volumes far larger than the average barrel, staves are thick—in some cases several centimeters (5, 6.5 and 8 cm are the standard thicknesses)—with widths proportionally substantial. The behemoth of Byrrh boasts staves a half-meter wide and more, 16 centimeters thick, and 10 meters long. In addition, the classic barrel form is forsaken for a broader base, with staves tapering upward to a relatively narrower top. Depending on available wood and the joinery space to be filled, staves are sometimes inverted, with the narrower end placed downward.

Some foeders are cylindrical, with several encircling adjustable clamps holding their staves together. Others are oval and horizontal, requiring two different angles of joinery to assemble, one for the top and bottom curves and another for the sides. The construction of these more closely resembles that of conventional barrels, but requires greater contrast of shaping in order to accommodate their size—sometimes as much as a third of the wood is removed on the stave's inner surface to create the curve, and staves are dramatically broader in their middles than at their ends. In addition, a broader bottom stave is required to mitigate the strain of incorporating the bunghole. Taransaud also makes quirkily beautiful egg-shaped foeders, fitted with stainless steel dish bottoms and tapered tops, their staves held together by an internal cable system likened to stringing pearls by their manufacturers. At that same fouderie we saw an ornately carved oval foeder presented as a graduation piece by a once-apprentice foudrier. Seguin-Moreau offers the option of the custom inclusion of a single Plexiglas stave for the display of contents in process. Like more conventionally modern steel tanks, foeders are fitted with manways for entry and cleaning, as well as sample cocks and any number of configurations of plugs, valves, and in many cases sprayballs for Clean-in-Place processes (CIP). Some have internal cooling systems, either coils or hollow fins through which propylene glycol or water are circulated to modulate fermentation and conditioning temperatures. The heads of foeders can be flat or convex, designed to withstand potential internal pressure, though aside from hydrostatic pressure exerted by the contents this would not be expected to be more than a few pounds. The heads of horizontal foeders of a certain age and hard use can sometimes seem alarmingly distended and misshapen.

Like the making of the strongest beers and wines, every phase of the construction of foeders is far longer than their smaller, more prosaic counterparts. Trees, first of all, must be older and larger to yield staves of necessary size. Extra care must be taken in sawing to incorporate as best as possible the desirable impermeable and unbroken medullary ray in each stave (because of both size and difficulty of orientation of these rays, the staves for foeders must be sawn); in fact, it's quite common for foeders to leak based on this shortcoming, in which case other measures must be employed (see chapter 4). Because of both length and width, other defects such as knots and the flare of the trunk both upper and lower are more difficult to avoid than with a barrel's smaller stave. Inspection of the stave ends is vital, as it can tell a story far beyond that of the construction of the humble barrel. A 10 hL foeder will have staves of 130 cm, but one of 500 hL requires staves of around 4.2 m, and thicknesses are commensurate, with staves often thicker at the bottom than at the top. As mentioned, the staves of the foeder in Thuirs were made 10 meters long, and would have been longer had rot during storage not taken its toll. Drying, steaming, and toasting times are protracted; an additional couple of years in the drying yard is required for the necessary seasoning to penetrate the larger staves, and hours amounting to a full day's work are needed to patiently execute the required degree of toast, during which fires must be continually fed and monitored and bending pressure painstakingly applied. Appendages such as manways, sample cocks, temperature probes, sprayballs, valves, and cooling inserts also have to be incorporated and properly mounted. And as with any construction project, scaffolds surround the vessel as it is being made. Several foeders may be under construction simultaneously, and they may be shipped a few or more at once, but they are most assuredly turned out one at a time.

Figure 2.6—Egg-shaped foeders by Taransaud are fitted with stainless steel dish bottoms and tapered tops. The staves are held together by an internal cable.

3

Wood & Wooden Vessels

I t's easy to forget in this age of stainless steel and electrical efficiency, even considering that the artisanal practices of hands-on brewing have been rediscovered in the last few decades, that nearly all processes of brewing used to be undertaken in wood. Brewhouse vessels were of wood, fermentation and aging vessels, too, and of course the barrels that provided the means for the brewery's beer to be transported and served in establishments other than what might adjoin the site of production. Wood would likely have fired the kettles— once they were made of copper or steel—and if not it would have been peat or coal. Every chute, barrow, and bin would have been of wood, as well. Of course, there are many wooden vessels remaining in older breweries, almost all of them in Europe and generally lined with steel, with the wood serving as insulation. The Guild House of the Brewers in Brussels has an all-wood mashing vessel on display, along with the traditional *stuikmande*, or wort-collecting basket, in which wort was dipped for boiling. Here and there, such as at Boon Brewery in Lembeek and at Rodenbach in Roeselare (both in Belgium), you can still find row on row of unlined wooden fermentation and conditioning vessels. Brasserie Vapeur in Pipaix-Leuze, also in Belgium, takes the old-timey thing to delightful extreme, with a wood-clad lautering system powered entirely by steam, the fuel for which, back in the day, would also have been wood.

Unlike other processes rediscovered by modern artisanal brewers, it's more difficult to imagine a wholesale harking back to the use of wooden mash- and lauter-tuns, though there are occurrences of their use. Ale Apothecary, just outside of Bend, Oregon, has revived the old Nordic practice of lautering some of its beers in a hollow spruce log through a lattice of twigs and straw. They also ferment in wood, though the boil is conducted in a locally-sourced copper kettle. Anchorage Brewing in Alaska also ferments in wood, as does Sante Adairius in Capitola, California, using both a Solera-style system of ongoing fermentation and simply straight-up fermenting in barrels, and there are others such as Bell's Brewery in Comstock, Michigan, rediscovering wooden roots by repurposing old tuns from a bygone age of American brewing. Happily, the list grows longer all the time, including Anderson Valley Brewing Company in Boonville, California, and Chad Jakobsen's Crooked Stave Artisan Beer Project in Colorado, but generally speaking stainless steel is the material of brewing's modern age.

Barrels are a different story. Nearly everywhere you go these days there are a few racks of barrels aging something or other, and a number of breweries have hung their hats on the large-scale production of beer aged in wooden barrels, sometimes thousands of them, as at Goose Island in Chicago and Founders Brewery in Grand Rapids, Michigan. Not that anyone is considering forgoing their stainless steel keg floats in favor of wholesale distribution in wooden barrels. This is an important distinction, as barrels these days are being used by brewers for aging and flavor enhancement, and almost never for the rolling-out of song. Oh, here and there you'll see them in use, as when the very modern-looking barman at the Schlenkerla taproom of the Heller Brauerei in Bamberg hammers home a rustic tap in an equally rustic barrel atop the bar, or at the ceremonial trundling and tapping of the Tuesday barrel at the Cascade Barrel House in Portland, Oregon. The modern near ubiquity of barrels used as aging vessels might seem to point out a paradox, given that the primary function of the barrel throughout all but its most recent few hundred years was as a vessel for transport. Barrels were used for moving things—beer, wine, and spirits among them, but including hundreds of other materials, liquid and dry. Aside from some notable and honored exceptions, it's only very recently that the techniques of wine and spirit makers have been adopted for aging beer in barrels. And speaking of those exceptions, crafters of *lambic* and other traditional sour beers do all sorts of things off the path of the average brewer.

But that path is meandering. And, really, that's why we're here. For it's only a step or two from bourbon barrel aging to long-term cellaring of sour beers, onward to picking up a foeder or two and really getting serious about a wood program. We've got a lot to learn from those lambic brewers, too.

In this chapter we'll look at wood, as it's grown, chosen, harvested, and used in making vessels, both for actual brewing's various processes and the uses to which the world has put it when made into barrels. We'll consider various woods, but mainly oak, and we'll get into why that wood has come to be dominant and what makes it uniquely suited for barrels in particular. And we'll spend some time considering all the brewing-related functions it has served throughout history, but with a focus on today. We'll also review the uses of wood of types other than oak, as well as other wood products, those both made of and influenced by wood.

Let's first take a look at some of the woods that have been used for making vessels of various types. You'll notice that when flavor characteristics are mentioned it is mainly in connection with wine.

- Acacia (*Acacia*)—Used in Austria for white wine and *eau de vie*. Gives a yellow color to pale liquid such as white wine. Chateau Montelena in Napa Valley has experimented with black locust or *Robina pseudoacacia* (not actual acacia)—also mentioned under other wood below—for Sauvignon Blanc, and is generally pleased with the lighter touch. Acacia can provide body and texture with some tannin without the sweetness and bigger flavors and aromas of toasted oak. Seems to be gaining importance in the world of wine as more barrelbuilders are producing barrels from acacia as a subtle-touch alternative to oak. Used for dowels in France.
- Ash (*Fraxinus*)—Used for the aging of genever spirits, giving color and taste to the distilled liquor. A strong and substantial wood, also once used for packing meat. Some dowels are made from ash, as well as baseball bats and the legendary jousting lances of medieval knights. Along with oak and thorn, a mystical wood in Celtic lore.
- Beech (*Fagis*)—Once common in Chile, but has largely been abandoned for barrels as it grows too fast to be suitably watertight. Its most widely advertised use is in shaved form as a clarifying agent in conditioning for Budweiser beers at Anheuser-Busch breweries, though this was

more practically necessary in the age before sterile filtration and centrifugation, and today is practiced mainly to justify the use of the term "beechwood aged" in labeling. Similarly, pure alpha cellulose from beech can be used for filtration, and has been certified for use by the Forest Stewardship Council, an international sustainability organization. Aged beechwood is also used to smoke malt, mainly in Germany.

- Cedar (*Cedrus*, or *Cryptomeria japonica*)—Used for aging sake, and subsequently at the Kiuchi brewery in Japan for production of its Classic Japanese Ale, as well as for Brazilian cachaça. Somewhat resinous and repellent to insects.

- Cherry (*Prunus*)—Still used in some European countries. Italian ripasso-style wines are aged in cherry. Black cherry is mentioned in old Interstate Commerce Commission (ICC) regulations for tight barrels (Hankerson 1944).

- Chestnut (*Castanea*)—Used in the humid marl cellars of wineries in the Loire valley. It has also been used for lambic production due to being cheaper than oak. Traditionally popular for long oval casks used in the Rhone valley, Beaujolais, and parts of Italy and Portugal. Generally more sharply tannic than oak and not as watertight, so sometimes lined with paraffin or silicone. Probably the second-favorite wood used for barrels.

- Cypress (*Taxidium dichtum*)—Usually pitched, used for mashing, fermentation, and storage vessels, but also once considered a viable alternative to oak for use in barrels (Schenk 1908). The Dixie Brewery in New Orleans had cypress fermenters. August Schell's brewery in New Ulm, Minnesota, has removed the pitch from some cypress foeders of 160 hL for use in making sour beers, and Bell's Brewery has, within the last couple of years, acquired decommissioned cypress vessels from the old Stroh's brewery in Detroit for use as fermenters. Cypress logs raised from the Shawnee River, an old southern logging route, were used to construct fermenters for the Four Roses Distillery in Lawrenceburg, Kentucky.

- Douglas Fir (*Pseudotsuga taxifolia*)—Mentioned in ICC regulation for tight barrels and in Schahinger (1992). Used in fermentation at Dalwhinnie Distillery in Scotland and Four Roses distillery in Kentucky.

- Eucalyptus (*Eucalyptus*)—Once used in its native Australia, but must have been coated internally (Schahinger 1992) due to structure and strong flavor and aroma.

- Jequitiba-rosa (*Cariniana legalis*), Freijo (*Cordia*), Garapa (*Apuleia leiocarpa*), Cedro Rosa (*Cedrela odorata*), Cabrueva (*Myroxylon peruiferum*), Balsam (*Ochrama pyramidale*), Vinhatico (*Persea indica*), and Amburana (*Amburana cearensis*)—All are used in barrels for aging cachaça, the fresh-pressed sugarcane rum of Brazil. Amburana, in particular, is noted as imparting spicy notes of cumin and cinnamon. Many have been used for aging beer by the Bodebrown brewery in Curitiba, Brazil.
- Juniper (*Juniperus*)—Related to cypress, and these days seeing some demand, according to the Rocky Mountain Barrel Company.
- Larch, aka Tamarack (*Larix*)— Grown at northern latitudes and high elevation. Siberian-grown Larch is used in fermenters at Dalwhinnie.
- Oak (*Quercus*)—As mentioned, oak is the dominant wood for barrels. We'll come back for a more in-depth look, but for now we'll observe that it's light compared with some other woods, is malleable, and has high tensile strength. Because of its unique physiology it is relatively impermeable to liquid (within parameters of species) and semi-permeable to air, and has beneficial flavor compounds that can be brought along through heat treatment and extracted when desired. These include flavors of wood, coconut, vanilla, sweetness, butterscotch, clove, and other spice and smoke.
- Palo Santo (*Bursera graveolens*)—Extremely hard wood, with an aggressive and ponderous flavor effect, pioneered for a beer of the same name at Dogfish Head Brewery in Milton, Delaware, which had a 9,000-gallon foeder of the wood constructed at great adventure and expense. Small cubes and blocks are emulatively used by homebrewers for notable flavor contribution. An interesting article appeared in *The New Yorker* in November of 2008 chronicling Dogfish's introduction to and use of the wood, its founder, Sam Calagione, and extreme brewing in general.
- Pecan (*Carya illinoinensis*)—Hard wood found in abundance in the southern United States. Several breweries and a number of homebrewers have used pecan wood in a variety of styles but it is primarily used for smoking barbecue or, in the case of brewing, malt.
- Pine (*Pinus*)—A soft, harshly resinous wood, used for wooden water tanks such as those on top of buildings and in the chemical industry due to its resistance to acid. One of the fermenters at the Dalwhinnie Distillery in Scotland is of Oregon pine. The Greek wine *retsina* gets

its resinous flavor from contact with pinewood. Its porosity and high terpene content demand for it to be lined when used for making barrels, which these days is rare to nonexistent.

- Red Gum (*Eucalyptus rostrata*), Blackwood (*Acacia melanoxylin*), Karri (*Eucalyptus diversicolor*), Australian "oak" (*Eucalyptus regnans* and others), Jarrah (*Eucalyptus marginata*), Birch (*Betula*), Maple (*Acer*), Elm (*Ulmus*), Redwood (*Sequoia sempirvirens*), Kauri (*Agathis robusta*), and Black Locust, or False Acacia, (*Robinia pseudoacacia*)— Many of these are mentioned (Schahinger, et al) for use with wine, but often with negative flavor comment, and hence are sometimes lined. Pseudoacacia is mentioned above in connection with use at Chateau Montelena near Calistoga, California. Redwood is noted as being difficult to bend. Scratch Brewing in Ava, Illinois, has experimented with Shagbark Hickory (*Carya ovata*), Eastern Red cedar (*Juniperus virginiana*), and Sycamore (*Platanus occidentalis*), as well as more conventional maple and oak in many different ways, including adding nut hulls of hickory and oak to boiling wort and enacting spontaneous fermentation with burr oak (*Q. macrocarpa*) acorns.
- Spruce (*Picea*)—Another resinous conifer, sometimes used for fermentation vessels and tanks. Anchorage Brewing Company commissioned a foeder of Alaska white spruce in 2015, and Ale Apothecary in Oregon uses a hollowed spruce log for lautering one of its beers. Some of the world's oldest individual trees are spruces, including one in Sweden of nearly 10,000 years.
- Walnut (*Juglans*)—Still used in Europe.

In addition to woods used for making actual vessels, many woods—oak primary among them—are shaved, chipped, cubed, powdered, or spiraled for use as flavoring aids. Planks or staves can also be used, placed within aging tanks, either loose or on racks installed for the purpose. These products can also be toasted to levels correspondent to those enacted upon barrels. This process has the added benefit of taking less time than barrel aging to impart associated flavors. Interesting work has been done by the Independent Stave Company to assess the effects of these treatments with oak in wine, and both analytic and sensory tests in New Zealand have cast light on the use of native woods from that country in similar fashion, such as *totara, kahikatea, manuka,* and *pohutukawa,* also comparing them—in some

Figure 3.1—Sake barrels used at the Kiuchi Brewery in Naka, Ibaraki Prefecture, Japan, for aging their Classic Japanese Ale.

cases, favorably—to American oak (Mahajan 2008). As a side note, totara (*Podocarpus totara*) is of limited practical use as it is a protected species, while manuka (*Leptosternum scoparium*) is also used for smoking bacon. Some of the New Zealand woods tested, in fact, never reached the sensory stage, as they combusted during the toasting process. Cigar City Brewing in Tampa, Florida, has taken an aromatic and resonant page from its hometown's cigar-making heritage by using the Spanish cedar (*Cedrela odorata*) best known for packaging and aging cigars for flavoring some its beers. Cigar City has also aged on lemon and grapefruit woods, after taking a full year to accumulate enough of them for effective use.

While this list is long and a little overwhelming—all those woods used for *cachaça!*—it's edifying and interesting to see the resourcefulness people have employed in finding and using wood for storage and functional and flavorful use in connection with beer, wine, spirits, and other liquids. And of course, back to *cachaça* for a moment, alternative woods must be used to make barrels and other vessels where there is relatively little naturally occurring oak. But we're getting ahead of ourselves. Best to start at the beginning.

The Wood Before Time

Oak as such made its distinct appearance on Earth around 60 million years ago, when it genetically separated from chestnut. It's tempting to wonder if the dinosaurs coexisted with oaks, but we won't indulge that Flintstone fantasy for more than a moment. The first North American fossil record of oaks is from 55 to 50 million years ago, and various oak (*quercus*) species separated from each other between 22 and 3 million years ago. A symbiosis between hominids and oaks arose perhaps 30,000 years ago, which is not at all to say that oaks were cultivated at this point, but people of whatever sort did gravitate to where oaks grew, mainly for the nutritive value—if perhaps not delicacy—of acorns, but also, no doubt, in order to hunt the animals attracted by the food source. Both humans and animals amassed great stores of acorns for later, seasoned use. Some of these caches were here and there discovered by farmers in North America decades after the Native Americans who had gathered them had been forced to move on. Animals still do this, of course, but use of acorns in foodstuffs has devolved these days to specialty use—flours and jellies, for example. In addition, the trees themselves provided shelter, and the leaves could be fed to domesticated animals (Logan 2006).

As tectonic plates moved, mountains rose and landmasses altered and as glaciers appeared, encroached, and receded, oaks, along with everything else, found their homes as circumstances allowed. Life flowed back to where the glaciers had been. Having once formed great populations in regions now more arboreally inhospitable, such as those now composed of the Negev and Sonoran deserts, oaks pushed northward (and to some extent southward) along the Pacific coast and into the vast region closer to the Atlantic in North America, upward from the Mediterranean across Europe, and throughout much of China and Japan. These regions continue to be where nearly all oak is found. There are some 600 oak species in total, with around a quarter of those in evidence in Mexico alone. The United States boasts about 90, and there are 100 or more in China.

Oak has occupied spiritual space in cultish civilization. Along with ash and thorn it is one of the three celtic magical woods, favorites to the fairy folk. It is also endowed with specialized significance due to its symbiotes, druidic mistletoe and the truffles of Perigord. Oak is neither the oldest, the strongest, the largest, nor the most precious of woods, but throughout human history it has been plentiful and of great use, emblematic in heraldry, place, and family name, occupying something of a special position in consciousness and history.

As a plant, oak exists as a tree or shrub. The genus has two main genera or subspecies, *Quercus* and *Cyclobalanopsis*. *Quercus* has a number of subdivisions such as *alba* and *robur* (the white oaks of Europe, Asia, and North America), *mesobalanus* (Hungarian oak and its relatives in other Slavic countries and Asia), *cerris*, *protobalanus*, and *lobatae* (a red oak also used in cooperage). With 600 species, this clearly constitutes only a few. Oak is wind pollinated and hence lends itself to hybridization between various species of *Quercus* and *Mesobalanopsis*, the two main types used for tight cooperage. *Quercus* is sometimes also referred to as *Lepidobalanus* or *Leucobalanus,* but *Quercus* will be the term used in this book. *Quercus* species are primary in use for cooperage, but veneer is the main use for oak, with furniture trailing barrels in usage. Roughly 5% of American-harvested oak and 20% of French-harvested oak these days ends up being made into barrels.

Oak has many properties especially suitable for making barrels, all of which are a result of its physiology and the way it grows respective to other woods. It is a relatively slow-growing wood, contributing to a tight grain, which gives it strength and resists the free flow of liquid through it. In addition, it has two unique characteristics that set it apart from nearly all other woods. Its sap channels, which during the early growing season allow movement of nutrients throughout the tree, later fill with material called tylose, degraded from the passage walls and rendering them nearly impervious. This combined with the occurrence of substantial medullary rays radiating from the tree's center to the new, outer sapwood contributes to eventual watertightness. The medullary rays in conifers can be only a single cell thick, but those of suitable oak are far more substantial and easily visible to the splitter in the cooperage. Each stave should ideally have a span of medullary ray across it to act as a barrier to liquid, hampering leakage that would far more readily occur with other woods. Not all oaks have medullary rays of sufficient thickness to serve. Only about 20 oak species are so suited. Chemically, oak is a particularly pure wood, without much resinous content that in many other woods can carry unpleasant astringent flavors. It is considered lacking in odor or taste and has a pleasant, mild, "carpenter shop" smell, which is associated with 9-carbon gamma lactones (more on this later). The location where oak is sourced will influence the type, the flavor, and the price of the wood. European oak for cooperage tends to be grown in fairly small forest plots of 100–200 hectares, particularly in France. American oak forests are relatively vast even in this age of endemic depletion. Oak is typically harvested when it is about 80 years old, but less carefully husbanded areas harvest it younger. Conversely, it can grow to hundreds of years in age.

Much is felt, said, and studied about the differences between American oak and European oak for their respective use in cooperage and later effect on alcoholic liquids stored in barrels. Within Europe, as well, there are differences as to species and character. Some of these differences are based on analytic study, while others have more to do with sensory perception. As time passes, however, these sensory differences are also being quantified by analysis.

European oak carries 2.5 times more phenols and water-soluble components than American oak. This can contribute a flavor of raw "oakiness" or general wood character and is the reason European cooperage has striven over time for a more neutral character. European oak also contributes more brown color to wine (or sprits or beer) than American. American oak provides more aroma and flavor-rich components, while European oak has more flavorless carbohydrates. American oak gives more oakiness per unit extracted due to a higher non-tannin phenol fraction—21% non-tannin phenols in American versus 14% for Limousin oak, where European oak is higher in overall phenol content. As observed, these differences can be a matter of taste over time. For their differences in early use, European oak and American oak yield similar levels of flavor after more than three uses.

Seasonal Growth Differences in Phenol Content

Some differences as to growth and how they might relate to the above qualities are outlined in this chart:

Source	European	American	Unit
Growth	2.7	3.3	(mm/year)
Density spring	0.49	0.6	(mm/year)
Density summer	0.73	0.84	(mm/year)
Extractable phenols			
Spring	7.3	1.9	gram gallic acid equivalent/100 g
Summer	4.8	1.5	gram gallic acid equivalent/100 g

You'll note that American oak shows greater overall density, with a higher proportion of growth coming in the spring. Potential differences in flavor pursuant to this will become evident later. The far higher levels of extractable phenols in European oak are also striking.

If as we move forward it seems that some predisposition shows even in statements of numeric analysis, it's because it surely exists. Connoisseurship is, after all, a human condition. You no doubt already have some of your own ideas; some of them likely justified. Still, with oak as with so many other things, beyond toxicity and other universal unpleasantness there is no right or wrong. There are merely more choices to be made.

American Oak

Although oak of various type grows pretty much everywhere in the United States, white oak used for wood vessels is found mainly in the eastern part, an area of around 45 million hectares. This area runs from southern Minnesota and Wisconsin to eastern Texas, all the way eastward with the exception of the Mississippi Delta, Florida, and northern New England. *Quercus alba* is the dominant species. Little effort is made to identify American oak by its specific area of origin within the United States. The closest one can usually

American White Oak *(Q. alba)* Distribution Map - U.S.A.

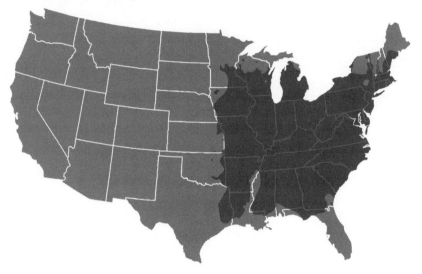

Figure 3.2—Distribution of American White Oak in the United States.

get in origin determination is in identification of the mill where the wood is worked and staves are cut. Because of obviously more compressed growing seasons, oak from the northern part of the United States is harder and more dense due to tightness of grain. Most oak is harvested on private land, and forests are naturally seeded and pollinated, typically in mixed woodlands with different tree species growing side by side.

Oak for cooperage in the United States is called white oak. The easiest way to differentiate between white oak and the less suitable red oak is by looking at the end grain of a cleanly cut, dust-free piece. Red oak will show dark sap pores compared to the more grayish-white tylose-blocked channels of white oak. See? Even within otherwise similar-seeming oak species differences of suitability exist. Another easy test is to blow air through a piece of wood in the direction of the grain. If bubbles appear the piece is likely red oak, since air can pass through the unobstructed sap channels. An exception could be chestnut oak, considered a white oak but still somewhat permeable. Additionally, looking at the faces of oak boards will show dark brown streaks running with the grain. The length of these streaks in red oak will rarely exceed .75 in (19 mm), whereas in white oak they can be substantially longer.

A list of American oak species variously suitable for cooperage follows:

- Burr oak (*Q. macrocarpa*)—Found along the bottom of the Ozark valley.
- Chestnut oak (*Q. prinus*)—Low branching oak grown mainly in Appalachia, usually with not very straight trunks, but if grown under good conditions can produce good wood. Lacks tyloses so needs to be split like French oak, and has a different flavor profile than both American and French oak (Swan 1997).
- Chinkapin oak (*Q. muehlenbergii*)—Found on the well-drained slopes of the Ozarks.
- Durand oak (*Q. durandii*)
- Overcup oak (*Q. lyrata*)
- Oregon white oak (*Q. garryana*)—Has been used experimentally in the past and is now used by Clear Creek distillery in Portland, Oregon, as well as in barrels manufactured by Rogue brewing and distilling at their Rolling Thunder Cooperage in Newport, Oregon. Closer in character to European oak.
- Post oak (*Q. stellate*)
- Red oak (*Q. rubra*)—Not not to be confused with European *Quercus robur*. Not watertight in itself, so needs pitch or other lining. Listed in ICC regulations. Was once good for shipping heavy dry goods since it's of great strength and cheaper than white oak barrels.
- Swamp chestnut oak (*Q. michauxii*)
- Swamp white oak (*Q. bicolor*)—Tried out by one of the Scottish distilleries for aging barrels (at least for heads).
- White oak (*Q. alba*)—Most used, native to eastern and central North America.

Much American oak is destined for export, particularly to Europe from eastern parts of the United States, and primarily to winemakers in France, Spain, and Italy, since whiskey producers in Scotland and Ireland deal mainly in second-use bourbon barrels.

European Oak

As some older references point out, barrels made from oak used to come from all over Europe, as local demand required production closer to home. Time, politics, centralization of markets, and the efficiencies and durability of modern materials such as plastic and metal have since taken their toll on

Sessile Oak *(Q. patraea)* Distribution Map - Europe

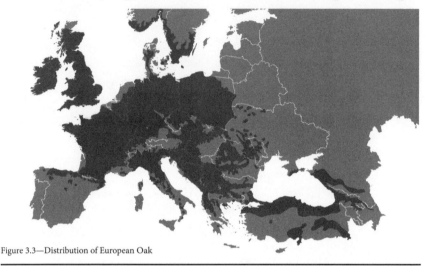

Figure 3.3—Distribution of European Oak

the artisanal production of barrels. Estonia still has oak branches in its coat of arms, and was once a large exporter to Australia of barrels made from Memel oak, so named for the Lithuanian city now known as Klaipeda (Schahinger 1992). Wars hot and cold have also altered priorities and curtailed widespread production, effectively reducing areas in which barrels are made to France, Germany, Portugal, and parts of some Balkan countries.

The following oak varieties have commonly been used for making barrels in Europe:

- Durmast oak (*Q. petraea* or *sessilis*)—Winter oak, slow growing (1mm/yr). Found in Europe and Western Asia. Like *robur*, it can be found from the Atlantic to the Ural Mountains.
- Summer oak (*Q. robur*)—Grows fast, up to 10 mm a year, with a low trunk and a wide crown. Found in Europe and western Asia. Other names sometimes used are *quercus pedunculata*, the penduculate, and English, Limousin, or French oak. This species is widespread from the European Atlantic coast to the Ural Mountains in western Russia. Less used for wine cooperage, although it is the dominant species in Spain and outpopulates sessile oak in France.
- A few other varieties of lesser importance: *Q. afares, Q. macranthera, Q. longpipes, Q. imeretina, Q. iberica, Q. pendunculiflora, Q. lanugnosa, Q. farnetto,* and *Q. mirbeckii.*

As delineated above, the two main oak types used for making barrels are often referred to as *sessile* and *pedunculate*, the latter describing a structure with a stalk or stem, the former mainly composed of a base structure. One datum of Pliocene trivia explaining why there are so many fewer oak varieties growing in Europe than in either Asia or North America is that as both the Alps and the Pyrenees are mountain ranges running east to west, botanical migration was kept from running as strongly in its usual north-south climatic pattern, resulting in the localized extinction of much plant life, including oaks.

French Oak

France has a fairly large growing area for oak, around 4.13 million hectares (10.2 million acres) of *Q. petreae* and *Q. robur*, with proportionally more oak going to cooperage than in other countries. Still, it is dwarfed by the oak-producing area of the United States. The management of the forest is mainly under control of the *Office National des Fôrets* (ONF), a French government organization. Around 2 million cubic meters (850 million board feet) of oak is harvested every year. Cooperages submit bids on specific hectares of forest after assessing the quantity of cubic meters of wood they can harvest from the straight trunks. At least 200,000 barrels made from French oak are sold annually, with the United States the primary customer (Robinson 2006).

The first record concerning the condition of the French national forest dates to 1291 with mention of *maitres des forêts* (masters of the forest) in the royal ordinances. The regime of Colbert in 1669 also had ordinances ordering a systematic replanting of oak trees for use in shipbuilding, and established the Office National des Forêts, which owns 70% of the forests. As with many monitored crops, the trees in government-owned forests are carefully managed and farmed to grow straight and tall. Each tree is sold at auction, standing uncut in the forest. The first commercial cut comes when trees are 80 years old and follows in 20-year intervals thereafter. Older trees are deemed the best for cooperage, but are generally not older than 150 years. France is the only country that identifies regions of origin, or *terroir,* for their oak. The species and their hybrids may be the same as in other regions, but it is the growing conditions that are considered to be of influence on the wood. The website of today's ONF lists 26 distinct regions of supervision, including the colonial lands of Guyana, Guadeloupe, and Martinique, where oak and presumably other woods are husbanded.

Some of these regions are:

- Allier—Grown south of Nevers, fairly similar to the oak in Nevers.
- Burgundian—Just east of the upper Rhone valley. Similar to Limousin oak.
- Limousin—Predominantly *Q. robur* grown around Limoges in the southwest of France. Poor growing conditions in rough, hilly, granitic and sandy terrain lead to tough, coarsely grained wood. The stocky, tortuous trunks are almost exclusively used for the maturation of Cognac, but some chardonnay is aged in this wood as well.
- Nevers—Around the city of Nevers, in central France. Gently rolling rich and moist soil grows tall, straight trees. This area grows predominantly *Q. petraea* that form tall straight trunks when grown in forest conditions. The wood is close-grained and mild in flavor.
- Tronçais—A specific forest in the Allier region that was planted as a strategic reserve in the 17th century for warship building. Rich, deep soil leads to a spectacular forest of trees of great size. The wood is fine and long and relatively soft. The barrels are used for premium winemaking in France, and also for Pinot noir in California. Very highly regarded.
- Vosges—This low mountain area in northeastern France is a relative newcomer (since the late 1970s) to supplying oak for barrels. In demand in the area of Burgundy.

While these regional differentiations are interesting, they are naturally not completely homogeneous. Variations in locale, soil, altitude, orientation, and micro-climate exist. Trees on the edge of a forest are substantially different from trees further within it. The 40 or so staves of a barrel can come from many trees within the same area, contribute idiosyncratic differences, and effectively even out to a common character. Some experts state that the way trees are grown is more important than the region. In France there are three different distinctions as to how a tree is grown:

- Coppice (*Taillis sous futaie*)—Wider spacing of oak trees with lower growing trees of other types between. The advantage for the grower is that there can be a faster harvest of the smaller trees for the ready generation of income, but as the economic viability of firewood as a crop has declined, this method is disappearing.
- Grove (*Futaie*)—Densely grown forest. Due to density of planting, the trees do not develop much in the way of side branches, resulting in long, straight trunks desirable for cooperage, essentially uninterrupted by knots.

- Rural growth (*Champêtre*)—Oaks grown on their own in fields, typical for Limousin. This can result in the most spectacularly branched trees, but the short trunk does not yield much straight-grain wood.

Regional differences can further be confused by cooperage. Demptos and Nadalie are well known in Bordeaux, where Taransaud, Vicard, and Seguin Moreau are in Cognac and François Frères, Billon, and Damy are in Burgundy. Many coopers operate facilities in a number of different regions, as well as internationally. Coopers are generally careful to receive specifications as to origin, shape, thickness, and other attributes of the wood, including new or used, from producers of the liquid destined for their barrels, though they will of course provide guidance based on their experience and knowledge of the market. The customer may not always be right, but they do have right of refusal should barrels not be manufactured according to agreed-upon specification.

The Oak of Other Regions

While both supplies and management have been uneven over the past couple of hundred years, oak in a number of former Soviet bloc countries—Hungary and the Baltic states, for instance—has enjoyed popularity and demand, and is still used by some Italian winemakers for larger barrels due to its tight grain, low aromatics, and medium tannin levels. Both *Q. robur* and *Q. petraea* are included. Seguin Moreau continues to buy oak from Romania and Russia.

Other countries where oak was once vigorously harvested mainly tell a story of decline. The oak of the United Kingdom, for example, once protected and held so dear by Henry VIII and others is nearly all gone, though the brewery of Innis and Gunn uses Scottish oak for the chips in their "oakerators." The oaks of Germany have mainly been replaced by pine trees, presumably to be harvested for construction. Spanish oak is still used by the Macallan distillery in Scotland, and some oak and chestnut barrels are produced in Portugal. Misunara oak (*Q. mongolica*) is used in Japan and China; the Suntory Hakushu Distillery boasts it provides strong coconut and vanilla notes, is low in tannins, and has more aromatic trans-lactones than any other oak. It is tempting to wonder, given the Chinese tide of stainless brewing equipment being offered nearly daily via everyone's email inboxes, whether barrels of Chinese oak might eventually be considered worthy of production.

Harvesting, Splitting, Dressing, and Seasoning

Many of the words associated with the processes of readying oak for assembly into barrels and foeders reminds one of butchery—not the wholesale slaughter of armies or innocents, but the skilled reduction of hunted or husbanded and brokered animals, the cuts from which are differentiated as to grade and suitability, and then in some cases aged to invite slow microbial and enzymatic alteration en route to deliciousness—at least for those of us who eat meat. This may be forcing a comparison, but along with many other artisanal skills—farming, quarrying, pickle-making—they show the accrued wisdom and experience of the ages in developing the most fruitful and economical methods for bringing to humankind the bounty of the earth. There's a lot to be done, in short, before you're even ready to turn wood into a barrel.

As we've observed, the best oak for making barrels is of only a few different varieties physiologically suited to later requirement. It grows straight and tall under the patient and observant eye of its tenders, its brokers, and its regulators. And at a time when it is judged ready, it is felled and shipped to facilities prepared to take it the rest of the way. We've taken a look at what goes on in the cooper's shop, the joining, the scraping and planing, the raising, the toasting, and the rest. Let's back up a bit and, with the background of physical fact we've just gone through about what makes oak most suitable for making barrels, get a bit more into what makes the wood what it will be.

We're not really here to tell you how to cut down a tree. Some of you no doubt have experience along these lines. Typically, a wedge is removed by sawing in order to determine the direction in which the tree will fall. Sometimes the tree is topped to minimize damage to the trunk when it falls. Lines are attached just to take a little of the guesswork out of the process, and with a little more of this and that, down it goes, right where it was supposed to. Easy for us to say. There are any number of videos available showing you how it's done. Like raising a barrel, that doesn't mean we can do it ourselves, or need to.

In the Northern hemisphere, wood is typically harvested between December and March, since those are months when the tree carries the least moisture. In the United States this can extend throughout the year. As it is, moisture can constitute well over half of its mass. Once the branches are trimmed and the points are determined at which usable wood can be claimed—remember that trees flare at both crown and base, and the grain within those spans is correspondingly broadened and idiosyncratic—the trunk is cut into bolts of appropriate stave length. Most of cooperage, of course, is devoted to barrel making rather than the construction of larger vessels such as foeders, so these bolts are most often relatively short. It's tempting to liken the appraisal of logs of suitable length and evenness for the making of foeders to the sensing of the sculpture within a block of Carrera marble, but that would be forcing an already over-used comparison. It is a skill of envisioning, however, no doubt enacted before the tree has even been felled.

It is at this point that the staves are either split or sawn from the bolt. Splitting is far less efficient and more difficult than sawing, but more often necessary with European oak and its less robust medullary rays. Only 20% of the wood is claimed as staves when split, compared to 50% or so when they are sawn. Split staves are also more difficult for coopers to work later in the process, though they are more resistant to breakage when bent. As mentioned, splitting is far more often done in France, due mainly to the physiology of French oak, which generates less tylose for sealing of the sap channels, and generally has a more open and porous grain than American. More care must therefore be taken in order to ensure the occurrence and orientation of medullary rays for later effectiveness as a barrier to liquid in the barrel. Because of the length and thickness of the staves used for making foeders, splitting is impracticable and they must be sawn. They are therefore somewhat more vulnerable to through-wood leakage owing to difficulty of medullary orientation.

Splitting of staves for barrels can be done either vertically or horizontally, these days using lasers for plotting the pattern of staves to be split and hydraulic wedges that accomplish the splitting itself. At Tonnellerie Vicard in Cognac we saw the horizontal method employed, with the operator turning the wood just so by means of two foot pedals. Splits run along the radius of the wood, ideally maintaining a pattern with the medullary rays running across the resultant staves. The staves also come out somewhat wedge-shaped, and so must be trimmed at both the narrow and wider sides in order to achieve consistency of dimension. This is primarily where the inefficiency of splitting lies. In addition, the soft outer sapwood must be cut away and discarded. Sawing is also done with the aid of lasers, plotting the ideally efficient pattern along the end of each quarter bolt. The first stave is sawn, the wood is rotated 90 degrees for the removal of the next, and so on. They are similarly trimmed to remove the sapwood and render them consistent, but with far less waste than splitting.

Throughout the process of stave preparation the wood is inspected for flaws and blemishes. Knots are formed where the branches join the trunk, and are fairly obvious to detect—except when the branch has broken and ceases to grow, in which case the knot can be hidden inward. In the worst case the knot will fall out and leave a hole, but even in place will likely cause a leak. Conscious choices of planting density can reduce the quantity of side branches, and hence the occurrence of knots. As mentioned above, the soft outer sapwood must be completely removed from suitable heartwood. In addition to being insufficiently impervious to liquid it is prone to insect and fungal attack. Rot and fungal decay can occur either in living wood, such as when a branch has broken off, or when it is laid out for drying with insufficient ventilation. Many different grubs and insects like to bore and nestle in either dead or living wood. They can leave holes that will leak, though if there are only a few in a single stave they can be repaired and won't necessarily be rejected out of hand. Splits and shakes can occur along the grain of the wood and are the result of drying too quickly. This is one of a number of reasons wood in the drying yard is intermittently sprayed with water, especially in the early stages. Splits generally part along the medullary ray since it is of different material from the rest of the wood. They can also occur during felling or transport. And of course there can be foreign material left by the influence of man—nails, fence wire, bullets and their holes, even shrapnel. While most flaws are detected during the preparation of the staves, the wood is evaluated at every later stage of the cooperage process, and rejected if necessary.

The wood is now ready for drying, or "seasoning." Hardwoods such as oak are far more difficult to dry than softer woods used for lumber, as they are denser and more complex in structure, and because of their relative lack of permeability require greater time and patience to evenly give up their moisture. Wood is hydroscopic, and will balance its moisture content with its surroundings, shrinking and swelling as ambient moisture varies. Staves are traditionally dried in stacks that command a disproportionate amount of space at the cooperage. A rough rule of thumb is one year of drying for each centimeter of thickness, with the staves for foeders requiring four to six years or more due to their greater size. The thickness of the staves will also determine later oxygen diffusion in the barrel or foeder. Despite the ultimate aim of drying, the wood is allowed to be rained on and, especially in the early stages, is watered artificially. This helps leach harsh tannins out and keeps the ends of the staves, where the grain is exposed and drying is potentially faster, from cauterizing from heat and dryness to hamper the release of moisture and prevent splitting.

In addition to the reduction of moisture in the wood over time, microbial activity helps temper the wood and reduces toxins that could affect the eventual flavor extracted from barrels made with it. Molds have a hard time gaining a foothold in wood due to the presence of protective phenols, and it is common mildew (*Aerobasidium pullulans*) that takes the first steps in degrading phenols and the wood in general, releasing some sugars from the glycosidic bonds in lignin, but leaving cellulose intact. After some of this detoxification, other organisms can take hold, living on the autolytic remains of earlier degradation, creating a matrix important to the formation of flavor precursors to the toasting process later on (Vivas 1996). In addition to *Aerobasidium pullulans*, *Trichoderma harzianum* and *Trichoderma koningii* help to degrade lignine and coumarine to contribute later roundness and complexity as opposed to bitterness and dryness. Some studies indicate degradation of cellulose itself by the trichoderma species (ISC 1997). Exposure to smells or fumes during the drying process can also affect eventual flavor and aroma. We were impressed during our visit to Seguin Moreau in Cognac by the rich, gingerbready aroma we took to be coming off the drying wood, but were told it was from the caramel works next door.

With the world demand for barrels increasing, much research has gone into faster methods of air drying. Some of these involve watering techniques intended to pull sap out of the wood faster, vacuum drying, and microwaving. Staves for bourbon barrel production are both naturally and artificially dried, partly owing to the more forgiving structure of American oak. Natural air-drying does positively affect the balance and concentration of flavor components. Some materials such as gallic acid and the tannins castalegin and vescalegin reduce over time, while hydroxy furfural remains about the same during the process. Ellagic acid will increase for a time and then decrease. Vanillin as well will follow this pattern, but then increase again (ISC 2008). It's easy to imagine the difficulty of synthesizing all these inherently slow processes and maintaining the integrity of their interplay. Freezing and thawing also play their part in degradation and maturation.

Much care has clearly been taken to this point to bring the wood to a stable and workable state. It is here that the cooper figuratively snatches the staves from the drying yard and begins his or her work, in the course of which the other substantially transformative process—toasting—occurs. As this unlocks and develops substantial flavor components inherent in the eventual barrel, it is treated in chapter 5, "Flavors from Wood" (also taking into account its more general use in connection with wine and spirits). Similarly, the actual construction of the barrel is covered more completely in chapter 2, "Cooperage."

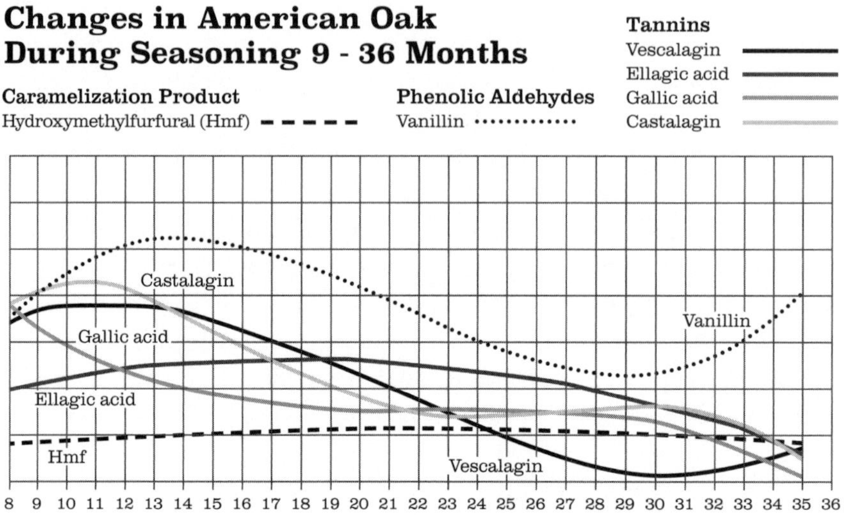

Changes in American Oak During Seasoning 9 - 36 Months

Tannins
Vescalagin ———————
Ellagic acid ———————

Caramelization Product
Hydroxymethylfurfural (Hmf) ― ― ― ―

Phenolic Aldehydes
Vanillin ·············

Gallic acid ———————
Castalagin ———————

Castalagin
Gallic acid
Ellagic acid
Vanillin
Hmf
Vescalagin

8 9 10 11 12 13 14 15 16 17 18 19 20 21 22 23 24 25 26 27 28 29 30 31 32 33 34 35 36

Figure 3.4—This chart illustrates the rise and fall of various wood components during the drying process. Chart courtesy of the Independent Stave Company.

Vessels of Wood—About the Size of It

There was a gradual standardization of barrel sizing during the middle ages, bringing the towns of a region into alignment in order to keep overall costs down and make pricing of contents comprehensible. Still, Europe has always been composed of many regions. The standard English barrel, decreed in 1543, was a different size from the north German standard Rostock barrel, and the Delft barrel, used in most of Holland, was another size as well. Even today, between the two preeminent wine regions of France, Burgundy and Bordeaux, a difference in standard barrel size exists (228 and 225 liters, respectively), with general differences in shape and toasting treatment as well. For all movement toward standardization, in fact, myriad barrel sizes and types exist today in various use and reference. Schahinger (1992), himself referring to the 1963 *Lexique de la Vigne et du Vin,* provides a list of common sizes, types, and measures:

- *Alsace*—Large oval foeders.
- Barrel (US) 190 liter/50 gallon—Used in the whiskey and bourbon industry in the United States. American wines used these barrels for a time in the 1980s when there was a decline in the bourbon trade.
- *Barrica Bordelesa* (Spain Rioja)—225 liter, modeled after *barrique.*
- *Barrique* (Bordelaise) or Château in Bordeaux area—225 liter/59

gallon. 93 cm/37" high, staves only 2 cm/0.8" thick, but export version may be lower and thicker. This cask has become a world standard for wine. Traditionally manufactured with wooden crossbars on the heads and a top and a racking bung. Often chestnut hoops were used, but functionally these are now of metal, with chestnut relegated to decoration. In 1866 the volume was standardized to 225 liter instead of between 215 and 230 liter. The 900-liter Tonneau is still used as a measure for trade in Bordeaux, as four barriques or 100 cases of wine, but this large cask does not exist anymore.

- *Barrique* (Cognac) 205 liter—According to Robinson (2006) now 350 liter.
- *Botti* (Italy)—400 liter, mostly made from Slavonian oak.
- *Bourgogne* or *pièce* (Burgundy)—228 liter, low and squat barrel made to go through narrow doorways with a deeper bilge to collect more lees. The staves are usually 2.7 cm thick. Traditional chestnut or black painted iron hoops. French oak, 265-liter casks with burgundy heads and Bordeaux staves.
- *Butt* (Cherry or American oak)—490 liter, later used in whiskey production for more rounding and sweetness.
- *Carato* is sometimes used for a barrique in Italy.
- *Caratelli*—Used for a smaller wooden cask in Italy. Can be between 50 and 225 liter.
- *Champagne*—205 liter, but the few houses still doing barrel fermentation now also use Burgundy barrels.
- *Demi-muid*—600 liter, in *Châteauneuf-du-Pape*.
- *Feuillette*—132 liter, or something more than half of the Burgundy *pièce*. Used in Chablis. Quite rare now, but still the unit for sales prices.
- *Fuder* (Germany)—1000 liter, with 500-liter *Halbfuder* along the Mosel.
- *Halbstück* (Germany)—600 liter.
- *Hogshead* (UK)—300 liter.
- *Lambic* barrel—A 200-liter stubby.
- *Leaguer* (South Africa)—277 liter.
- *Pipe* (Portugal)—522 liter, made from French, American, and Portuguese oak.
- *Puncheon*—475 liter, or 450–500 liter according to Robinson (2006).
- *Quartercask*—160 liter.
- *Quartaut*—57 liter, used primarily for topping up in some *domaines* in the *Côte d'Or*. In this area they also use a specific *feuillette* of 114 liter.

- *Stück* (Germany)—1200 liter, with 600-liter *Halbstück* in use along the Rhine.
- *Tini*—A larger upstanding cask in Italy.
- *Viertelstück* (Germany)—300 liter.

A vast number of other sizes are mentioned in various other sources (Lange 1894, Southby 1889). In addition, staves were made to different thickness. In England three different thickness standards are described as Stout, Intermediate, and Slight, with Stout being thickest for four different-sized barrels: hogsheads, barrels, kilderkins, and firkins (Wright 1897). He also mentions some slight differences concerning hoops, where the slight *kilderkins* have six hoops and stronger *kilderkins* only four.

You'll note that beer barrels are not mentioned in the above, mainly wine-oriented list. Considerations for their production, handling, and use are different, owing to the need to maintain carbonation, the frequency and roughness with which they were moved, and the fact that contents needed to be tapped for service. Staves, heads, and hoops are sturdier, there is a rounder, more pronounced bilge, and different machinery was employed in its construction. In addition, it is generally fitted with a brass bung for tapping, and lined with pitch in order to better hold pressure. Wood insulated and kept contents cool more effectively than the steel that replaced it, and required somewhat specialized cellar treatment to maintain proper levels of humidity. All of these factors of construction and intent make the humble beer barrel something unique and exotic, and in modern times essentially extinct, beyond some manufactured in Germany still used for serving beer in Dortmund and at some of the beer halls in Munich and Bamberg. There were two US types of beer barrel, one made of quartered white oak and another, patented as the Mullen Beer Barrel (US patent 2291980), made of bonded plywood (Hankerson 1947).

Barrels used for aging, transport, and dispensing are only part of the story where wood vessels and cooperage are concerned. In fact, a whole artisanal hierarchy existed for coopers and their relative levels of craft. First were the dry coopers, making containers for the shipment of dry goods such as nails, tobacco, fruits, and vegetables. These were not required to hold liquid. A step up were the dry-tight coopers, producing barrels able to keep dry materials such as flour and sugar, before they came to be packed in sacks, from taking on moisture from outside or allowing passage of vermin. White coopers worked in the pale woods that gave their subdivision its name, beech, willow, and fir, mainly to produce tubs, buckets, and churns—vessels that would hold liquid but weren't intended for shipping. And then the tight coopers did the fine work of producing barrels for beverages. At the top of the ranks were—and still are—the foudrieres, making the large and exacting wooden tanks used for the mainly air-tight aging of fine wines, spirits, and beer. As we've observed in chapter 2, these come in a variety of sizes and orientations, upright and horizontal, round and oval, cylindrical and tapering.

Vessels for brewing came out of the cooper's shop, as well, the simplest among them the open-topped tuns used for mashing and lautering, but also for fermentation, as at Pilsner Urquell in the Czech Republic, but also in the whiskey distilleries of Scotland, Kentucky, and elsewhere. These are still in common use for spirits production, and when encountered in the brewhouse are most often lined with mild or stainless steel. Peter saw some foeders being cut in half at the Bonny Doon winery near Santa Cruz, California, their bottoms to be used for open fermentation and their tops as hot tubs. In any case, after protracted use, the influence of wood on the flavor of finished beer, wine, or spirits would have reduced to nil. Foeders and other tuns are finding increasing use, of course, among American craft brewers for primarily aging and to some extent fermenting beer, though there is certainly further American and European contemporary precedent at such breweries as August Schell's in New Ulm, Minnesota; at Boon in Lembeek, Belgium, and other lambic producers; and at Greene King in Bury St. Edmunds, Suffolk, for the aging of their 5X strong ale. Like other beers aged in the rarified confines of wooden tuns, the 5X is also blended down to produce a range of products, including Strong Suffolk Ale. Rudy Ghequire, brewmaster at Rodenbach, suggests that Eugene Rodenbach visited Greene King prior to the most substantial expansions at his brewery in Roeselare.

Curiosities and Anachronisms—Other Wooden Vessels Used in Brewing

We've alluded once or twice to the Nordic hollow log traditionally used for mashing and lautering Scandinavian and Finnish beers. Sahti is the beverage most commonly associated with it, but it has historically been used in many northern countries in the production of rustic beers on a farmhouse scale. These days it also sees use by Paul Arney, brewer and owner of Ale Apothecary outside of Bend, Oregon. With it he brews one of his standard beers, Sahati, a Nordic play on the name of his flagship beer, Sahalie, itself in turn named after his daughter. As per variegated tradition, it incorporates spruce into the matrix of mash and layered materials for runoff. His is also fitted with wheels for mobility and display.

Quite a few accounts of this process exist, with certain elements variously stressed and the array of preferences as to woods, straws, and other materials in general keeping with idiosyncratic farmhouse procedure. The Norwegian ethnographer Odd Nordland offers one such account, mentioning twigs, straw, and horsehair used for lautering, with the eventual innovative addition of juniper twigs, which would of course also contribute flavor. Often sticks of alder were placed first in the trough, but hazel, willow, spruce, and rowan were also sometimes used in its place. Barley straw for the top layer was moistened in a hot decoction of juniper, with further flavor mentions of caraway, St. John's Wort, and Hypericum. Other accounts generally agree:

> "Then sticks had to be placed on the bottom of the vat. I used to go to the woods to fetch these sticks on the day they were to be used. They had to be alder. They were whittled flat on two sides, so that they were about 3 cm thick. The sticks were put over the whole base of the vat, with about 2 cm between them. A second row of sticks was laid on top of the first, at right angles to the sticks below, so that small openings of about 1–2 cm were formed. On top of the sticks juniper was put, and clean, washed barley straw on top of that. The layer had to be so thick that the grain was kept back."

—Jan Gelden, Årnal, Sogn, and Fjordane

Completely different in construction, geography, and stage of brewing procedure is the Burton Union system of primary fermentation once in common use in Yorkshire in the North of England. Sadly, the unions are now mostly gone, with the one long in use at the Bass brewery in Burton-on-Trent now relegated to display as a cultural relic alongside its parking lot (shades of Richard III indeed). Happily, the one at Marston's, also in Burton, is still making beer. We mention all this here since the primary vessels of fermentation are wooden barrels.

The system at Marston's links upwards of two dozen barrels of vaguely super-puncheon size (around 144 UK gallons, or 650-ish liters) into which inoculated wort is run for ensuing primary fermentation. As fermentation becomes sufficiently active, yeast and beer are forced upward through the barrels' bungs and out copper "swan's neck" tubes to fall into a trough open to the air, from which it is reintroduced into the barrels below. This method, of course, allows the influences of exposure to air, which certainly includes a microfloral element, and enacts a general blending of common contents throughout the line of barrels. The system was devised following the age of larger, single-vessel industrial production of traditional porters, when the paler and hoppier beers of England's north assumed prominence. The wood for the fermenting barrels was traditionally made from Lithuanian Memel oak, but by the time of a refurbishment at Marston's in the early 1990s the supply was shifted to forests between Frankfurt and Heidelberg, in Germany, and fashioned at Buckley's, a 200-year-old cooperage housed in an old cotton mill in Dukinfield, near Manchester (Jackson 1992).

Another, similar system was used in London, at the Whitbread and Godings breweries (and no doubt others), employing ranks of upright barrels from which yeast and fermenting wort was allowed to escape through individual spillways not unlike those used in Bavarian wheat beer breweries, to be captured in a trough for reintroduction. This construct was referred to as the Ponto system, probably somehow related to the word pontoon. It is referred to in the 1911 edition of *The Encyclopedia Britannica*. Inspiration for the Ponto system crossed the Atlantic, and is chronicled as having been used at the John Taylor and Sons Brewery in Albany, New York. The barrels are shown as straight-sided and tapering upward, and were of cedar. The following account, reproduced in Martyn Cornell's Zythophile website from December 24, 2009, describes it:

"Perhaps the most remarkable feature of Taylor's Brewery is to be found in the pontoon room. Standing on an elevated platform at one end of the vast apartment, the eye of the spectator passes over three hundred and sixty five white cedar vessels or pontoons, capable of holding twenty six hundred barrels, placed in regular order and divided into five sets. Between them wooden troughs are arranged which carry off the yeast as it purges from the new-made ale contained in them undergoing the process of cleansing. From each pontoon the creamy yeast, crowned with foam reminding one of white-capped billows, slowly pours itself into the receiving troughs. Heretofore this refining process was effected solely by hand, a slovenly and dirty process which, until this pontoon apparatus was introduced by Mr. Taylor in his present brewery, was the only one employed in this country. Even now the expense necessary for making the change deters many breweries from adopting the new and more perfect and cleaner process."

It may be interesting to the modern reader to note the pride of supposed purification of the yeast in such systems, knowing as we do that exposure to the air, while not necessarily bad, could only have increased adulteration. Perhaps it was considered that trub was drawn off by the process, or that yeast was isolated either by flocculation along the way or for top collection.

The Firestone-Walker Brewery in Paso Robles, California, also employs a union system, but with some variation from its Burton antecedents. Its barrels are smaller—standard 60-gallon wine barrels—and they are of medium toast, influencing flavor of the beer mainly destined for Firestone-Walker's DBA beer, which is a 20% blend, but a couple of other beers as well. In addition, the barm is kept from the air and reintroduced by a closed system, eliminating inconsistencies of outside influence. Beer is kept in the union for six days, where at Marston's it is only three, and in both cases the beer is then run to stainless for aging and blending. Firestone is, in general, committed to a substantial portion of its production to fermentation and aging in wood, both at its production facility in Paso Robles and at its Barrelworks, down the road in Buellton, overseen by Jim Crooks and Jeffers Richardson.

It's difficult to know where to draw lines of procedure, origin, manufacture, influence, and suitability where wood and beer is concerned. Elements of one necessarily spill over into another, and as time passes further lines are both drawn and effaced. Wood has had its place in the centuries-old traditions of brewing, winemaking, and spirits production, and these days the lines between those traditions are blurring. Brewers are borrowing from techniques of winemaking and distilling, and the favor is being returned, with single-hop-varietal spirits and hopped and smoked ciders and meads fermented and aged in barrels. It's perhaps of note that winemaking has so far been far less influenced by the worlds of beer and spirits than the reverse. In any case, the willingness of craft brewers to experiment and embrace the intriguing—wherever it comes from—has come to be a defining element of our movement. We'll no doubt see more of this as we continue our explorations of wood and beer.

4

Wood Maintenance

I conic and beautiful, defined both by its function and the constituent properties of the wood of which it's made and the specific treatments it has received in the course of manufacture, the barrel can seem daunting, even mystical. To the brewer contemplating its second use it is somewhat antithetical to customary sterile practice, often arriving wet, even sloshing with residual ingredients. Decisions bold and timid can be made—whether to clean at all before filling or to clean as much as possible within ordinary rigor. In any case, risks can be accommodated to get underway with one's own modest wood program. But what if a barrel leaks, or becomes damaged? An awful lot of used barrels do leak when received and filled by brewers; in many cases they've come a long way and seen hard use. What if an off-flavor or aroma develops in the course of repeated use? Without a lot of experience this can give one pause. Isn't it safest and easiest just to chalk such mishap up to education, to let the barrel in question go and move on to the next one with the benefit of possibly having learned something?

Well, sure. It's always easiest to move on. But commitment of any kind demands patience, tolerance, and a willingness to put oneself out there just a bit. The brewer took a chance back at the outset (right?) by allowing this sloppy, non-sterile vessel into his or her brewery in the first place. Not to minimize the importance of 50-odd gallons of production in this age of burgeoning teensy breweries, but it is only beer. Most of us can make it tolerably well. But the use of barrels managed properly—or even a bit haphazardly—can result in something with a unique and extra dimension. Besides, barrels these days are getting hard to come by. And they can be expensive. It's worth a little extra work and intellectual effort to keep them in the production stream, to address compromise and reclamation. Most of cooperage, after all, involves the repair and rejuvenation of old barrels. Not to at least learn about what can be done is to miss out on a whole realm of the fun.

In this chapter we will address the assessment and maintenance of wood, from the contemplation of acquisition and the wisdom of devising a workable storage system to the disassembly and refurbishing of barrels needing more than a rinse to be brought back into line. We will sniff and look into mirrors, hammer, scrape, wash and sulfur, chisel, plug, knock down, and raise up—all in the course of bringing the barrels and foeders that cross our paths up to the standards required for their productive and ongoing use in the brewery. We will also move them around, emptying and refilling them, giving them a home designed to bring out all their best aspects and to minimize those that are best suited to making vinegar. Along with a few specialized tools some courage is required. We know much of what it takes to be brewers and cellar people. Can we be coopers?

Cellar Design—From Zero to Infinity (and Beyond)

Most brewers getting started on a wood beer program begin with a barrel or two, stowed wherever most out of the path of normal operations. Mostly, in fact, they are placed right in the way of front-of-house business, between tables and right next to the bar, there for the world to see, a bit of collateral ambience often deemed at least as important as what may or may not be going on inside the barrel. Depends who you talk to. In any case, to refer to the resting place of a handful of barrels as a cellar is a bit of an overstatement. But it's been the way that most of us started in wood—a few barrels falling in our path and the determination to learn what to do with them.

In contrast with the past of even 10 years ago, most breweries these days begin operations with a plan to do something with beer in wood, and many design a cellar or barrel room into their premises. According to stat maven Bart Watson of the Brewers Association, 85.5% of all US breweries these days do something with wood and beer. The barrel-slinging pioneers of that earlier time can be ticked off on the fingers of a couple of hands—Todd Ashman of Flossmoor Station and FiftyFifty, Tomme Arthur of Pizza Port, Vinnie Cilurzo of Russian River, Matt Brynildson of Goose Island and Firestone Walker, Rob Tod, Jason Perkins, and the crew at Allagash, Will Meyers at Cambridge Brewing, Ron Jeffries of Jolly Pumpkin, and, of course, Peter and his core duo of Lauren and Eric Salazar at New Belgium. There are others, to be sure, and these are the people who led the way in American craft, borrowing techniques and practical know-how from the wine and spirits industries, as well as from the time-honored practices of European brewing exemplars, inspiring the rest of us to emulate the eye-opening beers they were able to produce. It is thanks to them that craft breweries these days are designating substantial space and attention to roomy, temperature- and humidity-controlled cellars, sometimes large enough to hold thousands of barrels, or forests of foeders.

For if the soaring fermentation tanks and stolid and sleekly functional brewhouses of the best of craft and industry are brewing's beautiful cathedrals, its classic cellars are the basilicas of an earlier, earthier form of worship. Not to flog the churchy imagery too much, but the snaking passages of the old gypsum mine through which some 5,000 bourbon barrels are cycled each year by Founders Brewing in Grand Rapids, Michigan, is reminiscent of the Roman catacombs employed by clandestine early Christians. Inspiration comes from other quarters, as well: The subterranean rotunda at Chateau Lafite Rothschild is a privilege to enter, organized into radiating rings of some 2,000 barrels of legendary first-growth claret beneath gentle and mildly mossy arches; the cellars of the KWV winery in Paarl, South Africa, with its beautifully sculpted horizontal foeders presented in a worshipful setting; similarly, the million-liter foeder standing sentry in its own room at the apéritif manufacturer Byrrh in Thuirs, France, looking for all the world like the weapon of mass destruction of some nineteenth-century steampunk supervillain. Add the cellars of red-banded foeders at the Rodenbach brewery in Roeselare, Belgium, receding from the visitor in ranks seeming in addition to offer a lesson in vanishing point perspective, and the warm and fragrant barrel houses in Kentucky's bourbon country, stacked high and wide. These are the sites of cellaring's pilgrimage road, places to stand in geeky awe of the wonders of wood.

Organization and Inventory

More prosaic than the mystical stirring stick of temperature, humidity, and the various x-factors of ambiance and urging generally associated with bringing along fabulous barrel-aged beer, simply putting together a system of organization for your cellar is a step not to be underestimated. The combination of space and time required for barrel aging necessarily results in a low output per square meter, and efficiency of storage must be balanced with the need for occasional access. Visitors to the Allagash Brewery of a number of years ago in Portland, Maine, were shown a barrel room stacked both high and deep with barrels filled with various beers, in varying states of age and readiness. To reach any given barrel buried somewhere within, it was admitted, could take as long as a day of forklifting, removing, and replacing. But this is what can happen when a brewer is bitten by the bug of barrel aging. An odd space given over to a few orderly racks can quickly become jammed, layered and virtually inaccessible. Space can't be created out of thin air, of course, but some foresight in layout and—it must be said—safety should at least have a voice in plotting what can realistically be done. Allagash, by the way, has since taken steps to address these issues.

Since they've been mentioned, let's begin with racks. When New Belgium purchased its first nine barrels in 1997—yeah, 1997!—even Peter didn't know from barrel racks. They slapped together 8-foot lengths of 2x10 and chiseled the depressions into which the vessels of their "cellar" nestled. If a barrel needed to be lifted or moved, it was with the aid of a lever, ropes, and two hooks, along with the careful effort of a few people. Peter's inspiration for this contraption may have been the logo for the Belgian brewer Alken-Maes, depicting a common method to lower barrels into the cellars of pubs, and, in fact, there's further historical precedent for loading barrels into the holds of boats using slings in a similar arrangement (Hankerson 1947). Less than a year later, while taking a course in barrel repair at Barrel Builders in Calistoga, California, Peter and his associate Robert Poland were astonished to discover that such things as barrel racks existed, each configured to hold a pair of standard-size barrels and easily forklift-able and made to be stacked. They bought a whole truckload of barrels to augment their modest cellar of (by this time) 12 barrels, along with sufficient racks for the whole lot. We could say that the rest is history, but that would be taking a shortcut.

While some store barrels stacked on top of each other and restrained only by chocks, it's far safer to use racks. Even as venerable a figure as Armand Debelder of Drie Fonteinen in Beersel was using the chocking method as recently as 2014,

Figure 4.1—Armand Debelder, *geuzesteker* at Drei Fonteinen stacks barrels in the basement with brewers. Note the chain and hooks hanging on the wall that are normally used to carry the barrels.

and, in fact, this practice is widespread among Belgium's lambic brewers, often in cellars with brick floors that do not accommodate a forklift or a pallet jack. When stacking without a rack a sort of pyramid arrangement suggests itself, with barrels in the upper layer settled between those below to spread weight and nominally hold in place, at the same time allowing space to get to the bunghole for transfers. Racks can be stacked in more stable multiple layers with the aid of a forklift (if you have a forklift, that is). Of course, they can be stacked in place by hand and then filled, but until emptied they are captive, and if leaks arise the only alternatives are to repair or transfer contents. Adapters exist for placement of a single barrel on a rack ordinarily intended for two. Racks also require a level floor for use, but it's difficult in any case to imagine much of a cellar existing on a slope. Vinnie Cilurzo of Russian River Brewing reminds us that there are actually a few different types of barrel racks, not entirely compatible with each other. Be sure to commit to consistency both for ease of use and safety.

Other methods exist, of course, such as that used at Chateau Mouton Rothschild in Pauillac, Bordeaux, involving the use of two raised concrete rails, along which barrels are rolled, in one side of the cellar and out the other side for emptying. We also saw a similar method used at Woodford Reserve distillery in Versailles, Kentucky, a rail system to transfer barrels from the filling station to the storehouses. The typical bourbon distillery method of long-term storage is worth mention, though not so much because it has applications for the average brewery. A separate rack structure is built to accommodate as many as several independent layers, often tied into the structure of the building, in order to make barrels theoretically more accessible and to eliminate the load on the barrels on lower layers. In such a setting the barrels manage to look effortlessly placed, but keep in mind that they must be rolled in and laid to rest with all bungs upward. Cascade Barrel House in Portland, Oregon, had a similar, if much smaller, system, with some racks freestanding. Wynkoop Brewing in Denver, Colorado, solved the dilemma of public display and practical use by building wheeled barrel carts from 2x4s that could be moved from its dining room to its cellars for the dirty work. While upright storage of barrels exposes greater liquid surface area to possible oxidation, some breweries have tried this, such as Crane Brewing in Raytown, Missouri, which waxes the heads and chimes to minimize leakage and penetration by air, and New Holland Brewing in Holland, Michigan, which stores its Dragon's Milk Stout for upwards of five months in stacks of pallets for maximum use of space. Similar to the upright barrel is the upright foeder, though with the volumes concerned proportionally less beer is allowed to come in contact with interior air, and especially if, as in many cases, the tank ceilings are bulged upward. Complete filling can also be aided by standpipes or other vents, including manways, or by placement along a slight incline as at Rodenbach and New Belgium. Horizontal foeders can be stored on big I-frame structures as they are at Boon Brewery in Lembeek, Belgium.

It should be mentioned that anywhere wood supporting systems are used for barrel storage, whether racks or pallets, the opportunity exists for mold and other contaminants to grow. Given the aging times devoted to maturation in barrels, as well as the need to keep things reasonably out of the way (and in many cases out of sight), such resolutions can be tantamount to asking for trouble. This also goes for some of the wood products needed in the course of barrel use and maintenance, such as bungs and reed flagging. All storage, in short, needs to constitute a reasonably mold-free environment.

We've alluded a couple of times above to the challenges of moving barrels, especially when filled, but it must be acknowledged that most small breweries don't have forklifts, or, for that matter, multistory keg barrel elevators such as at the old Tivoli brewery in Denver, a five-minute walk from where the Great American Beer Festival is held. Barrels are made to be rolled, of course, and while they may seem at times to have minds of their own and self-determining

Figure 4.2—Wynkoop Brewing in Denver, Colorado, solved the dilemma of public display and practical use by building wheeled barrel carts from 2x4s that could be moved from its dining room to its cellars for the dirty work.

inclinations for transit across the cellar floor, practice will be rewarded (reference the ease with which we all twirl half-barrel kegs on edge across floors and sidewalks). They are also made to be tipped upright, if necessary, by the efforts of a single person, though standard caution in lifting should be taken. Ramps can help in placing barrels in their spots of repose; though, as observed, some planning and experience may be necessary to ensure that once barrels are situated bungholes are facing upward. It should also be pointed out that as the bung stave is the weakest part of the barrel, care should be taken not to drop the barrel on it (or at all, to be obvious, but it happens). Foam cushions are sometimes placed as a safeguard, akin to the keg pads or car tires many of us have used in the course of day-to-day delivery. We saw an enormous one of these at Dalwhinnie Distillery in Scotland.

The moving of foeders is a subject on a whole different scale, of course. Invariably moved empty, care must still be taken for fork or hook placement and gentleness of lift and drop in order not to flex the overall structure too much. Horizontal foeders can be moved as barrels if the bottom pipe is removed. Foeders can be lifted from the top beam of the foeder or they can be picked up from the bottom. The forklift beam should be long enough to reach under all support beams if lifted from the bottom. Small foeders typically only have two beams, but larger foeders can have many more. The wood support beams should be perpendicular to and support all bottom staves. The forks of the fork-lift should support those beams to keep the integrity of the foeder. Ratchet straps should be used to tie the foeder to the horizontal part of the forks, so the whole foeder does not tip over when braking or going downhill. Put some cardboard between the ratchet straps and the foeder to protect your cute asset. Of course, the foeder should be light enough for the rating of the forklift, taking the center of gravity of the foeder into account. A dry foeder could use an extra ratchet strap around the foeder to keep it together. Staves should be numbered, so that when the whole thing falls apart you are able to reconstruct it easily. This can be particularly worrisome with dried-out foeders. A forklift, sometimes with extended forks, can be used with smaller foeders, though if hung from forks an extension may be necessary to allow them to hang free. For larger foeders a crane is generally required, preferably with a crane crew, unless your brewery has a maintenance department able to tackle such projects. Keep a pallet with timber and a manual jack around if you have to shuffle the foeder into the right orientation and right place in tight spots.

Sometimes vertical foeders need to be shipped horizontally to avoid special road transport. Tipping foeders back up is best done with two cranes with straps choked around the whole foeder. The two cranes first lift together, and then the crane on the bottom of the foeder lowers. This was tried at New Belgium with a strap through the bunghole, with the unhappy result of breaking the bung stave. In this aspect horizontal foeders can be moved far more easily since they can be rolled around, theoretically as easily as regular barrels. A brewery door of sufficient size is also desirable, lest you are forced, like Gabe Fletcher at Anchorage Brewing in Alaska, to disassemble and put back together the foeders you've brought in for installation. We'll speak more about Gabe's technique for reassembly later.

While you may start with a collection of barrels small enough to be able to indi-vidually name them, the day will likely come when some less idiosyncratic system must be devised in order to keep track of where everything is. You'll no doubt have barrels from different sources, and this might lend itself to loose catalogu-ing, but numbering and notebooks are simple and invaluable ways to keep things straight. When huge numbers of barrels are in question something else might be required, though the thousands of barrels held at Goose Island in Chicago—begun with a whimsical half-dozen in 1992—are kept in order essentially by a system of notes and maps (and even then an indeterminate entropy is admitted—more the rule than the exception where cellars in general are concerned). The bar code system employed by many distilleries and by Boulevard Brewing in Kansas City is something almost certainly beyond the reach of most small breweries, but it can be used to call up an astonishing array of data, including not only dates of fill and placement but of information as to barrel manufacture, even perhaps to the trees from which it was made. We are partial to the system used by Founders Brewing Co. in Grand Rapids, Michigan, employing 8½x11 color photocopies stapled to each barrel for reference by batch and type for the use of personnel not always supremely well versed in what it is they're moving around. One series bore pictures of old Detroit Red Wings greats, another, Detroit Tigers; others were devoted to wrestlers, rappers, and Pam Grier. The order to the storage facility employee to remove 50 of "Project Pam"—the one where she's wearing the Native American headdress—is something not likely to be misunderstood.

Figure 4.3—Founders Brewing Co. uses a system for labeling barrels by attaching 8½x11 color photocopies to each barrel for reference by batch and type. This barrel features rapper Sir Lucious Leftfoot. Previous barrels were identified by Detroit Red Wings greats, wrestlers, and Pam Grier in full headdress.

Cellar Ambiance—Temperature,
Humidity, and Other Factors

Traditionally—in Germany and other seats of classic lager brewing, anyway—cellars were caves carved into the earth by a combination of geologic time and human ingenuity. Temperatures were constant—generally somewhere below 12°C—as was humidity, and casks of lager beer, often lined with pitch, could be stored through the warmer months of the year for later release. The extensive cellars at Pilsner Urquell in the Czech Republic are testament today of the endurance of such methods, as are the cellars still maintained by many of the breweries in Bamberg, Germany, dug into the hilly outskirts of town, some of them with nice bucolic beer gardens to complement the scene. Brewers in the United States, as well, employed such methods, with the large breweries of St. Louis tunneling beneath the city for storage and maturation space, and August Schell in New Ulm, Minnesota, still using its cave cellars. The museum at August Schell also displays pictures of townspeople harvesting ice from the river for use in keeping the brewery cellars cold, and still today breweries are sometimes providers of local ice, such as at Namibia Breweries in the middle of the beautiful Namib Desert. Newer breweries have also adapted local caves and mines for beer storage, such as at Boulevard in Kansas City, and in the defunct gypsum mine in Grand Rapids, Michigan (already mentioned), where Founders stores thousands of barrels, artificially cooled to 3°C 100 feet underground. Historically, buildings were sometimes constructed to keep barrels cool with ice stored on the floor above. Somewhat related was the unfortunate collapse of the cellars of the old Rainier Brewery in South Seattle when, on its decommissioning, the matrix of frost holding the whole thing together was allowed to melt.

In addition to hampering the rampant growth of potentially harmful microorganisms, cool cellar temperatures encourage stability in the liquids concerned. It isn't an infallible shield, however. Not to suggest alarm, but Founders has encountered *Lactobacillus* even in the marked coolness of its mine storage facility. In the bourbon industry temperature fluctuations are embraced, as the resultant rise and fall causes expansions and contractions that allow the whiskey to penetrate deeper into the wood, and then correspondingly recede, resulting in further extraction of oak color and flavor. The early "cellar" at Pizza Port in Solana Beach, California, was, in fact, outdoors, behind the brewery, shaded from the sun, but subject to the sometimes-marked fluctuation in ambient temperature in generally summery San Diego.

This method isn't particularly recommended for just this reason, but many of the beers thus produced at Pizza Port were idiosyncratic and delicious, a mile marker in the education of us all. Alpine Brewing, also in the San Diego area, stores barrels outside, as well. Head over to Arizona Wilderness Brewing in Gilbert, Arizona, and you'll see barrels and its single foeder stored in a temperature-controlled area, and at Green Bench Brewing in St. Petersburg, Florida, a cooling jacket is used to temper fermentation in its foeder, with the room cooled to appropriate temperature for souring.

Along somewhat less vertiginous lines, lambic brewers also welcome seasonal fluctuation in temperature. As they brew only during the cooler months and age their beers for years, lower temperatures early in the process encourage the inoculation and growth of mainly desirable native microflora for slow fermentation without too many bugs taking hold. Subsequent warmer aging enables a sequence of dominance by initially less forceful bacteria, and provides a fortuitous ambiance for the introduction of fruit to the fermentation. Ron Jeffries at Jolly Pumpkin is careful to stack his barrels and place his foeders only so high, in order to avoid the warmer temperatures closer to the ceiling of his facility in Dexter, Michigan. The cellar keepers at Rodenbach are careful not to let temperatures drop below 15°C, employing steam-heated coils when things cool by even a few degrees. It all depends, of course, on the yeasts and other cultures under consideration and the flavors desired.

Practically speaking, not all of us have the capability of storing our barrels in a designated temperature-controlled facility, but as more breweries are opened with barrel rooms as part of the initial concept, such things are becoming more commonplace. The familiar scenario of a few barrels sitting out, wherever, will almost necessarily result in substantial seasonal temperature fluctuation and all that can come with it, good and bad. Smaller barrels, of course, are subject to the most frequent and precipitous change, although the wood itself acts as insulation. We all learn the vagaries of our spaces to hand, of course, and can generally identify places most appropriate for nominally cooler storage. Sometimes warm (roughly 53°F/12°C) cellars on an approximately English model can be just the thing. We are all accustomed to working with what we've got and improving where we can. Results will speak louder than technically parsed procedure.

From the time a tree is felled to the time finished barrels are received for use, the moisture content of the wood is falling by stages. At Brown-Forman's cooperage in Louisville, for example, logs arrive carrying as much as 65% of their weight as moisture. Once cut and aged four to six weeks, moisture has dropped to 20%, and further aging and drying drops this figure into the teens. A delivered new barrel should contain around a 16% moisture component, and pains should be taken not to let this quantum drop by further drying. Hence, time is of the essence in the commissioning of barrels once they are received, and humidity must be maintained even as beer is aging in them. Ambient humidity is something we are often dealt by geography, of course, and some climates are harder on wood than others. The dampness of Seattle, for example, might seem better suited to the easy maintenance of barrels than the dryness of Colorado, but there are also limits: Ambient moisture of above 85% can foster bacterial growth. Hence, a balance must be achieved. The ideal cellar should be humid enough to maintain equilibrium with filled barrels. If it is too dry liquid will be lost; too moist and bacteria will be allowed to grow, and perhaps even take control. Balance can be achieved through the use either of humidification or dehumidification systems. The following chart displays ideal balances of temperature and humidity for the cellar.

Cellar temperature	Recommended humidity	Very risky humidity threshold
10°C	72-85%	<64%
15°C	73-85%	<66%
30°C	75-85%	<68%

A barrel will absorb or give off moisture as it finds equilibrium within its atmosphere. Water is a smaller molecule than alcohol, and so will migrate more readily through wood. Conversely, increasing amounts of alcohol in solution will reduce the surface tension of the liquid, allowing easier penetration through even the tiniest passages in wood, such as pores and sap channels, as well as any gaps caused by damage or infestation. Both water and ethanol are polar solvents and can slowly dissolve wood components and bring them into solution, especially when aided by *Brettanomyces*. Black mold *(Baudoinia compniacensis)* and a disproportionate "angel's share"—the term given to the rate of evaporation of water and alcohol—can be hazards in cellars of high humidity, with more alcohol than water evaporating. Other more benign but spookier-looking molds—sometimes even a couple of meters long—can fur and festoon the relatively undisturbed cellars such as those of Burgundy, Bordeaux, and Napa Valley. These are generally *Penicillium* and *Cladosporium*, and can easily be wiped away, but are daunting to discover (witness Peter's experience as recounted later in this chapter). The sawn ends of staves are the places in a barrel or foeder most likely to leak and lose moisture. This condition can be remedied by the use of food-grade, watertight paint or epoxy applied on the stave ends, along the chime. It can be striking how quickly stave ends will swell back to a desirable plumpness once this problem is remedied.

Mention of the holes left by wood-boring insects as possible sources of leaks begs at least touching on infestation in general, as it can compromise both the general tightness of any wooden vessel and the cleanliness and soundness of the cellar. Wood-borers will leave little piles of wood dust as remnants of their activity, which can accumulate on the floor beneath the barrel or on hoops situated beneath their holes.

Fruit flies and wood-boring insects are both indications of cleaning left wanting and harbingers of possible contamination. Even snails can be an issue under damp conditions.

Ventilation can be a factor, as well. One volume of exchange per day should be sufficient, unless factors such as excessive CO_2 or sulfuring are present. While a stuffy and completely closed cellar may pose confinement issues for humans, barrels themselves, and their contents, are not necessarily at all unhappy under such conditions.

Inspecting New Barrels, and Barrels New to You

Few brewers buy new, unused barrels. We are most often eager to riff on what was in them before they came into our hands, to combine the flavors of our beer with remnants of whiskey, wine, port, spirits, or even other beer that might remain. Used barrels are also far less expensive than new. A new barrel, however, can provide a clean and oaky slate, appropriate for the right project where such flavors are deemed desirable. More options exist when buying barrels new. How many hoops would you like? How thick and what type would you like them to be? Any special interior treatments, such as grooves or a particular degree of toast? Wouldn't your logo look fine laser-etched onto the head? Isn't this already sounding pretty expensive? French barrels are generally made more by hand than those for the American bourbon industry, which, technically, are produced for a single use and are often manufactured in larger quantities and by more automated techniques. Bourbon barrels are also dried for shorter periods of time, and tend to be thinner. You can get whatever you like as long as you're willing to pay for it.

Even new barrels warrant careful inspection on delivery. Just because they're new doesn't mean something couldn't have happened to them in shipping, or in storage. Obvious things to look for are any signs of having received rough treatment—scuffs, scrapes, dents, or cracks. The exterior surfaces should be smooth, and hoops tightly placed. There should be no gaps between the staves, of course, but you never know—they may have been shipped on a hot truck, or spent days in the desert. If they are wrapped in plastic, leave them there until you are truly ready to use them, as this provides protection from UV rays and retains innate moisture. The cooperages of Zemplén in Hungary and Kelvin in Kentucky both recommend storage at 18°C and 75% humidity. Remember, also, that even new barrels can be subject to dampness in shipping; a good sniff in the bung should disclose the presence of any contaminating mold.

Used barrels have been around the block, which is one reason we like them, provided that block is in a nice neighborhood, say, near a distillery or venerable winery. Given their history, however, whatever it is, we need to evaluate their state and get them ready for use. Most of us acquire our barrels in dribs and drabs, a few hand-me-downs here from a friend, and perhaps a handful passed on there by a friendly distillery possibly interested in a joint project. Occasionally we might find ourselves buying enough from a single source, generally a cooperage, to have sufficient leverage to specify what it is we want, and to refuse delivery should the product not measure up. This is a privilege for which we pay, of course. Breweries that deal wholesale in barrels by the thousands certainly do this. Jason Yester, who used to work at Bristol Brewing and now owns Trinity Brewing (both in Colorado Springs), once had an arrangement with his local hardware store wherein he was given first crack at the used barrels as they came in in lots, otherwise destined to be cut in half and sold as planters. Obviously, this was when demand for barrels was not as high as it is today, and before more conventional channels were regularly used by brewers. Nonetheless, it took Jason a number of years to amass a mere 20 barrels, with a rate of accumulation of only a few barrels for each 50 to 60 he inspected—that's what you have to expect if you hold out for French oak. In any case, and wherever our barrels come from, we need to assess what we might be up against in adapting them for our use.

Aside from the evaluation of obvious physical condition, probably the most important thing you can do in judging the worth of a barrel new to your possession—once you've made sure it wasn't shipped after sulfuring—is to stick your nose right into the bunghole and smell what's inside. What you should smell is the clean aroma of wood and whatever other contents used to be in there. What you shouldn't smell is mold or any other off-aroma indicating some microbiological misadventure. A funky barrel isn't necessarily a lost cause; it will simply require some steps to bring it back into line. We'll talk about that later. Still, it's tempting at this point, should you encounter something rank, to ponder the wisdom of beginning a relationship already compromised. Approach the bunghole carefully, however—sometimes even used barrels are sulfured before shipping! Wave a hand toward your nose across the opening before going all in. Since you're already assessing the interior, shine a light in there and see what you can. A dentist's mirror is an extremely useful tool for interior assessment. If it's a bourbon barrel you'll see evidence of charring. Are there blisters, either from overzealous charring or from when the staves were bent? If it's a wine barrel you may see (beyond simple staining) the presence of wine stone. This is composed of glittery tartrate crystals—the same stuff that collects on corks and at the bottoms of wine bottles over time—and is really quite pretty, but to bring the barrel into use it will need to be removed. Ditto blisters in a barrel, as both are potential harbors for bacteria. Take a breath. This will involve removing the head, pressure washing and/or scraping down to the wood, and replacing the head. Before introducing them into his barrel-army, Chad Jakobson of the Crooked Stave Artisan Beer Project removes the heads from each new conscript and takes a good look, having lost any squeamishness during his earlier work in wineries. Don't worry—we'll get to that later, too. You might even encounter a barrel lined with pitch, in which case you've got another decision to make: whether to use it as is, as it doubtless was already used, to age lagers, for example, in a nonporous vessel, or to remove the pitch. We'll touch on that later, as well.

So, now you've had a look under the hood. Let's take the used car analogy one step further and see if you can tell if your barrel has been in any accidents and how serious they were. As with any other manual, a checklist might be the best way to approach this.

- Run your hand along all the exterior surfaces of the barrel. Are the staves tightly joined, or have some been banged out of alignment? A few whacks with a rubber mallet might be enough to settle things back where they belong. Don't worry—barrels are made to take a few licks.
- Are there gaps between the staves? The barrel might have dried during shipping, or been knocked about enough to loosen the rings. This, too, is easily remedied, with a few taps of a hammer on a hoop driver. If hoops are already well-placed, avoid the temptation to ritualistically hammer or tap on them, just because. This also applies to later, ongoing inspection once barrels are full. Tomme Arthur refers to this as "whistling while you work." He does not mean it as a compliment.

- Does the barrel seem watertight as you roll it around, checking its general integrity? Have the hoops been moved? Do you see the marks of hoop driver activity? Again, tightening the hoops before or after swelling the barrel should resolve this.
- Look for lateral cracks across the bunghole. This is not uncommon and need not be cause for rejection. Nor will it necessarily leak once filled. You can still use the barrel if it seems watertight and the channel will not admit air. Check on the sides of the bunghole as well to judge the severity of any cracking—it may not go all the way through the stave.
- Are the rivets on the hoops placed in a single line? If not, this would indicate that hoops have been moved or replaced by someone without the sensibilities of an actual cooper.
- Are the hoops galvanized or coated on their edges? Given their single intra-industry use, the hoops on bourbon barrels can be entirely uncoated and subject to rust.
- Are any hoop nails in the right place? Hoop nails are not generally necessary, but if they've been used to keep hoops in place they should be tight to the edges of the hoops, and there should be no additional holes from multiple placement.
- Does the head hoop sit flush to the end of the chime? Is the chime itself intact, without hammer marks? Any marks might indicate other trouble or repairs, or by placement indicate a cracked stave at the chime or croze, or an otherwise damaged stave. Cracked staves at the croze are easiest to evaluate if the head hoop is removed. Marks can also be the result of rough handling.
- Are the heads bulged? This is rare in younger barrels, and with age some truly remarkable bulging is sometimes to be seen, such as in large barrels in lambic breweries, and when pressure mounts within during unvented aging. Though they should be tested, bulged heads do not necessarily leak, and in such venerable sites are still entrusted to hold their precious contents.
- Is the bunghole burned out? This is a cauterizing method used to seal and harden the wood and preempt potential later leaks.
- Are there any inserts inside the barrel? These include cubes, chips, and spirals, sometimes used to speed and enhance oakiness and to extend the effective life of a barrel. You'll want to remove these, even if you choose to add your own later, or even to reuse what you find after cleaning and assessment.

We got our first lot of barrels at New Belgium in 1997; we checked them out with a light and a dentist's mirror. They were full of beautiful crystals so we decided to remove those, but had never worked a small barrel like that. We bought some stainless nuts, washers, and bolts, and we sharpened the washers. We fixed two washers on every bolt in place with the nuts and we threw four of these contraptions through the bung into each barrel. Then we went about and tumbled the barrels through the grass, making sure the bolts would hit as much surface as possible. The end result was that quite a bit of the encrusted crystals were broken off and washed out with a sprayball cleaning. But it is really easier to remove the head and pressure wash when the wine stone is severe, and/or to scrape to remove the last wine stone.

—from Peter's recollections

Testing and Hydrating Barrels

When testing a new barrel, place it on its side, introduce 10–20 liters of chlorine-free, iron-free water, and pressurize to around 0.5 bar. This is generally done with a rubber bung fitted with some kind of nozzle hooked up to an air compressor. CO_2 can also be used, of course, but is a needless expense at this point in the proceedings. Rock the barrel around to test. If you don't have the compressor setup, fill the barrel all the way up with water. It should seal within an hour. Or, if you don't have easy access to mineral-free water, you can use 5 gallons (19 L) of hot (150–165°F/65–74°C) water, sealing and rolling the barrel to test for tightness. Kelvin Cooperage in Louisville recommends putting around 20 gallons (76 L) of water in the barrel, then tipping it up onto one head for 12 hours and onto the other head for an additional 12 hours. A rinse afterward and it should be ready to go.

Used barrels are iffier, of course. Assuming some compromise, they should be filled entirely with chlorine-free, iron-free water to test. Hoops may need to be tightened to help the process along, or a variation on the tipping process can be used, but with water added on top of the barrel to aid in swelling and sealing the heads, in sequence. This can result in water leaking into the barrel, with the possibility of stagnation. Smell the barrel as you are filling it with water, in order to make sure no moldy smell lingers. Empty and refill the barrel daily, tipping as necessary to completely hydrate.

Cleaning Barrels

As brewers, we are used to cleaning. It's much of what we do, but mainly takes place within the confines of stainless steel vessels. Some of us have some experience with copper. But wood is a different story, and its very nature makes it difficult to clean and sanitize. Something that is truly dirty is one thing; barrels that have been exposed to weather, for example, will need to be thoroughly cleaned. But when aging beer in barrels that have been used to contain something else, and carry some of that residue, the term dirty begins to change, even to lose relevance. If you want to mature a higher alcohol beer, say, and want to pick up some of the flavors of the previous fill of bourbon or tequila, you'll probably barely rinse the barrel, if at all. You may not even drain the excess liquid left behind. Or if you do, you might drink it. Along with flavor uptake is, of course, the almost certain incremental pickup of alcohol, which, technically speaking, can become a matter of regulation. This, of course, assumes watertightness, which is often not the case if the barrel has been empty for a time or has been shipped over a long distance, as in the case of a lot of Honduran rum barrels we have heard of, which, after traveling overland (with military escort, no less), were left to dry for weeks on the dock before shipping. To assume tightness on delivery under such circumstances is, at the very least, unrealistic.

When cleaning a barrel you have just emptied of beer, you will likely have a little sediment and perhaps some beer stone to deal with, presuming that the barrel has not been used for primary fermentation. Beer stone builds up far more slowly than the stone from wine, and is far less tenacious. A simple rinse in this case will likely suffice, but the option exists to just keep going and refill. If the barrel has been used for fermentation it will have a far greater cleaning load, with yeast, kraeusen, and barm needing to be removed, probably by the use of a sprayball, at least, and perhaps with further chemical cleaning. The latter would be most advisable should you plan to use the barrel for clean fermentation.

Sometimes the barrels have been previously filled with strongly flavored liquids, such as soy or hot sauce—this barrel thing is catching on in other industries, as well. We had a very interesting beer called Takeshi Umami Stout at Against the Grain Brewing in Louisville, a portion of which had been aged in bourbon barrels used for fermenting soy sauce. In these cases flavors can be so strong and pervasive as to require fairly thorough cleaning, and, in all likelihood, pretty judicious blending of the resultant beer later on.

The following chart shows some basic guidelines for cleaning based on previous use.

Process	Previous use	Cleaning
fermentation		spray cleaning/chemical
maturation non sour	distilled wine beer soy maple syrup	rinse? rinse rinse spray cleaning rinse?
maturation souring	OK not OK	rinse? chemical

When a barrel you've used for a time has a souring effect that you like, you'll probably want to keep this going and won't aggressively clean between fills, with perhaps only a soft rinse to remove sediment and remnants of the pellicle, the gelatinous membrane that in the course of aging will have protected the surface of the beer within the barrel from oxidation. With a Solera system, where some beer is left in the barrel in order to inoculate subsequent fermentation and aging, your only option is simply to refill and run with it. This is a system employed to delicious effect by Cambridge Brewing Company in Massachusetts, New Belgium Brewing Company in Colorado, and Sante Adairius Rustic Ales in California. Prudence would dictate careful inspection and some removal of the leavings of time in order to avoid buildup. Souring can also go wrong, and bolder cleaning might be required for reclamation of the barrel, if success under such circumstances is even possible. If things go way off you can always just burn the barrel in order to get it out of your cellar once and for all, preferably with a beer in hand. While certainly a challenge, such barrels can often be turned around and brought back into use, though Peter does recall some difficulties he once had with some 150-year-old barrels.

Apart from the fairly straightforward methods of mechanical and chemical cleaning, there are any number of ways to bring a barrel back, all the way to scraping and even re-toasting and charring the inside, either by your own efforts or by hiring out for such a service. Rinsing with beer is a far more benign and simply executed option, especially with a beer of high bitterness or high alcohol, or perhaps one made with dark malts, as all of these conditions are unfriendly to beer spoilers. The older books show barrels rotating with hot water and a chain, as you still can see at Oud Beersel and Cantillon. Hot water and steam is another option, though it can take time to reach temperatures approaching pasteurization. Goose Island in Chicago has a nifty portable ARS Enterprises steam generator with brass wands that are inserted for varying times, depending on need, into the barrels they use for their femininely-named sour program (e.g., Matilda, Sophie, Gillian), as well as for their Bourbon County Stout and Barley Wine. Jason Yester at Trinity Brewing has devised another type of wand system using a pressure cooker as a steam generator. It should be remembered that barrels so treated should be refilled right away, as the dampness of water and steam present fine conditions for mold and bacteria. Wood is also a good insulator and offers plenty of opportunity for hiding spots. Peter remembers it taking days, when he was at Rodenbach, to heat up a foeder with 5 cm thick staves to even 113°F (45°C), as measured on the outside surface. Such extended high temperatures are not good for long-term wear. Gabe Fletcher also steams the interiors of his foeders at Anchorage Brewing. If the vessel in question is to be used for clean fermentation—whether from pitched cultures or the result of spontaneous inoculation elsewhere—using steam to sterilize it is probably a good idea.

Any visitor to the public brew day at Cantillon in Brussels has probably noticed the barrel cleaning device on display, bucking and whirling as though trying to escape its continuum. Also on display are the abrasive chains that are inserted into the bunghole, flung to and fro in the course of operation, loosening any barm or other residue while still essentially respecting the interior wood. These were the devices and treatment Peter was trying to synthesize with his bolts and washers. Also traditional is the method of half-filling the barrel with boiling water, adding a handful of pebbles and rolling, rolling, rolling to similar effect. Most of us are better able to employ the simple sprayball or whirling spray nozzle, inserted upward through the bunghole and pulsed with water pressure from a pump. Not much in the way of generally available barrel cleaning machinery exists to our knowledge, but Belle-Vue in Sint-Pieters-Leeuw has a fancy setup involving a grilled false floor and a sprayball onto which a barrel can be rolled, enacted by a proximity detector to start hot water cleaning. Thonhauser, an Australian company, produces a dosing system involving high-pressure caustic and hot air that can be adapted for use with barrels.

Chemical cleaning can be mild or aggressive, depending on the challenge at hand. Should your brewery have an ozone generator for treating water for sanitation this can be a simple solution. Sodium percarbonate, soda ash, citric acid, and potassium metabisulfite are other chemical options. Sodium percarbonate

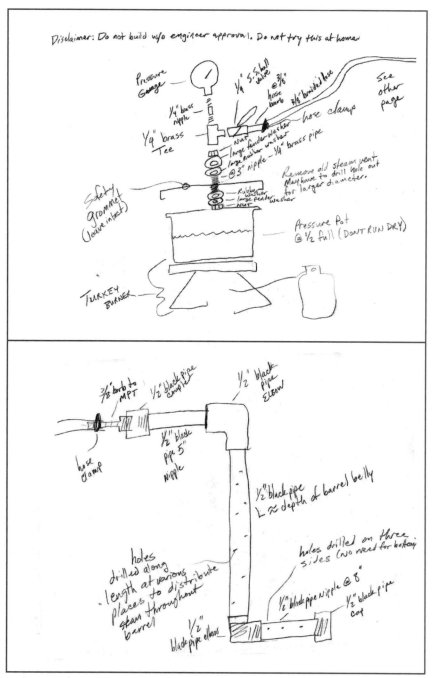

Figure 4.4—Sketches for a "clean steam machine" for barrel sterilization, as designed by Jason Yester at Trinity Brewing in Colorado Springs, Colorado.

is a mixture of sodium carbonate and hydrogen peroxide ($2Na_2CO_3$ & $3H_2O_2$) and cleans aggressively enough to eliminate wine stone buildup, as Peter saw at the Bonny Doon winery in Santa Cruz County. It can also be used to bring back tainted barrels, mixed into solution at a rate of one tablespoon per gallon of water (3.9 mL/L) and with 24-hour contact time, then rinsed and neutralized with mild citric acid. Various commercial versions exist. Soda ash, or sodium carbonate (Na_2CO_3), requires a similar process. Strong acids and chlorine-based cleaners are to be avoided when treating wood, though it is said that a 48-hour treatment of 0.5% sulfuric acid followed by a 0.5% rinse of sodium carbonate can eliminate mold. Chemical vendors can be consulted on such matters, but then you'll need to decide whether they actually know anything about barrels. In wine areas they are no doubt best informed. Remember as well to mix and dilute chemicals before their introduction into the barrel.

When not in use barrels should be stored either dry with a sulfur treatment or filled with a solution of 0.1–0.2% potassium metabisulfite (KMS). The latter might require a citric acid rinse or 0.05–0.1% citric acid to lower the pH, but opinions are mixed as to its necessity. Wineries avoid citric acid since it can promote *Brettanomyces*. Rodenbach only used 0.1% to good effect in foeders 100–655 hL, but the surface-to-volume ratio was lower than barrels. Experience indicates that as long as potassium metabisulfite is well mixed it should suffice. The Four Roses distillery stores its Red cypress and Douglas fir fermenters filled with water and lime when they sit idle over the summer. Both foeders and barrels should be visually inspected between fills, even to the extent of partial disassembly from time to time.

Sulfuring is a traditional method to hold a barrel dry when not in use or to create a nominally sterile step in the process. The most common method involves burning 10 grams of sulfur wick held inside the (225-liter) barrel. The burning consumes any oxygen inside the barrel and generates poisonous sulfur dioxide (SO_2), which sterilizes the inside surface. Sulfur dioxide gas can also be injected for 3–5 seconds to the same effect, should you have an exterior source. Once sulfured, the bunghole should be plugged with a paper cup or a plastic or wooden bung wrapped with plastic. Check sulfur every few weeks. Take care with sulfuring, as SO_2 is a poisonous irritant to the eyes, nose, and throat. Checking concentration by smell can be risky, especially for those with asthma or other respiratory conditions. SO_2 can also be generated by adding 500 parts per million (ppm) of KMS and then citric acid to lower the pH of the solution sufficiently to release the gas, which dissipates over time. Barrels so stored should be checked every few weeks for smell.

Sampling from the Barrel

Once filled, you'll want to periodically check on the contents of your barrels. This should not be done too often, but as you get going with your wood program you won't be able to help yourself, and especially not with particularly lovingly conceived experiments. Some barrels are installed with sample cocks, or with spigots hammered into holes in the heads, often above the lowest points in order to avoid pulling any lees. In a sealed barrel flow may need to be increased by loosening the bung to admit air. Hankerson also suggests the use of a ten-penny nail along an upper stave. The simplest and probably most traditional method is from the bunghole with a "wine thief"—a tube inserted and then stoppered at the top with the thumb to keep the trapped contents from simply flowing back inside. In an aging sour beer, however, this intrusion will likely compromise the protective pellicle on the surface, a matrix of filamentous yeast and other organisms that protect the beer from oxidation and, hence, acetic acid formation, as well as reducing ethyl acetate. You'll also need to have extra bungs on hand, as repeated removal with tools will no doubt compromise their integrity.

Our friend Vinnie Cilurzo of Russian River in Santa Rosa has a well-known method for sampling. Here is the info (he writes) on the stainless steel nail in the barrel head acting as a poor man's MacGyver sample port:

We drill a hole using a 7/64 drill bit on the barrel head of each barrel. The hole can be drilled while the barrel is empty or even with beer in it. You just have to be ready with the nail if you are doing it with the barrel full. The hole is so small that there is no problem with losing too much beer at this point.

I have two sizes of stainless steel nails that I purchase from McMaster Carr.

1½" 2D smooth common nail – 316 stainless steel McMaster Carr # 97990A102
2" 2D smooth common nail - 316 stainless steel McMaster Carr # 97990A104

I use the smaller nail, but, I keep the larger ones around just in case a hole gets bored out too large. It hasn't happened yet, but I'm just playing it safe.

I do use barrel wax sometimes (www.barrelbuilders.com) around the nail after I have pulled a sample. We have never had a nail blow out due to pressure; they are pretty snug in there.

You can pull a sample and actually have the flow stop coming out of the small hole in the head of the barrel because the barrel is not vented, but there is no issue. It is such a small hole that you can't harm the barrel. If anything, it makes it easier because you can control the flow by removing the bung and putting it back into place. I usually drill the hole about halfway up on the barrel head.

Recently we've started to drill the barrel out after the barrel has beer in it as opposed to before. Sometimes you don't get the small hole drilled out all the way. You won't know that this is the case until there is beer in the barrel and you see that you don't even have a small stream of beer coming out of the hole.

I've also taken to the practice of having a backup nail in my pocket when I'm pulling samples, just in case you drop the nail on the floor by accident.

The hole at the bottom of the head of the barrel (six o'clock if you are looking at the head of the barrel straight-on) for removing beer with fruit in it is a 15/16" hole, the tubing that you use to remove the liquid and fruit is also from McMaster Carr. A Belgian Oeneo beer bottle cork like we cork with fits in the 15/16" hole. Here is the part number from McMaster for the tubing:

15/16" OD tubing, McMaster Carr # 5231K944

It takes a little practice, but you can remove the cork quickly and push the 15/16" tubing in the cork hole. The tubing is then run down to some sort of strainer that you would need to fashion and from the strainer it is pumped to a tank.

Vinnie Cilurzo
Brewer/Owner
Russian River Brewing Company

Basic Cooperage Tools

The tools required for building barrels from scratch are many and arcane, and include planes, knives, scrapers, irons, borers, chisels, hammers, drivers, pullers, benches, and horses, to say nothing of the specialized bits of equipment for flagging, toasting, charring, branding, scoring, riveting, welding, raising, and pressure-testing. These days many of these are relegated to brewery museums, especially as now much of the work is performed by machinery, lasers, and computers. For basic maintenance only an awkward handful are required. Many of them still look fairly esoteric, but with a little instruction you'll see that their function is simple enough, even if a little practice is required to gain facility.

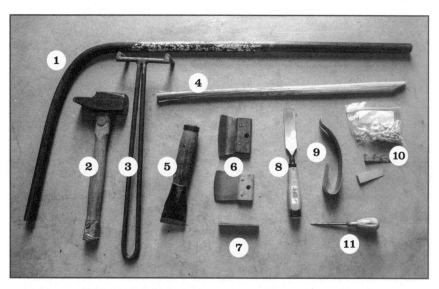

Figure 4.5—A sampling of cooper tools. 1.) Head hammer 2.) Hoop hammer 3.) Flagging tool 4.) Cattail stem 5.) Hoop driver 6.) Scraping knives 7.) Wedge, used for foeders 8.) Chisel 9.) Head puller 10.) Different types of spiles and wood wedges used to stop leaks 11.) Awl

First and most obvious is a hammer. Any small sledge of a couple of pounds will do. This is the implement to drive the others—the chisels and drivers—to effect repairs and set the hoops. Also essential is a mallet of some softer material, such as rubber, leather, or plastic, in order to be able to knock things about and set them back in place without marking the wood.

Next up is the hoop driver. This is configured similarly to a chisel, in that it is composed of a wooden handle fitted to a broader and somewhat concave, or grooved-bladed iron. This concave groove offers solid purchase to the hoop as it is driven in or out of place by the hammer. They are available for purchase from specialty cooperage suppliers such as Barrel Builders or the Vintner's Vault. You could make one yourself with the lightest (3 lb or around 1.4 kg) iron square head wood-splitting wedge, cut off on the top and file a groove in it to sit on the hoops.

The head puller looks curious at first, until you recall its functional similarity to the levers used to prize bicycle tires onto and off of their rims. It can look like—and often is—a piece of hoop with one pointed end curled slightly back on itself, or it can be fancier and more specifically dedicated, a flat, hooked piece of metal that holds the head in place between the head and the staves as the head hammer works to place the bevel along the head in the croze. This hook needs to be of enough substance to hold the head up, but not so wide as to be difficult to get out of the gap once the head is placed. Some head pullers are shaped like a squared Z with hooks on either end, while others have a 180-degree bend in the non-business end in order to facilitate hanging it in odd places (such as out of your back pocket). It's a simple enough implement. This is easy to make from a spare hoop, cut of a piece of 40 cm or 15" and cut all corners a bit off. Then bend it as in the tool picture. If it does not work well enough, adjust the angle that has to fit in the croze between the head and staves.

A skilled cooper can pull a head into place simply by benefit of his or her experience with only a head puller. It looks amazingly easy. Many of the rest of us, however, may find a head hammer necessary. This is an L-shaped steel implement, with one end shorter than the other. The short end is the length from the bunghole to the inside of the head. This is the end inserted into the bung and pointed upward to push and strike the head into place with the steadying aid of the head puller. The longer end sticks outside the bung so the cooper—you—can manipulate it by standing on the bung side of the upright barrel and tapping upward as best you can. To explain further at this point will only be confusing. Refer to the section, Head Leaks, and Head Removal and Replacement, for more information on removing and replacing heads. It won't make your first attempts any easier, but it's at least presented in step-by-step fashion. This, again, is a tool you can make yourself or have made by someone who can bend steel pipe.

Another type of tool useful for the removal of material residual or wooden is the scraping knife. This is another implement of the chisel type, with a typically wooden handle fitted to an L-shaped—and hence, perpendicular—blade. You'll find this useful in removing wine stone and other leavings, as well as smoothing and scraping wood for possible resurfacing.

Enough illustration and theory. What do you say we fix some things?

Repairing Leaks in Barrels

Leaks in barrels are of a few basic types: through the wood, between staves, in or around the heads, and at the bung. Each has its own methods for repair, from a little dab of this or that to disassembling and replacing damaged parts. In this section we will address all of that.

Through-Wood Leaks

On its surface wood is composed of a bundle of capillary tubes that carry nutrients upward from the roots to the leaves of the tree. This outer, sap-carrying part of the tree is appropriately called sapwood. As the tree grows thicker and the outer layer is replaced by newer sapwood, tyloses generated by the inner cells block these tubes, yearly converting the inner layers of the tree to heartwood. This heartwood constitutes the sturdiness of the hardwood tree—and particularly of oak—and protects it from rot. This process also makes oak better suited than any other wood to wet cooperage. American oak, in particular, has a high density of these tylose blockages, maintaining the relative impermeability of capillary tubes even when they are sawn through. European oak, on the other hand, generates less tylose and is more prone to through-wood leaking. This is why European oak is more often split than sawn for barrel construction, in order to avoid cleaving the tubes. Larger wood vessels such as foeders and other tanks are necessarily made of thicker staves (5–8 cm). The length of the staves pose an additional challenge to cutting, in such a way as to make them more prone to through-wood leaking. Because of size, their staves, too, must be sawn.

Small leaks can be difficult to specifically identify. A whole area might appear to be wet, but by wiping it as dry as possible and shining a light across it the extent of the leak may be better assessed. It could be a single capillary, or it could be more. Very small leaks can sometimes be stopped with a wipe of bentonite solution on a rag or sponge. This is a material most often used in wineries for clarification. A cut clove of garlic might also do the trick, as might chalk, simply rubbed over the affected area. The brewers at Cigar City in Tampa have borrowed from their local beach culture by using Sex Wax®, ordinarily used on surfboards, to seal barrels, though it must be observed that the use of any such product should include an assessment of any fragrances or other additives.

To those accustomed to other, more once-and-for-all kinds of repair, the home-spun methods employed in this kind of wood maintenance no doubt seem casual and slipshod. But this is wood we're talking about, having been fashioned to hold liquid as perfectly as practically possible, but subject both to change and the hand dealt it during growth and its life as a barrel. The ongoing job before the cooper and repairer of barrels is to keep the liquid within inside as long as it needs to be there, and then to evaluate and act on the situation once it's emptied. And then to do it all over again, as needed. An old barrel is like an old person: This or that has broken down with the years and healed or been repaired, not always perfectly. Its appearance is testimony to long and functional service to what is inside. It doesn't have to look pretty or perfect to perform sufficiently well.

If these simple methods are insufficient, a bit more fun is in store. With a chisel in hand try to assess where the capillary tube is coming from, looking closely at the wood to see if it's been cut or interrupted. Sometimes looking at the end of the stave toward the outer edge will show more, particularly if the head hoop is removed. If you're not overly concerned with the aesthetics of the barrel you can scrape with a scraping knife in the direction of the grain across the leak, then feel the wood with your finger in either direction to determine which side is smooth and which has a little lip. The place to set your chisel is an inch or so from the leak in the direction the lip is detected. This can be more difficult than it sounds, and sometimes trial and error, one side or the other, will serve, as well, with a light tick of the chisel to crush the offending capillary to stop the leak. If one side doesn't do the job, the other might.

Figure 4.6—Peter Bouckaert driving a spile to stop a leak.

Larger, more perceptible leaks require bolder measures. A peg or spile can be used to plug a hole, as can a wedge, depending on the shape of the hole. Remember that a wedge can be any shape it needs to be. The hole may need to be worried larger or into more regular shape with a nail or a knife. Then, when the plug has been tapped in, any remainder can be shaved off and sanded smooth, if desired or feasible. Lest all this seem daunting or overly intrusive, keep in mind once more the basic function of a barrel—all you're really trying to do is get it to hold liquid. There are certainly other, tougher, through-wood leaks you may have to deal with. Wherever wood has been cut there can be issues, particularly at the ends of staves, at bung or nail holes, or where manways have been worked into foeders. A combination of the above skills will be your arsenal, along with good luck and patience.

If you live in an area of low humidity food grade epoxy applied at the ends of staves can mitigate the drying of stave ends that can lead to leaking. It's surprising how quickly the gaps between staves can close as the wood swells once epoxy or other sealer has been applied. In central European areas such as Hungary or the Czech Republic red or green paint is often used, applied when the barrel is empty so that the paint holds and internal pressure is low. If you find yourself using either of these methods, remember that care must also be taken not to get paint or epoxy under the hoops, as they are meant to slide freely when removed and replaced.

Pests such as beetles and borers can also create leaks. There are a few different types prone to infest the oak of barrels, particularly the lead cable borer *(Scobicia declivis)*, which is attracted to wine-soaked barrels; the common house borer *(Anobium punctatum)*, and even the deathwatch beetle *(Xestobium rufovillosum)*. The larvae are what do the damage, arriving sometimes in old wood—particularly in foeders where the heartwood has been allowed to dry—and boring holes of a millimeter or two in diameter. Aside from the presence of holes, a little spilling of wood dust on top of the hoops or on the floor can be a tip-off. Warm water will sometimes kill the pests, but rotenone added to linseed oil can also work. In the wine industry mildewcide is sometimes used. The holes are generally fairly straight, and can be plugged with a narrow spile or toothpick. The fancy chestnut hoops sometimes added to wine barrels can seem more appealing to pests than the oak of the actual barrel (this is actually part of the idea). If such an infestation is seen the barrel can simply be removed and discarded.

Between-Stave Leaks

The first line of defense for between-stave leaks is your hammer and hoop driver. The barrel should first be swollen by moisture and the hoops driven evenly along the belly to tighten the fit of the staves. Doing this with a full barrel can be risky as shifting staves can result in further gaps opening up, and, when the barrel is under pressure, sudden escape of the contents, imposing urgency. Indeed, this can happen without even touching a barrel. Avoid concentrating on a single hoop, as this could loosen others. After some work on one hoop move on to the others on the same end of the barrel. This progressive tightening is like systematically working the nuts when replacing the wheel on a car. Tap on hoops only enough to tighten them—not simply to give them "just one more tap."

If all this does not close gaps sufficiently to stop leaks you may need to resort to flagging, which employs the inner spongy and sticky flesh of a common cattail *(Typha latifolia)*. A special and fairly simple tool is required, a flagging iron. Tipping the barrel on end with the leaky part upward and then removing all but one hoop above the belly should open the gap sufficiently to get a little working room. The head should stay in, but the integrity of the barrel will be loosened. The cattail should then be cut to appropriate length and peeled to allow removal of the soft, somewhat sticky center which is the part you will use. At this point further space between the staves must be created, which is where the flagging iron comes in. The central hoop can also be carefully loosened. The flagging tool uses one stave as a lever, while pushing against a stave next to the leak to open the gap with the other stave. Use the butt of a your flagging tool to keep the gap open until some cattail can be wiggled into the gap. Once this is situated the process is reversed, with hoops replaced and brought back into position. Admittedly, this is more easily said than done. Above all, though, avoid allowing the barrel to fall apart or "fall in staves." There is a Flemish saying along these lines, meaning that your plans just aren't working out. Or so Peter says.

Figure 4.7—The flagging iron is used to pull the stave next to the leak out enough so that there is room to add the soft, sticky cattail material.

Other methods for closing gaps between the staves of an empty barrel involve strips of cotton and melted wax, which can aid in blocking capillary leaks. Sterilized strings from a new mop are even mentioned (Ashley 2015), the gauge of which might be more appropriate for gaps between the staves of foeders. With wing-and-a-prayer methods such as these it's important once more to remember—and especially with barrels full of liquid—that sometimes temporary measures are good enough for the time being. Once barrels are emptied the job can then be done properly, or at least better.

Figure 4.8—After filling the gap with cotton strips, use melted beeswax to seal the gap between the staves.

Head Leaks, and Head Removal and Replacement

Methods such as those immediately above will often be the first thing you try when encountering leaks around the croze or between staves in the head of the barrel. A certain amount of directional hammering with a mallet might also be sufficiently effective. If on a head stave, a chisel placement parallel to and 8–10 mm from the leak could create enough additional wood pressure to close it, and if large enough this pressure could be maintained by the insertion of an appropriately sized wooden wedge. Remember never to chisel between staves or on heads. It may be that the head will need to be removed once the barrel is empty in order to recreate the seal within the croze, to tighten the joinery between head staves, or simply to maintain the barrel's inner surface. Of course, this involves the development of new skills.

In order to remove the head, first upend the barrel with the non-leaking head facedown. Make a mark on the head and chime so you will be able to replace the head in the same position. Typically, this is the bung stave and the top of the head. Remove the chime hoop and loosen all other hoops on the top half of the barrel. You may choose to remove those above the belly altogether to get them out of the way and loosen the integrity of the staves. If the head is fitted with a crossbar this should be removed, typically by wiggling free the wood pegs that hold it in place. Softly hammer on the head inward toward the barrel. Sometimes it will stick and the chime will need to be hammered, as well, or you could use your flagging tools for staves that are stuck to the head. You will gradually feel the head slide loose, and most likely fall into the barrel. If this happens the smell coming out of the barrel will tell you everything about it. We'll leave aside for the moment that a practiced cooper will probably not drop the head, using the head puller to maintain control. Remove the head from the barrel, taking care to align the head staves vertically so as not to risk damaging the head's integrity—or even pulling it apart. Head staves are joined by grooved joints, pegs, nails, or glue, and are somewhat vulnerable to structural disintegration. Set the head aside

Observe the inside of the barrel. For most of us this is virgin territory, but once the threshold is crossed a whole new level of maintenance and control is within easy reach. The first thing that will strike you is the wonderful smell, and the immediate view of the barrel's interior condition. Check the barrel's

Figure 4.9—After removing some of the hoops, the head can be softly hammered until it falls into the barrel.

general integrity, the tightness of the fit of the staves and the state of its inner surface. You may choose to tighten the belly hoop a bit just keep things solid. So exposed, any evident tartrate crystals can be simply scraped free of the wood, or a pressure washer may be used—carefully so as not to damage the wood by excessive pressure and closeness. In Figure 4.11 we found some crystals on the head and scraped those off with the scraping knife. Check, too, for any blisters that may have formed—in a bourbon barrel, but also sometimes in wine barrels—during charring or bending. Scrape and chisel these away, smoothing and evening the wood with your chisel and scraping knife. This is also the time to assess the condition of the chime, to see whether stave ends or croze have been compromised. Broken chimes are easy to find now.

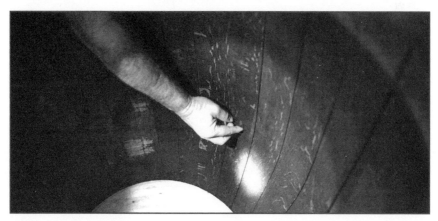

Figure 4.10—Inspect the barrel for wine stone and blisters. Blisters are nice hiding spots for microorganisms and should be opened and smoothed.

Figure 4.11—Scraping crystals off the head using a scraping knife.

In its state of structural dishevelment, our theoretical barrel is prime for repair and refurbishment, whether flagging, scraping, or cleaning. So let's skip ahead to the really difficult part: replacing the head. Be prepared for the kind of frustration inherent in having one hand too few to effectively do a job, like when replacing a bike tire on a rim. One essential tool for the task is the head hammer, an iron bent at a right angle that, when having its shorter end inserted through the bung, is used to steady the head and tap it upward into the croze. Meanwhile, the head puller is employed at the top in the cooper's other hand to aid in guiding the head into place. But perhaps we're getting ahead of ourselves.

Figure 4.12—Having all your tools accessible when putting the head back on alone is very important. Note the belly hoop is loosely on the barrel and can be adjusted as you work to either tighten or loosen the hold on the staves. Keep the hoop driver and hammer handy, the head hammer in the bunghole and the head puller can be kept in the back pocket for easy access.

While barrels are intended to seal with a simple wood-on-wood croze-to-head connection, in the case of a leak some kind of resealing may be necessary. A simple wheat paste, brushed around the croze, is an easy solution, or the edge of the head can be rolled in wax. Another possibility is 360 degrees of flagging, but that would require the maintenance of another ball in the air, so to speak, while enacting the already ticklish procedure of head replacement. Another option still is a paste made from sawdust and water. In any case, the head should be inserted into the barrel's open end, tilting downward, away from the cooper, with its staves once more oriented vertically and in alignment with the marks previously made, and some resistance felt against the opening. If not, the belly hoop may need to be tightened a bit. With the head hammer inserted through the bung and at the ready, likely held between the knees and against the bung, and with a hoop driver, loose hoops and hammer within reach, insert the bevel on the near side of the head into the croze and pull upward on the opposite side, as far as space allows with your hand. You thought that was tricky? Now try hooking the head puller where your fingers previously held the head and use your other hand to tap upward with the head hammer to attempt settling the head into the croze. What? You dropped it? It may be time for a beer as you prepare for your second attempt. Remember that cooperage is a skill, and that skills require practice, sometimes lots of practice.

Figure 4.13—This is the moment you will wish you had a third hand. If you end up hammering the head back into the barrel, you join many a good brewer in good company. It is a learned skill that takes practice.

Figure 4.14—Once the head is in place, lower the belly hoop softly and add the other hoops. No hammer needed at this stage, just gently push the hoops lower until they sit firmly in place. If the head puller is still present, it can be removed at this time.

As you begin to succeed in seating the head within the croze, tap around inside, left and right, with the head hammer to complete the placement and satisfy yourself that all is as it should be. Then exchange the head puller for your hoop driver, while holding up the head with the head hammer, and tick down the belly hoop without a hammer, just with the hoop driver. Don't worry if at this point the head puller seems stuck; all you're trying to do right now is lightly secure the head in the croze with the pressure of the hoop. You can leave enough play to eventually extract the head puller as you finish the job. Tick the belly hoop into place first, and then add the next one and tick it into place. Now would be a good time to extract the head puller, prior to placement of the final head hoop. If you earlier had to remove a crossbar, it should be replaced before final hoop placement. Now go to town on the hoops, hammering them systematically into place, taking care on the head hoop not to damage the chime.

Voila, as they say. If you've done everything properly—and why not?—you once more have a rehabbed and watertight barrel. You'll want to test the head with water—as you did when it first came into your possession—to make sure everything holds. And then you'll want to finish your beer.

Intermezzo: the Cooper's Dance

It's almost too obvious to state, but when hammering hoops down (or up) with a hoop driver never hold your fingers in between the barrel and the hoop driver. Hold your thumb towards you, your fingers on the other side of the hoop driver, so that it falls out of your hand if you do something wrong. Do not clamp your finger around the holder of the hoop driver, however natural this may seem. Similarly, make sure that your feet are not underneath the hoop driver, even if you wear steel-toed shoes. Place the hoop as level as possible on the barrel, and push it as low as it goes. When you work on a hoop, walk backward (taking care not trip over other tools or hoops on the floor) or forward as you hammer every 15–30 cm on the hoop. By doing so your feet are not underneath the potential dropped hoop driver. Keep moving around and around, moving from one hoop to the other in full turns. When the hoops are still loose you will only have to tick on them; if you hammer too hard at that stage the hoop will bounce up on the other side. This is why you sometimes see two coopers moving around one barrel, especially big ones. Keep going around and hammer until the hoops are firmly in place. Take a bow! You've done the cooper's dance!

Figure 4.15—Cooper's dance. See how he holds the driver.

The barrel should be dry during this stage, for optimal friction between wood and hoop (wet barrels are really hard to dance with). Varnish, paint, or oil can also reduce necessary friction too much. If the job becomes too hard you could use chalk on the inside of the hoop or by drawing underneath the hoop to facilitate driving. Chalk will reduce friction and is often used to drive hoops on foeders. For foeders the tools just described are almost toys. We will get to describing some serious tools for foeders later in this chapter.

The chime hoop is usually driven with the hammer alone, therefore your hammer needs a wide surface so as not to locally dent the hoop or damage the chime. But on more slack barrels the hoop driver will likely be necessary.

First, hammer the bilge hoop down, then the chime, and then the quarter hoop(s). Hoops need to be firm on the barrel. When driving hoops, proceed patiently and use judicious force, since as with any other progressive tightening the others will loosen or provide uneven pressure. Swelling during filling can also lead to excessive pressure on the staves and hoops, risking breakage. Getting the hoops firm will come with experience. Keep on dancing.

Bung Leaks

As barrels are generally stored on their bellies with the bung upward, leaks at the bung often go undetected, or are a bit of a non-event. They can, however, compromise the integrity of a barrel intended to hold pressure, or when contents are stored with the barrel in upright position. Wooden bungs should be set with the grain of the wood in the same direction as that of the stave, and driven with firm but judicious force in order to avoid this kind of damage. Cracks may be closed sufficiently by employing methods similar to those outlined in the paragraphs devoted to through-wood leaks—chiseling and inserting a wedge, for example— but in more extreme cases the stave may need to be replaced. Care should also be taken when cleaning the interior of the barrel to dilute any chemicals used before introducing them through the bunghole, as even carefully pouring them undiluted is certain to damage the wood, both within the barrel and at the bung.

Replacement of Staves and Other Cans of Worms

Staves can break due to rough handling. They can also split during bending, or become damaged by overzealous bung placement. Broken staves can sometimes be hard to detect, as cracks may only be evident from the inside of the barrel, or if at the bunghole may settle back to invisibility when the bung is removed. Sometimes a hoop can also hide stave damage, especially at the chime. Pressure can compromise both heads and staves, so if primary fermentation is conducted in the barrel pressure-relieving bungs should be used, of a type able to relieve the sudden extremes generated by beer fermentation. Many barrels normally intended for use with wine are easily fouled by beer and can eventually blow once pressure mounts. Actual replacement of staves is generally a job for a skilled cooper. This constitutes much of the work of refurbishment undertaken at cooperages such as Speyside in Scotland or Kelvin in Kentucky. It involves finding a similarly sized stave on hand, perhaps culled from a sacrificial barrel designated to give new life to others. Then the barrel must be reduced practically to shakes and subsequently reconstructed through re-raising and assembly (industrial cooperages have windlasses and such for this task). It is conceivable that hoops could be loosened sufficiently to work a replacement into position. Selection of the replacement stave is probably the most exacting decision to be made, given that once designated it must be incorporated by the complete process of construction. Flagging might be employed to compensate for less-than-precise joinery. In short, there are no tricks to be imparted. Should you be determined to try working from a raw and unbent stave and feel like trying out shaping and bending for yourself, specialized tools will be required, for starters. Check the rundown in this chapter of basic coopering tools. One bending method for non-industrial coopers involves placing a weight on the center of the stave and giving it some time. Or an appropriate vise could be used, putting pressure on the ends. Oh, and there's toasting. See what you've gotten yourself into?

Since we're on the subject of difficult and ambitious tasks generally enacted by professionals, we may as well touch on the notion of interior resurfacing. This might be undertaken in the case of extreme buildup of wine stone or bacterial contamination (should sulfuring prove ineffective), or simply when the inner wood is sufficiently extracted and you want expose new surface. Basing procedure on that employed at Barrel Builders, the barrel is first allowed to dry out somewhat and both heads are removed. The interior is then shaved or planed to remove the pigmented or otherwise affected wood, and re-toasting is undertaken with chips and cresset in order to avoid excessive astringency from the newly exposed wood. It may also take a wasted first filling after such refurbishment to season the barrel. Remember, as well, that with the removal of inner material the staves are thinner and more fragile. Take care not to remove material that may compromise the croze. If you're even attempting such treatment, you're beyond any instruction by us on reinstalling the heads.

It's worth mentioning that as an alternative to attempting resurfacing and its attendant risks, a whole range of products exists for imparting controlled wood flavor. These include chips, cubes, diamonds, spirals, staves, and planks. In the case of the latter two, one head would need to be removed to facilitate insertion (and later removal); otherwise they can just be dropped through the bung and either secured with string (as with spirals or bags) or simply rinsed free on emptying and cleaning. These products can also be used to impart oak flavor in vessels other than barrels, such as stainless steel tanks. In the wine world such treatment is sometimes paired with micro-oxidation in order to mimic prolonged contact with wood. All of this is more completely covered in chapter 5.

Pitching and Lining Barrels—Further into the Wormhole

Nearly all of our treatment of the use of barrels for beer, wine, and spirits has been based on the assumption of direct contact between the wooden barrel and its contents. Throughout most of history, however, barrels have been used to ship and store other materials, including foodstuffs and decidedly non-consumable liquids such as chemicals and petroleum. Viewers of Michael Jackson's Beer Hunter series are also familiar with the practice of lining barrels with pitch for the aging and dispensing of beer, such as at Pilsner Urquell in the Czech Republic. For the sake of academic interest we'll run through some of the materials used for the adaptation of barrels for industrial use, and then get into a bit about pitching.

Paraffin is probably the simplest and most common lining material, used for the storage of water-based products and food. Heated to 180°F (82°C) and mixed with 10% micro-crystalline wax, a sufficient amount is poured into the barrel, which is then bunged and rolled around to coat. The pressure generated in the hot barrel aids in forcing the wax into the wood and between staves to effect a seal. A glue mixture can be used for non-edible and alcohol-based products, based on equal parts water and glue and brought into solution by slow heating to 180°F. This mixture is then augmented by an addition of potassium aluminum silicate to increase viscosity. As with wax, the barrel is rolled around to coat and then allowed to dry and cool. Silicate and soda is a mixture used for oil-based products.

These days most of the breweries still using pitch to line barrels are found in Germany and Central Europe. The process is enacted in two steps: first removing the old pitch and then recoating with new. Brauerei Maisach, outside of Munich, recoats its barrels after four or five fillings, removing old pitch with 180–200°C water and then adding new pitch made from pine and larch heated to 85°C. Caution should be exercised at that temperature. Consult with your pitch manufacturer for recommendations. The bung explodes from the barrel, so this is not a beginner's process. Other practitioners, such as Alfred Schneele, prefer their pitch somewhat cooler to avoid coloration. The pitching of barrels is generally an all-hands-on-deck affair, as timing is essential and steps must be undertaken in succession. A skilled crew can pitch 200 barrels in a day. As with other coatings, the pitch is introduced hot and the barrel then rolled to coat. Care must be taken due to pressure buildup in the hot barrel, and the layer applied kept to an effective minimum to ensure accurate volume. Once pitch is applied and the excess removed, cold water is introduced to both cool and check for leaks. Properly executed, the pitch-lined barrel should impart no flavor of its own and retain full carbonation in beer. Pitch can also be used to line fermenters and aging vessels, such as at Augustiner Brauerei in Munich, which also dispenses some of its beer in pitched barrels. Fassbüttnerei Weis and Schmid, a cooperage still active in Franconia north of Bamberg in Germany, still produces pitch-lined barrels, as well as mock versions employing Durolit plastic, and stainless kegs sheathed in oak or acacia.

Believe it or not, brewer's pitch is still available for sale in the United States, from a company called Jas (James) Townsend & Son, which seems mainly to offer clothing and equipment for historical reenactments. Its slogan is "Where Ben Franklin would shop if he were alive today!" Its pitch is a food-grade pine-based product, the same stuff once used for shipbuilding as well as the lining of barrels. Especially for carbonated beer, pitch lining strikes us as an interesting artisanal niche market. Keep in mind, however, the flammable nature of pitch products.

Evaluation and Care of Foeders

While there is no official size at which a wooden vessel used for holding wine, beer, or spirits ceases to be referred to as a barrel and takes on another name, 600 liters seems about the point at which proportion and construction present enough difference for another designation. Barrels smaller than this are generally made by assembly line methods, whereas larger vessels, or foeders, are made individually and usually in a separate shop. Many of the general themes of construction and maintenance are the same for barrels and foeders. They are, for example, made from essentially the same trees. Effort is made to find spans of uncut wood that will lend themselves to the manufacture of larger vessels, but there is no unique species of oak correspondingly suitable and such things as knots and the natural flare at crown or root are more often tolerated in the interest of securing staves of sufficient length. This in itself can lead to very specific challenges of function and upkeep, but generally speaking, methods of evaluation, cleaning, scraping, and use of foeders is similar in most basic ways to those employed for barrels. One obvious departure is that one can get inside a foeder in order to effect much of this work. In this regard, greater familiarity can be gained with a foeder's inside surfaces than with a typical unopened barrel. Few, however, would say that maintaining foeders is easier, if for no other reason than that the stakes are higher. Some challenges and procedures are more obvious than they are with barrels, others more arcane and daunting. In any case, we are here to help you gain familiarity with foeders as well.

Inspection of Foeders

Many aspects of scale and construction where foeders are concerned have been addressed in chapter 2, but a little review is necessary in order to fit with the mindset of evaluation and the anticipation of potential challenges of maintenance. Sheer size makes the splitting of staves for foeders impracticable, and once sawn they must be slowly dried in order to avoid warping—typically one year for each centimeter of thickness. For economic reasons not all defects can be avoided when the wood for staves of such length is selected, as mentioned above, and vagaries of grain are more common than in a shorter stave. Such things as through-wood leaks can result from some of these irregularities, and so an evaluation of the staves in a foeder is likely to tell more than in the nearly hermetic barrel. Straight grain along the full length of the stave is, of course, desirable, with the growth rings in consistent alignment amid the other visible lines. Focus on staves that don't show this ideal pattern, as they are the ones that could compromise integrity and function. Knots will show as a disturbance in straight year rings and could allow through-wood leaking. The pale lines that might seem to weave between the grain are cut medullary rays, vertical lines in the tree that radiate from the center of the trunk to the outside that, when properly aligned, inhibit the flow of liquid through the wood. When these lines describe anything other than a full diagonal across the width of the stave, attention may need to be paid to enhance impermeability.

As with barrels, one's senses of smell and observation are important tools in the evaluation of foeders, but so is consideration of the environment in which they have likely stood stationary for years. Is the room damp and smelly? Is it stuffy and close, poorly ventilated to encourage excessive growth of mold? Or is it too well-ventilated? In some climates this could lead to drying of the wood. Little piles of wood dust, either on the floor beneath the stave ends or along the top edges of the hoops, could indicate the presence of wood borers, even if the holes themselves are not evident.

It may seem verging on superstition, but a foeder should look solid the first time you see it. With their broad wood surfaces and the imposing strength of dressed and painted hoops, a lot of makeup can be applied to mask defects. The gloss of linseed oil or an evenly applied coat of polyurethane can kindle an atavistic appeal, but they do nothing to close leaks or repair degraded wood. The rings should be solidly in place, ideally with no evidence of damage or repair. Is there evidence of old or ongoing leaks, such as staining and streaking, across or between staves? Unlike barrels, foeders are usually fitted with manways, ports, sample cocks, and other utilitarian penetrations. These can all constitute substantial potential for compromise. How does the wood look around these breaches, especially around the manway? It can be useful to test the solidity of the wood with a knife or screwdriver, almost as though testing a cake for doneness. Any place the grain has been cut has potential for failure by through-wood leaking. This process also extracts polyphenols, further weakening and otherwise compromising the wood.

Repairs are a fact of life and are not, of course, in themselves a detraction, especially in vessels as long-lived as foeders. It is necessary, however, to get an accurate read of what has been done and its degree of effectiveness. Epoxy paint can be an effective re-sealant, but it can also cover evidence of both damage and repair. Used across staves it is likely to fail when the vessel is moved. Evidence of chiseling and the insertion of wedges shows that leaks have been addressed. Have they been sufficiently repaired? Through-wood leaks and their repair can be hidden behind hoops. Staining will sometimes be the giveaway. If you find that you need to shift the hoops for watertightness, will placement of ports, etc. present a problem?

As you feel the thickness of the staves with your hand around the bottom of the foeder, do they feel solid, in place, and aligned? How does the bottom itself look and feel? Are the staves still sitting on the rim of the tank bottom, or is there some indication by discoloration that they have been moved? With the way the wood shrinks the problem will not be on the longitudinal side of the stave, but look in-between the bottom staves and on the edges of the shortest staves. Can you find any loose or broken chimes? If the bottom hoop is below the level of the chime, this can indicate breakage or compromise prior to its lowering. Feel all the way around the circumference. Once again, test the wood with a knife or screwdriver, especially around the bottom valve. Are the support beams in contact with all the floor staves, and if not, how are any unsupported staves holding on? With the volumes, weights, and pressures inherent in foeder use, the floor is the first place to give.

Seven of the foeders at New Belgium are fitted with stainless bottom manways; they have remained in place despite the near total replacement of the bottoms around them. For obvious reasons a flat-mounted manway is more solidly effective than one on a rounded surface. Take a look at the mounting of the manway. Does it suggest any potential leaks? The short staves below a side-mounted manway can easily loosen. Are they solid? A fact of stainless manway installation is that surrounding wood needs to be removed and then replaced. The places where the wood has been cut or adapted to fit the manway will have a higher likelihood of leaking. How does the grain integrity look on these short staves? The foeders at Rodenbach are fitted with square top wooden manways, bolted with a cross bar. An interior seal sits between the ceiling of the foeder and the manway edge. They are authentic and easy to make, but according to Peter, not ideal. Winemakers seem to like large top manways—sometimes as much as a meter across—but increased risk of exposure to oxygen makes these less suitable for use with beer. An upwardly bulged top can make for more effective filling and ultimately less oxygen exposure, especially with a top-fitted manway. Broken or damaged chimes are more forgivable at a foeder's top.

Open up the foeder and get a feel for its look and smell. Heavy buildup of wine stone can make it difficult to accurately assess this, but a clean wine smell is good. Look around the openings, and around the rim at the top and bottom. Test the wood to see if it remains sturdy. Some foeders are fitted with inserts, stainless racks to hold staves for additional flavor uptake or cooling or heating plates used to regulate wine fermentation. Will you leave them in place? If you decide to remove them can they be extracted without deconstruction of the foeder? Will holes remain that need to be plugged?

Intermezzo: See for Yourself!

I once was shown four decent-sized foeders in Napa Valley. They were in a dark brick building with a dirt floor. The whole room was damp, but the foeders looked OK on the outside, as far as I could see, anyway, since I could not crawl around the whole foeder. The winemaker insisted they were sulfured from time to time, so I should not open them since they were fine and the sulfur was dangerous. I stated clearly that I would not buy foeders without seeing the inside. So I pulled the manway open and found beautiful, long, hairy mold covering the whole inside. I had a look at the wine-maker.... I left with a bottle of wine, but did not drop off beer.

—from Peter's journals

So far we have mainly considered vertical foeders. Horizontal ones are con-structed more like barrels with oblong heads. This necessitates two different angles in stave joinery, one for the sides and one for the top and bottom. In order to support greater weights and pressures than conventional barrels, the staves for foeders need to be thicker. Warping and inward bending can occur, and the top and bottom staves are naturally compromised by the placement of bung and drain holes, respectively. Test the wood around these holes; make sure it is not turning to mush. Take a good look at the heads. Increased pressure on the heads makes the crossbars with which they are usually fitted more than merely orna-mental. As with other foeders, manways are potential spots for leaks. Sometimes these are made of wood, sometimes of stainless steel secured with bolts, which can themselves constitute leaks. We watched the installation of the manway of a new horizontal foeder at Seguin Moreau in Cognac, destined for the Chateau Ste. Michelle winery in Washington State. Beautiful work.

Rehydration of Foeders

Foeders should be kept filled at your brewery. This will keep them hydrated and in good shape. When emptied of beer they should be filled with KMS (potassium metabisulfate) solution. Given the seasonal nature of wine production, foeders in wineries are often kept dry for months between uses. Ambient humidity in such situations should be kept above 70%. Even so, rehydration is undertaken a couple of weeks before harvest, with good, chlorine-free water at 20–30°C. This applies, of course, to your own rehydration prior to the introduction of beer.

A few years ago New Belgium took delivery of several used foeders in April, but the area in which they were to be installed would not have floor drains until November. In the meantime they were stored empty in a dry warehouse nearby that also had no drains. By the time they were ready for installation they had each lost a thousand pounds in weight due to drying. Colorado is drier than many places, of course, but the fact is striking, nonetheless. As a side note, New Belgium blender and cellarman extraordinaire Eric Salazar has since observed enhanced oak character in beer aged in these foeders, due, no doubt, to new surface having been exposed during drying and subsequent contraction.

As observed, putting vertical foeders up dry can be risky. Tank bottoms can shrink to an oval as wood shortens inconsistently as it dries. Support of the bottom is also critical, and the fit of the bottom into the staves can be compromised, as greater shrinkage will occur along the year rings and medullary rays than along the length of the stave. This can also create a dangerous situation, as the weight of the foeder is not evenly supported. If the fit is not sound when rehydration occurs, and the lower hoop is tight, the expanding bottom has nowhere to go. One possible solution is the placement of a car jack—or two, across from each other—along the side staves to take the weight off the bottom sufficiently to allow the bottom to pop back into place. This two-jack method is also used at Rodenbach to shimmy tanks incrementally into place. Better to keep foeders hydrated and everything where it belongs.

Not surprisingly, the ceiling of the foeder is liable to be its driest place, and in drying these staves, too, may come out of the top croze. It may be possible to push upward from inside to get the head/ceiling to reseat, or if there are bolts or eyes installed on the top, to pull upward to the same effect.

When hydrating, close all manways, doors, valves, and ports. Fill the foeder as best you can with some water and recirculate with a pump and top sprayball so that all walls are covered—two hours on and two hours off until the bottom holds liquid. At Anchorage Brewing they run a hot water (180°F/82°C) CIP loop overnight. When the bottom no longer leaks, fill the foeder to somewhere below the side manway. Check the croze for leaks. They could indicate an imperfect seal with the bottom, or that staves have moved in the course of swelling.

Light hammering might bring staves back into alignment. You could also fill leaks along the croze with cattail flagging. Wax and flagging can also be applied between staves, from the inside or outside of the foeder. Lowering the hoops can also sometimes help, taking care not to lower the bottom hoop below the level flush with the chime, as this could put undue pressure on the chime, or even break it in places. Lowering of hoops in general may be challenged by placement of ports and other hardware, and it may be necessary to break the hoops and weld fittings in place to accept bolts for tightening adjustment. In a way this synthesizes the systems used for straight-sided foeders, where several encircling spans of threaded material similar to All-thread are loosened or tightened according to circumstance.

While we're on the subject of leaks discovered during hydration, we may as well treat through-wood leaks that present themselves at this stage, or with greater urgency when the foeder is filled with beer. Recalling that due to both the length of the staves and the fact that they have been sawn rather than split, growth rings in the staves of foeders are likely to be less constant and straight, through-wood leaks are more common than with conventional barrels. Methods for dealing with them are similar, but the angle of the grain may be far steeper—and certainly longer—thereby necessitating more aggressive penetration by the chisel in order to break the sap channel and close the leak. This angle is easily appreciated were one to have the luxury of removing the stave and looking at it, but in place the scraping method described earlier in connection with barrel maintenance can be used. By scraping with a knife across the grain the growth rings will present themselves texturally, and a chisel placement an inch or two from the leak can be made. Now comes the bold part, for with the thickness of the foeder stave it may be necessary to penetrate the wood one half to three quarters of the way through in order to break the leak channel. This being the case, a wooden wedge will likely be necessary to hold the gap open and maintain the repair you've effected. And, of course, if you've guessed wrong and the grain runs in the other direction you may need to apply the chisel on the leak's other side. Courage!

Commissioning and Cleaning of Foeders

The first thing to be done when preparing either to clean or hydrate a foeder new to your possession is to satisfy yourself that the interior surfaces have been cleared of wine stone or other buildup. This is generally brought about by a combination of scraping and pressure washing. It's surprising how much material can be scraped free. It can also be daunting how small foeder manways often are, as much of this work must be performed from inside by a brewer or cellarperson who, obviously, can fit through the hole. A great deal of rinsing is required once wine stone is removed, thereby getting a procedural jump on hydration. Cleaning with common cellar chemicals such as caustic is not recommended, as they can dry and otherwise degrade the wood, not to mention create a residually unpleasant environment. Once surfaces are cleared and the foeder is judged sound, there are other means to effect anti-contaminant treatment.

Foeders used either for primary fermentation or prolonged aging require special measures for cleaning, of course, as the byproducts generated can be both prodigious and tenacious. It should come as no surprise that the big foeders at Rodenbach provide special challenges due to the densely integrated filamentous layer, or pellicle, that sits atop their contents during two years of aging.

Intermezzo: Yuck!

At Rodenbach we always emptied the foeders. The slimy tough top layer of around 1 cm thick would at that point lie on the bottom, the diameter a bit smaller than the bottom, since the foeders were slightly conical and it would simply sink as the foeder was emptied. The foeders had a manway at the top, so we first gave it a rinse from the top and tried to cut some of the filamentous layer with water pressure. We had to get in with a ladder that could bend in the middle (due to cellar ceiling height restraints). You drop one half in and then lower it with the other half. At the end you swing it so it stands at a good angle to descend into the foeder. We had a stainless DN25 pipe of around 7 ft long, with one side flattened and welded closed on both ends. This was our knife and scraper. We used the flattened part to cut the layer so it could get through the bottom butterfly valve. We had to replace the conical bottom outlet where the cap could be unscrewed with DN100 stainless butterfly valves that were bolted to the bottom. Of course, these strips of slimy mold would wrap around the butterfly valve when the layer was nice and solid, and a second person was needed to pull them from around the butterfly.

Once the whole vessel was rinsed, we scraped off the beerstone with the same DN25 scraper. Everything was removed from the vessel, and a bucket with amphoteric protein came in with a brush on a long stem. The whole foeder was covered in this slightly foamy product and then rinsed again. The foeder was cleaned as such between uses.

—from Peter's journals

As observed, Rodenbach cleans with an amphoteric protein. This is a substance able to function either as an acid or a base, and as such is suitable for treatment of that brewer's unique cleaning challenges.

The US wine industry commonly uses a chemical compound with the trade name Proxyclean. This is a granulated form of hydrogen peroxide combined with sodium carbonate (sodium carbonate peroxihydrate). It is recommended as a substitute for more aggressive chlorine-based cleaners, and breaks down to simpler compounds after use to remove tartrates and to reclaim "off" barrels. It is also used for general cleaning. In France a hot solution of tartaric acid is commonly used, or an alkaline solution of potassium soda (K_2CO_3) followed by neutralization with citric acid. Less invasive is a rinse of clean 140°F (60°C) water through a sprayball inserted through a top bung.

As with barrels, a wet interior of any wooden vessel left alone will soon harbor mold and bacteria. After rinsing, doors should be left open and heat and ventilation applied to remove any standing water. This should be repeated after a couple of days, as moisture may also come out of the wood. Steam cleaning in larger wooden vessels is less practicable than for barrels, as the prolonged contact times needed for effectiveness can soften the wood and make it that much more susceptible to contamination. Anchorage Brewing, however, does this immediately prior to the introduction of wort for fermentation.

Sulfuring is not mandatory. Some breweries and wineries will simply introduce beer or wine for seasoning, often electing to discard the result, as it will likely have leached disproportionate flavor following cleaning and commissioning. Or a beer type could be first introduced that will bear and likely transfer the desired flavor appropriately. When choosing to sulfur, care must be maintained and cellars ventilated and left to clear in the interest of safety. And speaking of safety, do not burn anything inside a barrel holding any residual bourbon or other spirit—explosions and injuries have most definitely occurred.

Recommendations vary as to the amounts of sulfur to be used. Barrelbuilders is most aggressive, prescribing 1200–1400 ppm, or 7 kg per 100 hL of space to be sulfured, diminishing to 800 ppm in a few weeks. Conroy suggests a mere 2 g/hL. Peter recalls using 0.5–1 kg/100 hL at Rodenbach, placed atop burning newspapers in a metal bucket and hung within from the top manway, closed up and keeping a careful eye—and nose—to make sure of SO_2 generation and in case of fire. By the next day the area was ventilated and within another day was safe to reenter.

The reclamation of barrels and foeders that have "gone acetic" or otherwise foul, usually by prolonged and excessive exposure to oxygen, might necessitate the use of steam—desperate measures, etc.—but sodium carbonate is probably more safely effective. Or there's the Rasputin treatment of chloride and lime whitewash succeeded by muriatic acid and sulfites, each applied with steam. A milder treatment Peter has seen reported recommends a good soaking in strong bicarbonate of soda followed by rinsing and the introduction of water acidulated with hydrochloric acid, the idea being that freed CO_2 will drive out putrescent matter. Permanganate of potash is also mentioned as a desirable alternative. These rough treatments may not literally constitute a nuclear option, but their extremity is certainly an indicator of willingness to take on risk.

While largely cosmetic, a little outward treatment can help preserve the wood of foeders and mitigate discoloration due to leaks. A yearly coat of linseed oil will keep the wood sealed and protected while allowing it to breathe. It also looks nice. You may need here and there to do a little scraping and sanding prior to its application.

Maintenance of Foeders

Many of the maintenance techniques already described in connection with barrels also apply to foeders. One advantage to the repair and general shoring up of larger vessels is that you can get inside of them in order to effect flagging and other gap-stopping. Or you can work both sides, such as inserting cotton string or "wire" from the outside and applying a layer of melted wax on the inside that will both run in and later be forced by pressure into the gap to combine with the fibers to form a sealing matrix. The bold chiseling technique previously described to close a through-wood leak serves as a reminder that the grain of foeder staves is less reliably tight and straight than in barrels, and that greater grasp and visualization is required in assessing and effecting repairs.

And speaking once more of getting inside foeders in order to repair them, Peter offers a cautionary tale from his experience at Rodenbach:

> *The day was almost done. The cellar operators and I were chatting about what we were up to tomorrow, on how to work through the sequence for moving beer. We were only missing Filip. As a matter of fact, the other cellar guys did not recall seeing him much today. They saw him this morning when he was heading out to clean a foeder in cellar 8, but otherwise, no, and he was not there for lunch. Maybe we should check cellar 8 to see if he is still there somewhere. Indeed, water was still running out of one of the foeders. When we made noise, Filip answered, yelling from inside the foeder. We went*

to the top of the foeder and there he was. Next to him was a broken ladder. The upper part of the folding ladder had broken in two pieces. He had still tried to reach the metal threaded wire that stuck out of the foeder next to the manway with one of the rungs of the broken piece of the ladder, but he was not able to lift himself onto the lower part of the ladder. He was somewhat wet and cold, with a mixed feeling of being angry that it took us so long to find him and being happy that we finally did. He was hungry, but not thirsty, since he had plenty of water.

We changed our safety procedures after this incident.

Tools for the maintenance of foeders are, in general, simply larger versions of the ones used for barrels, though in truth a hammer is a hammer. Larger and longer drivers and pullers in solid iron to increase weight and effect will be required for the loosening and tightening of hoops, as work will often need to be done beyond arm's reach.

Figure 4.16—Tightening or loosening foeder hoops can be done using a heavy metal rod with a flat plate welded to it. The tool can be used from the ground or from the top of the foeder. The tool is heavy to allow for additional momentum when hitting the hoops.

Phil Burton of Barrel Builders in California's Napa Valley has devoted many years to the assessment, maintenance, and brokerage of barrels and foeders. His own words on the repair and placement of foeder manways are no doubt more reliable than any narrative paraphrase.

> *Most all tanks have either stainless steel or wood manways (we call them gates) installed, and one common problem is with leaks. Here's how to maintain and repair wood gates.*
>
> *To tell if the gate needs refitting, set the gate without any wax or sealer. If you can stick a knife blade through any gaps at the top or bottom, it's time.*
>
> *First, clean the residue of old wax or sealer from both the gate and the opening. Feel around the opening; it should be smooth and even. If it needs a little dressing, use a rasp or coarse file to trim it up, although typically this isn't needed. Then, using a piece of chalk, put a heavy bead over the entire sealing face of the opening and set the gate.*
>
> *Carefully pull the gate and, using a rasp or an angle grinder with coarse paper, remove all the chalk marks from the gate. Re-chalk the opening and repeat. Do this over and over until the bead of chalk extends all around the gate. If you've got the cojones to use an angle grinder, this shouldn't take more than an hour. Your gate will seat well for several more years.*

Simple, right? As noted earlier, manways in foeders are susceptible to all kinds of compromise—sort of the essential, much-used, and vulnerable knees of wooden tank construction. Their placement also compromises stave integrity, as the shorter staves often placed on one end or the other of the vertical foeder or top or bottom of the head on the horizontal are less sound and solidly placed than is ideal. This also results in the tendency of manways to drift, so to speak, and their need to be monitored and occasionally shored up.

As with barrels, staves can be replaced and repaired, though once again it is not work to be taken lightly. At times, replacing the whole stave isn't necessary. In the case of partial stave replacement, the scale of the work can be an aid, as an angle can perhaps more forgivingly be contrived for joinery with the stave remnant and its replacement segment, with a properly placed hoop keeping everything in place and properly curved. All critical considerations must be observed, of course, such as the angles on all sides of the stave, the distance and curve between the two crozes, and all relevant thicknesses, planings, and hollowings along the stave.

Much repair work has been done over the years on the oft-mentioned foeders at New Belgium, mainly enacted day-to-day by staff dedicated to their maintenance, but also at times by foudriers flown in from France and California. A fun detail is the new name sour beer czarina Lauren Salazar once gave a foeder that needed a completely new stave, or rib: Eve.

Gabe Fletcher at Anchorage Brewing has more experience than most at knocking down and reassembling foeders owing to brewery doors too small to otherwise admit entrance to his foeders as he's received them, or at least when he was housed in the basement at the Sleeping Lady Brewery in Anchorage, Alaska. He once had to do this to six 70 hL foeders, one after the other. Each was a little different in its behavior and in the experience gained, but he and his crew got it done. He offers a few hints to keep things from totally falling apart and making more work—and more uncertainty—for the brewer potentially concerned. Before disassembly, he recommends drilling a hole in every third stave at the level of the bottom croze and placing a screw in each hole to maintain general shape when the hoops are removed. In addition, wrapping duct tape toward the top of the tank will maintain the taper to the tank and keep it from springing open. Naturally, the staves will eventually have to be broken down, moved along with everything else, and reassembled, but doing it in stages is better than playing Jenga® to begin with. Further, and recognizing that the side manways of foeders are invariably set parallel to the direction of the staves in the floor, he also suggests spreading the few floor staves on the manway side slightly—a half-inch or so—in order to leave enough room to fit in that last stave. Beginning the reassembly with the manway staves and working back around to the manway's other side will make it easier to finish loose assembly. Then, when the hoops are replaced and tightened, the whole thing should pull back together, perhaps with the aid of a couple of hammer-taps.

Gabe's good-news-bad-news story? The good news is that his new digs have doors big enough to fit foeders through them. The bad news is that in order to get the ones in that he already had, he had to knock them all down and reassemble them all, again.

When any work is done on a foeder it is likely that the rings, or hoops, will need adjustment. This is especially true around the top and bottom, since those should sit on the bevel, at the croze. Often a new ring is made in a workshop with such capability, or a larger ring left from some other foeder can be adapted. This involves measuring the diameter of the foeder (D) at the appropriate height with all other rings tight. The thickness of the ring (d) must also be taken into account. The resulting diameter of the hoop needed should be the circumference of the tank + 2 π d (D+2 π d). L-shaped pieces of steel are welded to the ring ends and threaded for bolts, which are then used to tighten the ring into place.

Once again, Peter's experiences at Rodenbach serve as an illustration of proper maintenance of foeders as well as a statement of the truly awesome level of expertise and accomplishment in evidence at that brewery and in its beers.

Remember that Rodenbach keeps a cooper on permanent staff and generally has whole tree trunks at the ready for the fashioning of new staves. Note, as well, that the removal of material from the edges of the staves is cumulatively sufficient to require the introduction of a new one simply to maintain original circumference. Presumably, over time all staves would be winnowed to nothing as they are gradually replaced. But, of course, that would take hundreds of years. It's also comforting to note, reviewing the above methods of foeder reassembly, the old and new worlds coming together over the use of duct tape in effective foeder maintenance.

5

Flavors from Wood

U sing and devising techniques for imparting wood flavor to beer can be simple, or it can be complex, based mainly on one's desired level of awareness. Naturally, you can't literally taste awareness, but with it choices can be made that can impart specific flavors of determined strength and complexity. It's easy to get started with wood, simply by getting your hands on a barrel, filling it with beer, tasting it from time to time, and deciding when it's ready either to drink as is or to be blended off with something else. Or so one hopes. Or you can take it a step, or two, or six, further by weighing all the variables and making choices. What wood is it made from? Is it French, American, or from someplace else? Who made it? When? What degree of toast did it receive in the cooperage? Was it charred? What was in it prior to your acquisition? That's a lot of questions to be asking, and a lot of information to be gained, without even really knocking yourself out.

It can be daunting, as a beginner, simply to look at the various options available from supply houses for staves you can use to flavor beer in tanks—never even mind actual barrels yet. American? French? Limousin, or perhaps Vosges? Light, medium, or heavy toast? Size and shape? Grooved staves, thickness of the staves? To say you're feeling your way as you get started is an understatement. What you're doing is guessing, going with your gut, and probably being bolder than absolutely required. You didn't get where you are by being cautious, right? No light toast for you. Heavy, heavy all the way. Anything worth doing is worth doing boldly. And many of the barrel-aged beers in the infancy of modern rediscovery—say, 15 or so years ago—showed this kind of heavy-handedness. Naturally, it isn't quite that simple. You can get nice flavors from some staves, or barrels, subjected to heavy toast, but there's a lot to be gained from learning the differences. And that's only one variable. But it isn't a bad place to start. We'll check back in on the subject of toasting later, but for now let's use it as an introduction to the kinds of things one can weigh when deciding how to treat a wood- or barrel-aged beer.

One could do worse than beginning with a look at the website of the French cooperage Nadalie and seeing what words they use to describe the differences in toast levels. According to them, light toast "brings fruit aromas to the wood." Well, that's a start, isn't it? That's something you can get your head around. Subtle, pleasant, aspirant, appropriate for some beers, but maybe not for others. Medium toast comes in two degrees, regular and plus, with the gradations of description you'd expect. "Fruit is dominant; very intense aromatic complexity," runs medium regular—so far so good, a stronger variation on light, I'd say—while medium plus is, well, bolder: "Fruit mellows with empyreumatic flavors." Oh boy. Already you're getting the idea that more toast doesn't just turn up the volume on qualities earlier expressed. It can change things. And what about that "empyreumatic?" There's a word that leaves Dictionary.com in the dust, but a little more digging and Webster gives us "being or having an odor of burnt organic matter as a result of decomposition at high temperatures." You could get into this, right? Not so hard if you can just keep your wits about you. From there, heavy toast is practically a layup: "Spicy, grilled aromas predominate." Well, duh.

Look at the words and flavors described. Fruit, aroma, intense, complexity, burnt, spicy, grilled. Already a vocabulary presents itself. Already you're getting the idea that degree of toast carries a spectrum that isn't just a cumulative progression. There's a metamorphosis along the way. And this is just toast. Recall other words that are often used to describe oakiness, raw to incinerated. Remember vanilla? Remember coconut? Does butterscotch ring a bell? Clove? Smoke? There's a lot to be perceived and discussed, just in plain English, or the plain version of whatever other languages people speak who are these days getting into aging beer in barrels. And there are other woods, as well, though as we go along it turns out there aren't as many viable options as one might think.

We don't want to alarm you, but each of these descriptors can be attributed to specific chemical compounds, which have names and other properties beyond simply giving flavor to beer and other alcoholic beverages(we can't forget our vinous and spirituous brothers and sisters). The way they interact with wood can teach us how different combinations of wood, water, alcohol, and other materials such as fruit behave over the course of time, also based on what processes have been enacted prior to and during this period of contact. Add that to the fact that it's highly likely the barrels we put beer into for aging have already enjoyed a relationship with either wine or spirits. In short, there's a lot to think about if you choose to learn what's really going on inside that barrel. And once you've begun to think about all that there's really no turning back. You can't unring a bell.

While there are several dozen flavor compounds that can be picked out of oak by analysis—typically gas chromatography and mass spectrometry—five basic groups contribute the flavors we most commonly associate with oak as they show up in beverages. In sensory analysis they become evident, by definition, because they exceed thresholds. Vanillin is perhaps the most obvious one, and its name suggests the flavor it produces, vanilla. Lactones, such as cis-oak-lactone and trans-oak-lactone, provide the coconut flavor that, along with vanilla, can dominate a heavily oaked bourbon barrel stout or porter. Chromatographic analysis, in fact, reads lactone from oak the same way it does from actual coconut; they are literally the same compound. More controversial, given our brewerly training of avoidance where flavors of caramel or butter are concerned, are the furfurals (furfural and 5-methyl-furfural). These flavors have been a matter of fashion, prized in Chardonnays, for example, as the California wine industry was taking flight in the 1970s and '80s, but generally frowned upon in beer because of association with diacetyl. A marker of poorly managed fermentation, as well as simply a flavor characteristic of particular yeasts (a couple of classic English ones come to mind), diacetyl in evidence is one of the fastest ways to get a beer eliminated from competition. The wine industry has generally moved on from this penchant from earlier decades, as well, but a touch of caramel in an India Pale Ale or a sturdy white Burgundy need not wrinkle the nose of the would-be (or actual) aficionado. This is a good illustration of some things simply being a matter of taste. More prolonged toasting will bring out the clove and spice flavors and aromas of eugenol and isoeugenol, dominant when one walks through a cooperage while barrels are being toasted. And then, most obviously, when barrels have been charred for use with bourbon, guaicol and 4-methylguaicol emerge to create a smoky and charred effect beyond that of actual burning wood. These are the main building blocks of the myriad structures constituting the beers, wines, and spirits that come into contact with oak, and, to some extent, other woods.

We've begun this look at the flavor and aroma compounds evident in oak—and perhaps more to the point, as they are displayed in beer aged in barrels—with perhaps too close a concentration on toasting. For, in fact, all these flavors and more exist in different balance, based on additional factors. The origin of the wood and the very physiology of the individual tree also contribute to the intensity and the balance of all of these characteristics. The video shown at the visitor center at Vicard Tonnelerie in Cognac shows representatives of the cooperage tasting from a bore in individual trees as they are standing in the forest. Individual cooperages, and, for that matter, coopers, will produce barrels from the same wood with different flavor and aromatic interplay, much the way different brewers can work with precisely the same ingredients—even from the same recipe—and produce markedly different beers. Throw in climate and the patterns of growing seasons over time and throughout the world, and the list of variables inherent in wood and the beers it can engender defies numbering. But we still have to try, not so much to count but to appreciate the choices made in the course of aging in barrels and the blending of contents that often comes later.

Materials Extracted from Wood

A few further substances naturally inherent in oak should be touched upon here, partly because it's interesting material, but also to inform later vocabulary and to suggest the origin of some of the above compounds. Be warned: This will seem like wading at first, but it will explain a great deal as further variation is explored.

Cellulose: A linear polysaccharide chain that can be a thousand or more units long. It does not have a direct effect on flavors released in beer. Rather, it is the chemical structure that keeps the wood together and is probably the most widely available natural polymer on Earth. Some *Brettanomyces* can consume cellobiose, a glucose disaccharide reducing sugar that can come from cellulose through acid hydrolyses or through cellulose chains that are broken up in the seasoning of the wood or in toasting. Not all opinion is unified on this possibility, but Peter recalls a batch of Rodenbach Grand Cru in 1991 that showed an increase in alcohol that could perhaps have partially come from the reduction of a disaccharide like this, which in turn could have come in part from wood sugars. Given Belgian humidity, it would not seem that the beer would simply lose so much water. If anything, high humidity would have made alcohol evaporate, *reducing* the beer's strength. A substantial increase in alcohol is unlikely, but Holmesian deduction would indicate that wood-related reduction might have been in play in this particular alcoholic increase.

Hemicellulose: Short, two-dimensional, random amorphous structure containing different sugars such as xylose, mannose, galactose, rhamnose, and arabinose, and more complex molecules such as xylan, glucuronxylan, arabinoxylane, glucomannan, and xyloglucan. Upon heating in the toasting or charring process hemicellulose breaks down sugars and caramelizes them through Maillaird and other reactions, contributing flavor. The breakdown starts around 284°F (140°C) and becomes exothermic above 437°F (225°C). Toasting byproducts are furfural, hydroxymethyl furfural, maltol, cyclotene, and a whole range of other products, similar to what happens with malted barley in kilns or roasters.

Lignin: One of the most abundant naturally occurring materials, but not well understood. Hardwood lignin consists of two building blocks, guaiacyl and syringyl structures. These structures disintegrate through thermal depolymerisation under the heat of toasting and charring. Some older literature also mentions that lignin is affected by mild acid attack from beer stored within oak; once again, opinion is divided, with some analysts, such as Andrei Prida of Seguin Moreau, feeling the assertion of beer-related degradation of lignin insufficiently documented. In any case, when heat gets too intense some volatile phenols are formed, evinced in smoky, burnt wood, or medicinal aromas. The first guaiacyl structure will lead to extractable components as coniferaldehyde, vanillin, and vanillic acid. Syringyl structures will lead to sinapaldehyde, syringaldehyde, and syringic acid. Vanillin is the only one that exceeds flavor threshold in a 20% alcohol solution in water, but synergistic effects can come into play, as well.

Tannins: Tannins are perhaps most often associated with wine, with properties arising from the skins and seeds of grapes. In oak they are called ellagitannins, with the purpose of food storage inaccessible to predators such as insects. They are hydrolysable combinations of glucose with ellagic or sometimes gallic acid. Seasoning and toasting or charring breaks down the tannins and makes them more accessible. Tannins react with oxygen when catalyzing metals (the usual suspects being iron, copper, and manganese), forming mostly brown quinones and hydrogen peroxide that can react with ethyl alcohol to form acetaldehyde. Lower pH also creates an unstable environment for oak tannins. Ellagic acid is barely soluble and precipitates in the barrel. Generally speaking, tannins contribute less perceptible flavor than physical sensation of astringency. It is also possible in beer that malt and hop polyphenols could further mask this and confuse the palate. On this subject Prida also suggests that other sensory active compounds may come into play, such as terpenosides and lignans, but concedes that the research is as yet unproven. In very high alcohol concentrations, however, such as in spirits, reductive acetaldehyde combines with more alcohol to form diethyl acetal, a desirable and delicate top note for spirits.

Lipids: Oak lactones come from the small amounts of lipids (oils, fats, and waxes) present in the tree. Although the content in wood is small and generally neglected in analysis, the lactones are hugely flavor active. Already strongly present in green wood, their numbers increase enormously during both seasoning and toasting, although excessive heat, such as in charring, can decrease their content. In addition, some of their effect can be lost through evaporation. Oak lactones have a very low (sub ppm) flavor threshold and a very strong woody, coconut aroma. Trans oak lactone is sometimes described as more celery-like, with a flavor threshold in bourbon of 0.79 ppm, where the cis oak lactone is far more potent and rose-like with a flavor threshold at 0.087 ppm. Their differing names derive from varied molecular orientation. They are characteristic in bourbon, with concentrations around 10 ppm, due to the use of new American oak, which is especially rich in cis oak lactone. In wine, and likely in beer, they can be detected from 0.1 to 0.5 ppm, which is still substantial. Too high a concentration can be less delicate, even too cloying. Differences in the same variety of oak harvested from different regions in France show large variations in total extractions of lipids (highest in Limousin) and methyl-octalactones (highest in the central part of France and in the more easterly Vosges).

To put things in proportional perspective, heartwood, the solid, more mature wood used for barrels, is composed of roughly 45% cellulose, 25% hemicellulose (mainly xylans, which can hydrolyze to furfural), 23% lignin, and 3–5% extractives, including tannins.

All of this will help illuminate some of the variable properties inherent in wood itself. We've looked earlier in this book at how trees grow and what factors unique to oak make it the most physiologically suitable wood for making barrels. We've also looked at some of the different regions in which it is commonly grown and harvested for use. Now let's examine some of these differences that can contribute to identifiable balances of flavor.

Long bandied in wine circles, the concept of *terroir* has over time penetrated other realms of agricultural production. Simply put, it is the contribution of the growing environment and conditions (such as soil conditions and climate) to the ultimate character and quality of a particular crop and the products to which it contributes. Wine has its grapes, beer its barley and hops, and spirits its various fermentables ultimately destined for distilling. Oak as well can be thought to be the result of its terroir, the climate of its forests, the minerals of the soil in which it is grown, the rainfall it receives, and the readiness of its surrounding soil to retain moisture. While there exist a number of oak species used for making barrels, variations in character can be traced to individual regions of growth and even vary from tree to tree within a single forest, within a single species. The changes can vary minutely in the factors enumerated above, but also depend on such things as the straightness of the tree, its height, the consistency of its grain, and the placement of its branches.

As we've seen, the main regions of origin for the white oak used for making barrels are France and the eastern United States. Some Slavic countries, notably Hungary, are producers of suitable oak as well, but history and politics have conspired to render their contribution and productivity somewhat inconsistent. Within France, with its system of government management, origin is also designated by specific forest, province, or region, such as Tronçais, Limousin, or Vosges. In the United States things are less codified and overseen, but the oak from different states is sometimes delineated, though not infallibly. In all cases studies have been undertaken analyzing the presence and balance of specific properties, many of which have been explained above, differentiating them by geographic origin. In addition, subjective tests have been undertaken with panels of tasters to assess these differences as to preference.

Referring once more to fashion, there was a time when American oak was considered too fruity and raw for suitable use in wine, unless bleached with soda ash within an inch of its life. This supposedly unpleasant intensity of flavor was due primarily to lower levels of egallitannins (oxygen scavenging components) and higher levels of lactones in American oak as opposed to French. The oak of eastern and central Europe comes somewhere in between in both these categories, but shows higher levels of spicy eugenol and 2-phenol ethanol, as well as aromatic aldehydes such as vanillin and syringaldehyde. (Prida and Pueuch 2006). Times change, and preferences change with them, and, in fact, there have been times during which French and American wine-makers have preferred each other's oak to their own for barrel production. Difference, it turns out, need not preclude; it only offers more choice.

All this information and quantification only goes so far in determining the effect on beer, since the analyses we've mentioned are taken from oak itself. It's difficult, in fact, to determine by analysis of a liquid whether it has seen French or American oak. Other analytical differences between the two include scopolectin as a marker for American oak, which does not always survive toasting, more guaiacol lignins, including vanillin, in American oak, and more trans lactones in French. Using a statistical method known as Principal Component Analysis (PCA) designed to plot differences, more variation can generally be attributed from winery to winery than from the origins of oak. Colorado State University (Lewis 2009) drew similar general conclusions from beer evaluated from three different breweries in Fort Collins. As it turned out, it was the factors common within each brewery that carried more analytical weight than things that might seem more obvious, such as whether the beer was made with wheat. All this proves is that no single tool or method of evaluation can do everything. It turns out, somewhat comfortingly, that technique is of more concrete importance to the end result than supposedly knowing how things will turn out.

We've alluded to the importance of physiology on the differentiation of quali-ties from tree to tree and among different types and origins of oak. Let's take a look within the wood itself to see where some of these differences lie. Tightness of grain is probably most highly prized in the evaluation of wood in its suitability for barrels, and of oak in particular. It's a measurement of the thickness and density of the yearly growth rings in the wood, of how fast the tree is growing, pursuant to how well the soil in which the tree is growing retains moisture. One aspect oak has over most other woods is that it is ring porous. This means that each year two distinct growth bands are generated, an early porous layer con-taining the sap-carrying vessels followed by a tighter, denser band later in the growing season. This later band can vary in size depending on circumstances within the growing year, while the earlier growth tends to be fairly consistent. Depending on growth tendency, the sap-carrying rings can collectively com-prise anywhere from 5 to 50 percent of the aggregate wood. Not surprisingly, this porous ring is where the greatest extraction into beer, wine, or spirits occurs.

The later blockage of these passages by tyloses makes the wood less permeable by liquid, but does not diminish flavor components attributable to them.

The Buffalo Trace Distillery in Franklin County, Kentucky, once ran an experiment involving 192 barrels made in various combination with wood from 96 specific oak trees. Such variables were considered such as growth rings per inch, soil quality, whether the tree was situated north or south along a hillside, or whether the section was taken from the upper or lower part of the trunk. The precise French word *terroir* may or may not have been used to characterize the judgments carried out by the trials, but that's undoubtedly what was being explored. More subjectively, the legendary Buffalo Trace Master Distiller Elmer T. Lee was known to take particular barrels under his wing, producing single barrel experiments and limited releases with his "honey barrels."

Some forests are known for their slow growth, such as the Tronçais in France as well as forests in Michigan and the Missouri Ozark region. Research on both French and American oak has shown, generally, that a coarser grain provides more lactones and products associated with sugar caramelization such as furfural and hydroxymethyl furfural, while tighter grain has more lignin byproducts such as vanillin. Tasters have generally preferred flavors associated more with finer, tighter grain. (Newton and Thomas 1997)

Seasoning, Bending, Toasting, and Charring 201

Once the tree has been split into staves, its first transformational step toward becoming a barrel ready for use is the degradation of tannins wrought by mold, mildew, and other microorganisms in the long course of time in the cooperage drying yard. This is a process not to be underestimated. If it didn't make a difference years would not be devoted to it—up to seven or eight in the case of some of the large staves destined for foeders. It is here as well wherein one regional difference in treatment appears, for staves for bourbon barrels are aged only for a matter of months, due both to lower levels of naturally occurring tannin in American oak and the treatments these barrels will later receive uniquely suited to bourbon production (including the fact that within their own industry they will be used only once). Artificial drying will lead to more piney/resinous aromas and generally less aroma potential than seasoned wood.

This drying and seasoning of the wood also has a substantial influence on flavor. Oligomeric ellagitannins constantly decrease with time, also decreasing potential perception of raw astringency. This can be manifested as a sawdusty, raw plank, or cardboardy effect due to trans-2-nonenol.

Methyl-octalactone increases due to breakdown of its precursors (lipidic esters). The cis-precursor is less stable than the trans-precursor, resulting in more aromatic (3S,4S)-methyl-octalactone. An oxidative breakdown of lignin terminal molecules is also progressively underway, resulting in the emergence of vanillin and eugenol, but this formation is far less (only 20–30% of the total in the final barrel) than what will eventually occur when the barrels are toasted. Seasoning also allows for microorganisms such as fungi, naturally occurring yeasts, and bacteria to penetrate the exterior parts of the staves (0–4 mm). This microbiological activity is responsible for degradation of ellagic tannins, but also for the degradation of volatile and aromatic components. Freezing and thawing play their part, as well. All this having been said, it would seem that physical and chemical transformation during seasoning has greater effect on aroma than flavor.

The methods by which the staves are prepared for bending can have an effect on the flavor of the wood. This involves the application of heat to render the wood more pliable and varies by cooperage, with some proprietary methods. It can be administered by passage through a steam tunnel, by immersion in hot water, or by heating above a fire with water applied to keep the staves from catching fire. Each treatment has its effect on flavor, with immersion favoring vanillin and the fire method used for bourbon barrels providing more oak lactones.

While these earlier processes have bearing on flavors and aromas later to be imparted by the oak of barrels, there is no doubt that toasting is the most important and distinguishing step in determining flavors and their balance. We have taken a quick introductory look at factors both adjectival and chemical that develop during the various degrees of the toasting process. Now that we've developed a bit of a vocabulary, it's time to get a little more serious.

The descriptive words applied to levels of toast are traditional terms based on the visual appearance of the inside face of the staves. Light toast is a slight darkening of the inside wood, while heavy signifies dark to chocolate brown, but without char. Medium is supposed to be the color of toasted bread. Obviously some subjectivity is inherent in this interpretation and house standards vary from cooperage to cooperage. In addition, oak of different densities will be variously penetrated by heat, with the densest, such as many American examples, allowing greater heat penetration by greater resistance to coloration and charring. In all cases there is a gradient effect of heat penetration into the stave, varying by material and the intensity of the applied heat. The scale of light, medium, and heavy is really only a color-coding system indicating further changes going on in the wood. Another obvious clue to the chemical transformations being enacted is the smell of the wood as it is undergoing toasting. Results can be quantified and more closely standardized through the use of infrared sensors, applied either from time to time or throughout the toasting process.

Inconsistencies in the toasting process should also be addressed, given the typical single source of flame within the toasting barrel and the inevitable vagaries of convection within it. Temperatures can vary quite a bit from one end of a stave to the other, with surface differences noted as much as 24°C within a group of 40 barrels made in the same lot (Collin 2012). Penetration of heat into the stave will vary, as well, depending on the position of the barrel relative to the heat source, the air intake for the flame, type of heat applied, and any number of other factors. The method employed at Tonnellerie Vicard, where an approximately barrel-shaped metal vessel is inserted and radiates heat outward, as evenly as possible, is intended to render the toasting of its barrels more consistent. Toasting can be used by instrumentation, to be sure, but not to be underestimated is the sensibility of the master cooper monitoring the process, whose sensibilities of color, aroma, and their progress qualifies him or her as their industry's master chef.

Similar to the processes of cooking and, for that matter, brewing, when heat is applied to oak it enacts certain changes. Carbohydrate polymers such as the hemicelluloses and the lignin and egallitannin phenolic polymers are broken down in toasting, altering molecular structure. As more heat is applied over time and toasting advances, further changes occur, not all of them linear. Some aromatics are fragile and diminish as toasting proceeds toward heaviness, where others move into more prominent perception. Lignin degradation alone can run the gamut of flavor generation, beginning with vanillin and other aromatics as the result of phenolic aldehyde generation, with further toasting degrading those same aldehydes to produce volatile phenols evinced in the smoky and spicy aromas of guaiacol, 4-methylguaiacol and eugenol. The breakdown of carbohydrates begins quickly and forms furanic aldehydes (5-methyl-furfural, furfural alcohol, 2-acetyl-furan) similar to their formation in boiling wort, throwing faint toasty aromas. Maillard reactions also occur, further enhancing caramelization and its toasty aromas, and especially in French oak due to higher levels of 5-hydroxy-methy-furfural in the early-year porous ring. Other Maillard-related elements produced are cyclotene, maltol, and the sweet, fruity, toasty, caramel and vanilla aromas derived from variously numbered hydroxy-methyl furanones and pyranones, including a degradation of proline and glucose, which can give a burnt jam-like aroma.

The Independent Stave Company in 1998 conducted a subjective and descriptive test of aromas generated by various toast temperatures, both in staves naturally seasoned for 18 months and those kiln-dried. The first group of qualities is from slowly-seasoned air-dried staves:

- Oaky 200–300°F
- Sweet 280–360°F
- Vanilla, 360–480°F
- Almond: 480°F
- Acrid 480–520°F

Kiln-dried examples produced aromas associated more with green wood:

- Spicy 260–320°F
- Woody pencil shavings 300–380°F
- Toasty 400–420°F
- Green 440–500°F
- Sweet 520–540°F
- Acrid >500°F

Speaking to other regional differences, along with a generally denser grain, American oak shows a higher concentration than French of methyl-octolactones, allowing in both aspects greater application of heat for resistance and eventual reduction. This is the oak-coconut aroma, and is concentrated twice as highly in American oak, though it lacks the tannic component of the European. We observed earlier that the cis-oak-lactone is more aromatic than the trans-oak-lactone. Both are concentrated in the early growth ring, and so more will be extracted from wood of a tighter grain as this layer will constitute a greater proportion. It should be mentioned that the amount and presence of lactones in wood is still poorly known, and it is asserted that their occurrence is likely controlled by genetic factors. Woods of different oak species have different abilities to accumulate these molecules. For example, French sessile oak (*Quercus petraea*) is much richer in these components than the pedunculate (*Quercus robur*), individual examples of which could grow in the same forest (Prida 2015). These lactones are also more highly concentrated in wood that is air dried rather than kilned. Vanillin as well is concentrated in the early wood, and so tends to show more in American oak, and especially strongly in medium-toasted barrels.

Toasting alone influences 17 phenolics, 7 aldehydes and 7 lactones (Singleton 1974, Advanced Chemistry). Studies are many plotting the rise and fall of flavor and aromatic elements during toasting, thankfully due to the increasing interest among winemakers and distillers over the past decades, and more recently of brewers. Symposia held by the Independent Stave Company and the various winemaking and distilling organizations have provided a daunting amount of analysis and charting of the effects of toasting, and of the other oaking inserts available, such as cubes and spirals. These are resources worth consulting for further numeric and sensory evaluation of the effects discussed here. Talks on the use of barrels in aging have also increased in number at the Brewers Association's yearly Craft Brewers Conferences, though mainly with an emphasis on souring.

So, to review:

- Cellulose maintains the integrity of the barrel, and as cellobiose can perhaps be mildly degraded through hydrolysis by *Brettanomyces*.
- Hemicellulose is a group of wood sugars, subject to Maillard reaction yielding caramelization, color, furfural, maltol, etc.
- Lignin, with the application of mild heat and perhaps through acid hydrolysis, will produce vanillin and phenolic aldehydes. Under high heat to charring it will produce simple phenols, perceived as smoky, burnt, or medicinal.
- Tannins contribute astringency, but are reduced during seasoning, lessening raw plank or cardboardy aroma. They can produce an oxidative effect, reacting with metals and form hydrogen peroxide to create acetaldehyde.
- Lipids carry disproportionate flavor effect through lactones derived from oils, fats, and waxes in the wood, which are highly subject to development during toasting but degrade with further application of heat.

What Happens When Beer Contacts Wood?

Presume now that beer has been introduced to barrels made from wood properly seasoned, bent, and toasted or charred to a desired degree. Oak is the main wood used for all of this, but in the case of fermentation one can encounter such woods as cedar, fir, pine, larch, and even cypress or other regionally exotic woods, though this is more often found in the spirits industry. These vessels are also more commonly lined, with pitch or other material, and would therefore contribute no flavor either from wood or the lining material. We shall therefore concentrate more on the effects of pro-longed aging in wood. Keep in mind that it is relatively rare for brewers to use barrels for aging fresh from the cooper's shop, so subsequent use will show diminished effect from the wood itself. It will, in many cases, still be evident, however.

The most obvious of these effects is extraction of flavor from the wood. This includes all of the compounds treated above in the discussion of toast-ing and its effects, but also of charring, and of the residual flavor effect of whatever other liquid—beer, wine, or spirit—resided in the barrel prior to the fill in question. It is this latter effect, of previous contents—and bourbon, in particular—that first attracted many modern brewers to barrel aging. This extraction can be substantial, even setting aside spirits barrels that arrive audibly awash in residual previous contents. A 300-liter hogshead pen-etrated by wine for only one millimeter will extract 11 grams of oak material into its next use. Other barrel sizes produce proportional amounts of oak/wine extraction, up to about 100 mg/l, with minimum detectable taste dif-ference somewhere between 0.2 and 0.9 g/l. Another way to put it is in a standard barrel two to four liters of wine are taken up in the wood relatively quickly—in a matter of weeks—comprising around 1 percent of the total liq-uid carrying over to the next fill, whether rinsed or not. Having become wise to this wildly extravagant gift to later users of their barrels, bourbon distillers might rinse or otherwise extract the residual spirit for more economical use in watering their whiskey to standard commercial strengths. To date, some distillers do, and some don't.

Extraction is a diffusion process, with glucosides hydrolyzing by expo-sure to acids and enzymes. Its degree, sensibly enough, is relative to the ratio of exposure of liquid volume to wood surface. As barrels get larger the vol-ume per unit of wood reduces strikingly. A typical wine barrel of 225 liters represents an exposure ratio of 1.2 hL/m^2 of wood surface, but if the volume is increased 100 times to 225 hL, this ratio of liquid to wood increases to 5.2 hL/m^2. Extractive effect on the liquid, therefore, would be far less. Thickness of the wood also comes into play, as with more time beer and other liquids will simply penetrate further. The million-liter foeder at the Byrrh plant in Thuirs, France, though imposingly massive—the world's largest—provides the world's smallest wood effect on its contents. Never mind, by the way, that the Byrrh foeder has been out of regular use for decades and so is these days exerting zero influence on any contents. In fairness, it was in its day agitated for heightened contact. This is another technique that can increase wood extraction, even if simply by rolling. Formulas exist, of course, for the determination of the volume of a cylinder—or barrel—and its inner surface area. Such formulas would likely be found in any utilitarian technical reference pocket guide.

The table below shows that when the volume of a container increases 10x, the internal surface in per-volume units is a little less than half.

Volume liter	Barrel cm²/L	Cylinder cm²/L	Cylinder hL/m²
20	195	215	0.05
200	90	99	0.51
2000	42	46	2.17
10000	24	27	3.70
100000	11	12	8.33

The second table gives a rough idea of how the volume-to-surface ratio changes in common size barrels. This is just a guideline, since every barrel is slightly different, and the internal surface is relatively hard to calculate precisely.

Capacity liter	Surface m²	cm²/L	hL/m²
200	1.8	90	1.11
300	2.4	80	1.25
500	3	60	1.67

Looking at the makeup of a stave in contact with liquid, three main zones present themselves from inside to outside. The inner "waterlogged" zone comprises 1–3 mm, which will be stained by previous contents such as red wine. Its thickness is dependent on time and conditions of storage, as you'll see below. The next, fiber-saturated zone has a moisture content of around 18%, but is without free water, hampering the flow outward of larger molecules. Then there is the progressive drying zone on the outer layer of the barrel, holding 8–12% moisture and maintaining equilibrium with the outside humidity by possible passage of water molecules, either way depending on conditions.

Temperature and humidity can affect extraction. As touched on in the cellar section of chapter 4, cool and somewhat humid is best, in order to minimize the rate of evaporation of water and alcohol, or the "angel's share," lost to the cellar through the wood. The breaking point is roughly 65% humidity, with water evaporation occurring below and ethanol evaporation occurring above. Even a tightly closed barrel can give up 2–5% per year of its contents, and can create an interior vacuum as water and/or alcohol is pulled from the wood. Further, pressure can push contents one way or the other, depending on whether the barrel is over- or under-pressurized relative to its surroundings. High temperature also extracts more character from the wood in general. Fluctuation in temperature, as we've seen in the bourbon barrel houses of Kentucky, results in greater extraction due to the repeated ebb and flow of a barrel's contents into and out of the wood. Higher levels of ethanol can also increase the flow of liquid and level of extraction. Both water and ethanol are wood-extractive solvents. They just behave differently under different conditions.

The Cascade Barrel House in Portland, Oregon, produces a huge array of sour, wood-aged beers in a rustic urban setting. It sprang apparently fully-formed—even to those of us long acquainted with its founder, Ron Gansberg—from the brow of the more conventional Raccoon Lodge. Mentions above of matters relating to pressure and temperature call to mind a couple of aspects of Cascade's operation. Their barrel storage area—recently expanded to 23,000 square feet—is kept at a steamy 80% humidity in order to mitigate losses to the so-called "angel's share." In mockery of this, Ron and his gang do blends from barrels as they mature, calling such projects the "devil's due," as angels don't share, but devils do. Ron's first barrel project, enacted with compatriot Preston Weesner in mild breach of the dictates of Raccoon Lodge's principal owner Art Larrance, was an English-style IPA, dry-hopped in barrels and rolled for enhanced contact, allowed to warm and cool with ambient temperature and aged long enough to synthesize the storied sea voyages from Yorkshire to Calcutta. By "mid-voyage" the barrel heads were bulging from accumulated pressure, and Ron still bears a sort of slo-mo memory of one of the bungs blowing, sending a wreath of wet hops ceilingward along with a 14-foot geyser of beer.

Type, condition and treatment of wood have probably the most dramatic effect on flavor extraction. We've seen the influence of toasting where this is concerned, as well as the physiological differences and sensory manifestations inherent in woods from different growing regions. Once again, tighter grain results in a higher proportion of porous early wood, and, hence, greater extraction. Other heat treatments associated with bending can favor Maillard reaction and its resultant flavors. Physical alteration of the barrel's interior can affect surface area and other extractive-associated factors, such as the barrels we saw at Brown-Forman that were grooved on the inside for production of their Sinatra brand of Jack Daniel's whiskey. Other one-off variables such as the charring without toasting (also at Brown-Forman) of some tequila barrels would have their own flavor effects, though this particular treatment might clarify and color more than flavor a finished product. Different species of oak would, of course, carry somewhat different properties from each other, as would barrels made from other woods such as chestnut and acacia, or the barrels made from cedar and once used for sake, re-employed at the Kiuchi brewery in Japan for their Classic Japanese Ale. Inspired by this very beer and a suggestion by a local Tampa homebrewer, Cigar City Brewing began a tradition of aging on Spanish cedar, which they say provides notes of grapefruit and white pepper. Perhaps not qualifying as a treatment as such but nonetheless affecting extraction from the interior surface of a barrel would be any buildup of beer or wine stone, lessening the effect of wood and reducing oxygen diffusion, but almost certainly imbuing the contents with other residual flavors. Naturally, subsequent reuse of any barrel would generally lessen flavor effects, as well.

Some wood-aged beers never see the inside of a barrel. Instead, they are infused by various methods using staves, chunks, spirals, cubes, diamonds, and chips, and even powders (use caution due to allergies and breathing it in), generally of oak but sometimes of other woods. In most cases these other products have been subjected to toasting, and so carry the characteristics of degree along with the simple infusion effect of the wood. Most common is the passive effect of time and contact, but sometimes a more active approach is adopted such as with the so-called Oakerator at Innis and Gunn in Edinburgh, which circulates beer via a pump through a layer of oak chips in a steel tank. Cigar City uses a similar construct it calls Spinbot 5000, though it uses an array of woods for flavoring, including the above-mentioned Spanish cedar, the wood used in the construction of cigar humidors. The operative factor in all these cases is the surface area exposed to beer in a tank or keg. These treatments can also serve as an economy measure as the cost of actual barrels continues to rise. Wayne Wambles of Cigar City reports a reduction of wood usage of 30% when the Spinbot is used compared with more passive contact, and time needed for desired flavor development dropping from 7–11 days down to 24–36 hours.

Most scholarship concerning flavor effects from wood has been conducted in connection with wine. While many of the attributes of wines and beers aged in or on wood are generally common, there are differences in the balance of compound extraction based mostly on general differences of alcohol and pH (general since a sour beer, for example—or one extreme in alcohol content—deviates from the profile of more ordinary beer, and hence shows some results more congruent with wine). The presence of yeast can also affect this balance. Femke Sterckx, a PhD student at the Katholieke Universiteit Leuven, has conducted studies using different origins and toast levels of oak chips in order to study the extraction of monophenols from wood in beer. A corresponding study of lactones would also have been interesting, but as the research stands, the development of several specific monophenols were tracked in connection with the above factors, but also simply with amounts of wood added. Most monophenols increased, for example, when more chips were added, except for eugenol, thymol, 4-vinyl guaiacol, and 4-ethyl phenol—with the latter two perhaps not directly wood-related anyway, and familiar to brewers as part of ferulic extraction when mashing in at temperatures below 50°C. Temperature increase also enhances monophenol extraction.

And then there is yeast, a factor far larger in aging beer than wine, and something entirely absent in spirits. With lower alcohol content and the presence of nutrients such as free amino acids, our friend *Saccharomyces* is very comfortable reducing away in the medium of beer, with *Brettanomyces*, if present, choosing either to reduce or oxidize. We'll get more into the effects and processes of oxidation in a bit. One of the interesting flavor-related pathways yeast can take is the conversion of some of these nutrients into higher alcohols and sometimes esters. As brewers it is aldehydes and esters we are interested in, since with their low flavor thresholds they become readily evident in beer. The presence of aldehydes can be attributable to wood phenols, and when acted upon by yeast the result can be higher alcohols with flavor thresholds high enough to create a diminishing effect. This is especially true of vanillin, which is the most flavorful compound from wood extraction, but its alcohol, ester, and acid (itself perhaps also brought about by other microorganisms as well as oxidation) have a high flavor threshold. Poof! Vanillin is gone (or seems to be).

The following chart offers a far more concise summary of Sterckx's results.

Monophenol	Change during wood aging	Linear increase with amount of wood chips	Correlates with toasting degree	Correlates with wood origin	Influenced by yeast activity	Influenced by presence of oxygen
4-vinylguaiacol (4-VG) and 4 ethylphenol	-	-	-	-	+	-
4-hydroxybenzaldehyde and methyl vanillate	-	+	-	+	+	-
Eugenol and Salicyl aldehyde	+	+	+		+	-
Thymol	+	+	-	+	+	-
Syringaldehyde, Acetosyringone, vanillin, acetovanillone	+	+	+	-	+	+
Guaiacol and 4-ethyl guaiacol	+	+	+	+	-	-

A few other observations provide greater detail. Methyl vanillate and 4-hydroxybenzaldehyde barely increased by the addition of chips, but the increase was related to the amount of wood added, and American oak had more of those components than French oak. Eugenol, thymol, and salicylaldehyde increased with the addition of more oak chips, with more elevated levels seen for medium toast. Thymol was more an indicator of French oak, and especially wood of medium toast. Eugenol and thymol also increased when yeast was present. Heavy toast was mostly associated with acetosyringone, syringaldehyde, guaiacol, 4 ethylguaiacol, acetovanillone, and vanillin. Vanillin, acetovanillone, syringaldehyde, and acetosyringone reached the highest concentrations when oak chips were added. The toasting level correlated with the concentration of syringaldehyde and acetosyringone, and less with acetovanillone, which can also be formed by ethanolysis of lignin. The concentration of those four components also decreased with time, and especially in the presence of oxygen. Guaiacol and 4-ethylguaiacol increased similarly to beer on wood, except for French oak of medium toast. High toast levels increased those components, as guaiacol is a pyrolysis of wood byproduct. Longer aging also increases the resultant spicy wood aromas. In addition, and since flavor thresholds vary among tasters, synergistic flavor effects of multiple polyphenols can affect perception.

This is all pretty involved, and it may seem to require a codebook to make it all intelligible. Looking at all of these compounds in groups rather than individually can help make better sense of the flavor elements involved. As mentioned earlier, the website of the French cooperage Nadalie provides a good (and simple) adjectival rundown of options and effects where oak inserts are concerned.

More Arcane Processes and Effects of Extraction

Many of the extractive effects we've treated thus far could be attributed to simple contact between liquid and wood, the leaching of flavor and other properties in an essentially passive way. It should come as no surprise, given the myriad thermal, chemical, biological, and temporal considerations we've given other processes leading up to the manufacture and filling of barrels, to find that the reductive (from charred layer in bourbon barrels), reactive, and otherwise transformational steps onward do not cease once the filled barrel is lovingly patted and laid to indeterminate rest.

Wine scholarship at this point begins to mention oxalate and tartaric precipitation and tannin clarification, but as these are directly attributable to grapes they have little bearing on our inquiries with beer, aside from any residual effect from previous use. Most of the processes enacted within the barrel have to do with the introduction of oxygen, either through the wood over time or when the contents are introduced into the barrel or disturbed by sampling, topping, or simple movement of the barrel. Oxydation of vanillin, hydrolysis of acids, and ethanolysis are all things that can happen along these lines. Simple contact extraction is also augmented by hydrolysis as non-flavonoid phenolics are reactively pulled from the wood. It's no surprise that a second fill of a barrel of 16 weeks would show a reduction of phenols from one earlier given 12 weeks. Things just diminish with time, right? But give it a third fill and let it sit for six months and the phenols are back, indicating that hydrolytic reaction is aiding the effect of time (Rous 1983). Other directly extractable compounds from oak are vanillin, hydorxymethylfurfural, maltol, and ethylmaltol. Vanilla character comes from the oxidation of coniferyl and sinapic alcohol—themselves ethanolytical reductions of oak lignins—producing vanillin and syingaldehyde.

This effect would be far higher in spirits than in beer and wine (Prida 2015). Oak tannins (mainly elagitannins) have a very low capacity for oxygen reduction (redox), which demands, since such things must act in balance, that other factors in the liquid act to consume oxygen-freeing peroxide and acetaldehyde. Oxygen is. of course, also reacting with settled materials such as trub, yeast, and other lees and microorganisms. Vintners, in fact, have tried to synthesize slowly oxidative effects by micro-oxygenation through ceramic stones at a level of 1 mL/liter of wine per month (wine is somewhat more resilient to the effects of oxygen than beer). At one point Rodenbach attempted such a synthesis of oxidation by ultrasonic means, hoping to speed the souring process in its beer—it didn't work. In addition, enzymatic reactions can both oxidize and reduce inhibitors. Beyond the apparently easy balance of some of these oxidative processes, too much oxygen entering the barrel can lead to the formation of acetic acid, due to the presence of sufficient airborne acetobacter. Likely more than simply coming through the wood, oxygen could come via the bung, in between staves above the level of liquid or around the head.

This mention of a souring effect generally considered undesirable begs the discussion—brief at this point, as chapter 6 of this book will treat the subject in greater detail—of sour effects in wood-aged beer sought and desired. Oxygen is an essential part of these processes, as are time and the microorganisms present—perhaps in solution, but, more to the point, resident in the wood in question. The practice of kettle souring with *lactobacillus,* so popular among craft brewers these days, is essentially separate from this, but if the wort is not boiled prior to initial fermentation these bacilli could certainly come into play. Cellars of between 14.5°C and 16.5°C provide an ideal range of temperature for bacteria otherwise regarded as "beer spoilers" to work, nibbling away further at residual nutrients ripe for oxygen-related microbiological degradation. Once again, the key to this introduction of oxygen is that it be slow, a result of the barrel constituting an essential barrier between contents and the outside atmosphere, in order to create an environment where facultative aerobic and anaerobic organisms can strive. *Brettanomyces* can function either way. Microorganisms that have been hampered along the way by lack of nutrients or unfriendly extremes of alcohol or pH can still lie dormant in wood for later awakening. Finally, time can act to increase ester formation and subsequent aromatic effect. Foam in beer affected by these processes is generally reduced, but can be augmented by a grand cru-type blending with beer younger or of more active carbonation.

Other Wood-Related Products and Processes You May Not Have Thought Of

Natural cork is a wood product, in fact an oak product, deriving from the bark of *Quercus suber*, a tree found mainly in Mediterranean countries, and particularly on the Iberian peninsula. The thick bark layer is stripped from the tree every nine years in order to allow gradual regeneration without essential harm to the tree, resulting in a sort of arboreal shorn sheep look. No flavor from cork is desired, of course, but a couple of defects can occur, leakage and cork taint. The cork is boiled during manufacture for sterilization, but contamination can occur via reinfection. 2,4,3-trichloroanisole (TCA) is the most commonly designated culprit for cork taint, derived from chlorinated components used to treat cork in process, storage, or shipping. Tribromoanisole (TBA) has a similar effect on beer and wine. The indefinable mustiness sometimes identified by wine consumers can be confused with TCA taint. Leakage could also result in oxygenation.

Artificial corks from plastics are considered qualitatively more effective, but most consumers still prefer real cork. Nearly all corks used in beer are natural, and most innovation in the field is in connection with standard wine corks. One such innovation is the DIAM cork, where natural cork is milled to 2 mm granules and treated with CO_2 to reduce TCA before the granules are compressed to specification using an FDA-approved binding agent. Some brewers, such as New Belgium, have moved away altogether from the use of perhaps more aesthetically pleasing cork as closures for bottles, both for reasons of potential cork-related compromise and the determination that a properly seated oxygen-absorbing crown provides a superior seal.

The smoking of malt for brewing is a subject fascinatingly similar to the interior toasting of barrels, with the added advantage of wood variety for an array of flavors. Fruit woods such as apple, pear, and cherry are common possibilities, generally imparting mild smoke flavor, with oak itself often used, as well as beech, alder, mesquite, and hickory. The latter is, of course, commonly used for smoking hams and bacon, and so an associative effect can be marked, which may or may not be deemed desirable. Beech is the wood used in the classic smoked beers of Bamberg, such as Schlenkerla and Spezial, as well as the most commonly available commercial smoked malt, from the Weyermann maltings, also in Bamberg. Sabine Weyermann describes the aroma effect of the malt as "honey" or "vegetarian ham." Weyermann also produces an oak-smoked wheat malt initially suggested by Polish homebrewers eager for malt to use for the brewing of traditional Gratzer, and Briess Malting in Chilton, Wisconsin, smokes barley malt with cherry wood. Alder and mesquite are plentiful, fast-growing woods commonly available in the Northwest and Southwest, respectively, and as such find their way into regional smoked foods as well as craft-brewed smoked beers. Peat and straw have also traditionally been used. The British maltster Hugh Baird produces a fearsome peat-smoked malt, to be used with discretion, and the Crisp maltings once made a milder, peated distiller's malt, the secret weapon in early-1990s versions of Pike Place Brewery's Old Bawdy barley wine from Seattle. Because of their terpene content evergreen woods are considered too resinous and acrid to be desirable, though juniper is cited as an adjunct heat source for smoking peat (Daniels and Larsen 2000). Jos Ruffell of the Garage Project in Wellington, New Zealand, has smoked malt using the native wood Manuka.

Before indirect methods of drying malt were devised, products of combustion would come in contact with malt, generally imparting an incidental smokiness to it. While not necessarily sought, it nonetheless influenced the porters and brown ales of the day, and indeed all beer. Ray Daniels and Geoffrey Larsen, in their book *Smoked Beers*, further make the point that with fires also in use as a near-universal heat source, the world used to be a far wood-smokier place than we are accustomed to today. Everything—food, beer, and indeed the general ambiance—was rife with the touches of smoke and fire. While we consider smoked beers today to occupy a specialty niche, it's possible that prior to the advent of technology that made the production of pale malt more commonly possible and desirable, more beers displayed some smokiness than didn't.

We've examined the physical structure of wood, composed mainly of cellulose (40–45%), hemicellulose (20–35%), and lignin (18–38%). We've teased apart the transformations that occur when oak in particular is toasted. Like staves in a cooperage's drying yard, wood used for smoking malt is seasoned, in order to lessen moisture content and mitigate other possible extractives. When flame is introduced and pyrolysis occurs, the three above compounds degrade in sequence, with first hemicellulose and then cellulose leading the way, and lignin rounding out the process. The words used to describe the effects of this degradation are strikingly similar to those attached to the different degrees of toast in a barrel, and no wonder—they're from the same compounds. Sweet, bready, and caramel aromas are attributed to hemicellulose, with furans and lactones mentioned in connection with cellulose breakdown, among other components. Lignin combustion produces the spicier and more ponderous constituents, things such as our old friends vanillin, eugenol, syringaldehyde, and 4-methylguaiacol. Between them, they paint a smoky picture very similar to the different degrees of toast when oak is subjected to controlled heat.

Malt can be smoked in a number of ways, but the actual uptake of smoked flavors is a simple matter of condensation. Straightforwardly enough, the malt, whether dry or moistened, is cooler than the smoke passing across it, and this temperature difference causes the aforementioned compounds simply to condense on its surface. Other processes such as Maillard reactions and caramelization can also occur as a result of applied heat. Smokiness is a fleeting quality, and will diminish with time. Subsequent batches of smoked beers drawn from the same lot of malt will show lessening of smoke effect unless recipe proportions are altered accordingly. Against the Grain Brewery in Louisville, Kentucky, where smoke and char are part of local culture, has developed a nifty malt-smoking device based on a restaurant holding oven fitted with screened wooden trays. They specialize in the smoking of malt using the wood of local fruit and nut trees. Sometimes a hard sell in other regions, smoked beers are apparently fairly popular in Kentucky. Purely geographically related, Louisville is, of course, the home to the eponymous Slugger baseball bats, maple versions of which have been used—whole and unvarnished— among a coterie of breweries from far-flung corners of the country to age Homefront IPA in a program called Hops for Heroes.

Scratch Brewing is located on 85 acres of rugged land near Ava, Illinois, with trees of varying type interspersed with sandstone outcroppings. There Ryan Tockstein has taken his experiments with wood and its byproducts to a maniacal degree of inquiry, offhandedly mentioning that there are "lots of hidden flavors in nature." He has worked with oak, to be sure, but also with hickory, maple, cedar, birch, and sycamore, here and there adding sap to his brewing liquor, as well as bark toasted in the brewery's pizza ovens nearly to smoking, used for steeping in the brewing liquor. Effects vary, naturally, with hickory bark imparting a strong, incense-like aromatic reminiscent of marshmallow and vanilla, used in stout and wee heavy, as well as a lactic sour beer. Maple, oak, and cedar sap add a mineral note, and branches and chips of the various woods are sometimes added to conditioning beer. Not surprisingly, collected sap is subject to wild fermentation.

Whether verbal, sensory, biological, or chemical, it's doubtful how much of all this analysis crossed the minds of early makers of barrels, even when they began storing alcoholic beverages within them. Barrels just seemed like a good idea at the time, and filling them with wine, beer, and spirits merely an efficient way to set volumes of liquid aside for a while. With time, however, notice was taken and processes devised that made positive use of the effects of wood. Understanding these processes and having a grasp of the quantification of all these effects is what helps us begin to control their influence on beer.

6

Flavors in Wood

I t has long been established that wood in its many forms can contribute a great deal of flavor and aroma complexity to beverages fermented and aged within it. Every stage in its growth and processing contributes factors directly traceable to myriad influence by chemical compound, microbiological degradation, and thermal reaction, to say nothing of the effects exerted on beer, wine, and spirits in wood by time and environment. It's curious now to think that such effects were once regarded as incidental, things to be weighed, mitigated, and, if possible, eliminated in order to devise as neutral an environment as possible so as not to influence sensory effect on contents. Well, penicillin was sort of a mistake, too. Suffice it to say that a lot of things that start out being seen one way take on a whole different meaning once people get to thinking about them.

So it is with the aversions ingrained by our training toward becoming brewers. Flavors associated with infection and procedural misstep can be a source of shame to the fledgling brewer, once he or she becomes sufficiently schooled to recognize them—even more so, perhaps, to the brewer of some experience. But of course it depends what the flavor is, and what the intent of the brewer was entering into the project. Some things, of course, are anathema in finished beer. The corniness of DMS and the cloying butterscotch of diacetyl in excess turn pretty much everyone away. So too the generally procedurally derived effects of oxidation. But what if the flavors turn out to be pleasant, whatever window on perversity should be thrown open where convention is concerned? The beer writer Michael Jackson used to muse that sometimes it seemed the beers he most preferred were ones that were just a little flawed, ones not so unimpeachably made and conceived.

There's a tradition of sour beer, of course, and in itself it's been parsed and presented sufficiently for us not to need to do so now. But we've got a thing or two to say about beers that derive some of their flavor from cohabitation in wood with substances and organisms not literally of that wood. These can be things that, like the beer later introduced by wood-crazy brewers, once sat and aged within the containers in question, left over in residual quantity to exert nominal—or pronounced—flavor influence. Or they can be microbes, yeasts, and bacteria having taken up residence in the grain and gaps and residual leavings of prior agings of beer. We know that's why you're here.

Jumping back once more to the perspective gained by training we've all received both as hobbyists and professionals, a barrel is inherently a somewhat unclean thing. In most cases it arrives at our door with at least a bit of uncertain provenance. Who owned this barrel before me and what, exactly, did they do with it? What kind of brewer, or winemaker, or distiller were they? Can they be trusted? What am I getting myself into here? Well, there's evidence to be gained, of course. Whether new or used, it will almost certainly bear the wood-burned marks of the cooperage that produced it. In many cases it will show which winery or distillery saw its principal use. If from a bourbon distillery it was only used once, of course, so whatever's still inside (if it's coming directly from the distillery) can pretty quickly be determined. If from a winery it may well have been used multiple times, with the cumulative effect of penetration within the wood of the wines it's seen over time. It could have been reshaved or have oak inserts. If it's from whiskey, it could even have been reshaped, or have younger staves. If it's beer that was in there before it's likely you're the one that put it there, and it's to be hoped that not a lot of time has passed before you're able to fill it right back up again.

Nearly all of the scholarship we've cited in connection with our subject so far comes from the world of wine and spirits. It's all very interesting, of course, and provides a great deal of background for understanding what has happened to the wood in a barrel as it's manufactured and once it's filled with the beverage for which it is intended. Like the work done within the wine and spirits industries, research undertaken by coopers and their organizations has been devoted to determining how they can do the best job for their first-use customers. Then we show up, scavengers that we are—though these days generally able to pay a fair price—and muddle things with a slightly different set of expectations and aspirations. Both brokers and manufacturers of barrels seem to see this as a good thing. It does, after all, mean that the market has grown. At any given conference there they are, in greater numbers all the time, presenting wares in a range covering everything from inserts such as chips and spirals to brand-new custom-made barrels and tanks. But where the scholarship for wood-aged beers is concerned, there just isn't much. It would be collectively egotistical to say that we are these days inventing the category; sufficient precedent exists in Europe to dispel that notion. But like so much else that got us to where our movement is today, we are learning from what has come before, and from each other. Cue the micro-distillers, many of who come from a brewing background, and there's another layer to examine.

Beyond the fact that there's alcohol in it, beer bears little resemblance to its putative cousins, wine and spirits. We could get into distinctions of culture and perception, but what we care about here is that there are inherent chemical, biological, and physiological differences between beer and both wine and spirits that cause it to behave differently—and to change differently—when it comes in contact with wood. With some crossover exceptions, beer has lower alcohol content and higher pH than wine. It has far more protein, and more polyphenols due to the use of malt and of hops. It also has more variety. As complex and wonderful as wine can be, brewers have more latitude where conception and process are concerned, and produce a staggering array of variations on an initially basic theme. In addition to a vast range of traditional raw materials and a color spectrum ranging from pale straw to inky black and various other hues, they combine fruits, vegetables, spices, herbs, and almost anything else edible in beer. They range from accepting to embracing of microorganisms shunned by winemakers, even as they borrow other techniques from them. Ditto to all of the above with what they put into barrels, and the effects they hope to achieve with them. So, in a way we're on our own.

Will Meyers of Cambridge Brewing in Massachusetts captures both this aloneness and the dawning of collaboration and shared knowledge in his recollection of meeting like-minded colleagues on both sides of the historical line separating winemaking from brewing:

In 2003, just a week after the inaugural release of Benevolence, a winemaker from Sonoma County was at our bar. After several glasses of Benevolence (14% abv) he began boisterously demanding to speak with the brewer and I did my best to avoid him. Eventually he caught my eye while I was cleaning the brewhouse and began yelling "Hey man, do you know what this is? This is banyuls, man! This is banyuls!" Not knowing what banyuls was, and not yet having at my disposal a pocket-sized supercomputer with instantaneous search engine capabilities, I had to have him explain it to me. Banyuls, it turns out, is a fortified French aperitif or dessert wine which is maderised in barrels or glass jugs, exposed to air and direct sunlight and evaporation and heat. This California winemaker, it turned out, was an encyclopedia of obscure wines and techniques. I was intrigued, and I and the great Carl Sutton of Sutton Cellars immediately became fast friends. We spent hours discussing sherry and Madeira, solera systems, and Friulian orange wines fermented in amphoras. My head spun from all of these wines which seemed to break all the rules of solid practical fermentation science and I began to wonder which techniques could be applied to beer. The MBAA Practical Brewer warned against oxidation, light, temperature fluctuations and extremes, and beer "spoilers" like Brettanomyces, Lactobacillus, and Pediococcus. But this applied to contemporary beer styles in modern production facilities. I decided my passion was to pursue what I began calling "counter-intuitive ferments." Furthering this decision and also in 2003 (I think), I met Tomme Arthur of Pizza Port for the first time. As we discussed Benevolence and his Cuvee de Tomme, we were both struck at the similarities of our ferments and process over the previous several years without knowing of the existence of the other. If there were other brewers thinking the same thoughts as me, I felt I was on the right track.

Very few brewers put their beer into new wood. Odell's Woodcut of Fort Collins, Colorado, is one exception, and there are doubtless others. So, whatever other considerations there may be, previous fills loom large in the conception and execution of wood-aged beer. It all essentially began with bourbon barrels, since in this country they've been relatively easy and inexpensive to procure (never mind for the moment that with popularity they've become rarer and more costly). In their earliest examples some wonderful beers were produced, as well as many simply concussive in both their bourbon and wood effects. Both toasted and charred, bourbon barrels are made of already strongly flavored American oak, used once by the distiller and then passed on. The oak is quite rich in the so-called cis-whiskey lactone, which, with its low flavor threshold, is one of the dominant flavor attributes of this type of aging. In addition, of course, there's the effect of residual bourbon. As observed in chapter 5, this has been forced by temperature fluctuation in and out of the wood during aging at the distiller's, and, hence, is rich in its own right with oak character. This is an easy way to flavor beer, and typically these beers are sturdy and dark stouts, porters, and in some cases doppelbocks. It can happen cold and relatively quickly, and breweries that produce such beers on a large scale are often able to procure and dispose of used barrels through the same broker. They generally move onward to Scotland, sometimes Ireland, where in both cases the single-use requirement of bourbon doesn't exist. One has to muse on the possible eventual effect of all these barrels, used first for bourbon and then for beer, on the Scotch and Irish whiskey industries.

Aside from traditional European examples, these were the first barrel-aged beers to reach the US market. Big and bold, drenched with boozy flavor and the strong coconut and vanilla of oak, many were wonderful and many more were, well, a bit much. The alcohol soaked into barrels can be a substantial constituent of beers so aged, and can meaningfully boost alcohol by volume (abv) as much as 2–2.5%, according to brewers whose identities are safe with us. But as with beers whose acetic component first intrigued and then repelled aficionados, nuance came to be embraced where the flavors of wood and whiskey were concerned. During the late 1990s and early 2000s, Todd Ashman, was a pioneer with these beers at Flossmoor Station in Flossmoor, Illinois, and he's since moved on to FiftyFifty Brewing in Truckee, California, where such painstakingly constructed beers live under the Eclipse label.

Before we move on from bourbon barrels it should be noted that it can no longer be assumed that a bourbon or other whiskey barrel coming to a brewer straight from a distillery is necessarily simultaneously delivering to him or her a head start measure of spirits. As an economy measure it is these days becoming more common for distilleries to recapture and rinse out residual liquor for eventual blending down from cask strength. While perhaps a shame for brewers wanting that economical and flavorful touch of veracity, it's perfectly understandable. Who can blame thrifty distillers for making use of a flavorful byproduct that for years they've been giving away for free? Brewers eager to recapture the heady boost could always run out and buy a bottle of the spirit in question in order to re-whiskify the barrel's interior, but don't you dare tell the Alcohol and Tobacco Tax and Trade Bureau (TTB) we even had this conversation.

Since it's come up, however, prudence would dictate a look at current TTB regulation:

§25.15   Materials for the production of beer.

(a) Beer must be brewed from malt or from substitutes for malt. Only rice, grain of any kind, bran, glucose, sugar, and molasses are substitutes for malt. In addition, you may also use the following materials as adjuncts in fermenting beer: honey, fruit, fruit juice, fruit concentrate, herbs, spices, and other food materials.

(b) You may use flavors and other nonbeverage ingredients containing alcohol in producing beer. Flavors and other nonbeverage ingredients containing alcohol may contribute no more than 49% of the overall alcohol content of the finished beer. For example, a finished beer that contains 5.0% alcohol by volume must derive a minimum of 2.55% alcohol by volume from the fermentation of ingredients at the brewery and may derive not more than 2.45% alcohol by volume from the addition of flavors and other nonbeverage ingredients containing alcohol. In the case of beer with an alcohol content of more than 6% by volume, no more than 1.5% of the volume of the beer may consist of alcohol derived from added flavors and other nonbeverage ingredients containing alcohol.

You'll note the somewhat ambiguous language concerning "nonbeverage" contributions of alcohol to the finished product. One could interpret this in various ways, but it does seem to carry a letter-of-the-law-type prohibition against any knowing addition of other alcoholic beverage, however residual, to beer. We know of no active prosecution in connection with this, but wisdom would dictate judiciousness in deriving constituent alcoholic strength from vinous or spirituous leavings in second-use barrels. Practical, mainly conversational reports on such alcoholic boosting (conscious or not) vary widely, from barely measurable to substantial. Additionally, and happily only of historical interest, the state of California several years ago took a look at the potential tax advantage to be gained by categorizing beers aged in barrels previously having contained spirits as spirits themselves, barring thorough—and expensive—laboratory testimonial as to lower-than-threshold alcoholic supplementation. Fortunately for the 85% of us conducting experiments with wood, as well as the 100% of us who enjoy such products, the proposed law was not enacted.

Used wine barrels are decidedly more subtle in flavor, and a more delicate beer can benefit from some extraction of either white or red wine. If focusing only on previous flavor the extraction and aging can be done cold. Wine barrels are also higher than spirits barrels in microbiological load. The hops in beer will generally prevent the uptake of malolactic fermentation, fairly standard in many wines, but other organisms, such as *Pediococcus*, can survive. *Brettanomyces* is pretty universally anathema to winemakers, but it, too, can lie dormant in wood. Wine barrels in general are well suited for the souring of beer. Red wine barrels come far more commonly into the secondary market as they are cycled through more quickly than those used for white wines— often only a couple of uses before they are sold. White wine barrels typically hold their contents for shorter periods and can be used for many years with relatively less residual age to show for it. They can be a lot of fun if you can find them, particularly with some lees left inside. Russian River's barrel-aged Chardonnay Temptation is a fine example, and, in fact, Vinnie Cilurzo gave Tomme Arthur his first couple of white wine barrels for the production of the beer that would eventually become Lost Abbey's Red Poppy.

Bourbon and wine barrels are those most commonly encountered in the search for interesting places to put beer for extractive flavoring, but that certainly isn't where it ends. Other spirits, such as tequila, brandy, cognac, calvados, and gin, for example, can produce interesting flavors by residual and secondary effect. Imagine hints of agave, grapes, apples, and the myriad botanicals used in these liquors in a beer crafted to combine with them. One hears stories of empty tequila barrels shipped north of the border having holes drilled in them by customs officials looking for other potential exported contents. Indeed, we've since heard of barrels used for aging marijuana, presumably where such practice is legal, taking a page from the traditional barrel-aging of tobacco. Modern Times of San Diego ages the coffee used in its Black House in bourbon barrels. Barrels first used for port, sake, or rum (and its cousins *cachaça* and *pisco*) also become available, and with them their flavors—in the cases of sake and the southern sugar spirits, sometimes involving the use of less conventional woods such as amburana, cedar, freijo, or garapa, all of which have their own flavor contributions to the distillates and the beers that subsequently find their way into them. Allagash Brewing in Portland, Maine, has gotten its hands on Aquavit and Portuguese brandy barrels. Less exotic but interesting, nonetheless, was the distribution throughout the world in the late 1990s of barrels and fermentation vessels from the Pilsener Urquell brewery in the Czech Republic. The brewery would even custom shape the barrels to specification. A 10 hL bank of them appear in photos on today's version of the website of the De Cam geuze blenders in Belgium, originally acquired by De Cam's founder Willem Van Herreweghen and now plied by Karel Goddeau, who appears in a green shirt pretty perfectly matching the distinctive chime color of the former Pilsener Urquell vessels.

There are more offbeat previous uses for barrels into which beer is put. This is a conceptual harking back to the days when barrels were used to store and ship practically anything, and can include, following the almost inevitable previous use for bourbon, maple syrup, soy sauce, and even hot sauce. When at Founders Brewing in Grand Rapids, Michigan, we tasted a Mexican-style lager aged in second-use hot sauce barrels. When young it was reportedly not very good, but at six months it was showing a nice marriage of spice and crispness, with the mellowness of wood. Cross-town colleagues at Brewery Vivant once bought a lot of used barrels from Founders, one of which, they eventually discovered, was one of these hot sauce barrels, by which time they had filled it with a mango beer ultimately and appropriately dubbed Habanango. Down in Louisville, Kentucky, Against the Grain makes Takeshi Umami Stout, a beer aged in Woodford Reserve barrels in which soy sauce has been fermented. They also produce a beer called Monsterbator using pecanwood-smoked malt, *Brettanomyces,* and peaches. This is getting a bit ahead of ourselves, but it gives some idea of the variation and inventiveness explored by brewers these days using the products and attributes of wood. Given all this it should come as no surprise that at times brewers have resorted to fire to literally burn out the effects of previous contents.

All of this is extraction, of course, the flavor influence on beer of the vessel's previous contents, both in itself and as it has drawn wood character from the barrel or foeder in which it has previously taken residence. Far more must be said about the potential souring effect of other residents in wood, the yeasts, bacteria, and microbes that may have arrived with used barrels, but most likely have been consciously—even if spontaneously or by happenstance— introduced by brewers intending to influence flavors appropriately. Keeping in mind that sour beers as a larger subject have been treated by this imprint and elsewhere, we'll keep mainly to their treatment in wood.

Sour and Sour—Skinning the Cat

There are many ways to deliciously sour beer, from spontaneous inoculation in a coolship to sour mashing in the brewhouse on to pitching souring organisms in the kettle or in the fermentation vessel. Most of these have nothing necessarily to do with wood. Kettle souring, for example, enormously popular these days among craft brewers, is conducted at relatively high temperatures—86–122°F (30–50°C)—with inoculum coming either from the surface of grain or by pitching a known strain of *Lactobacillus* into the kettle. The main work of this type of sour fermentation can be essentially concluded in a matter of days. Souring in wood is typically done over longer periods—months to years—and generally within a temperature range of 50–70°F (10–25°C), allowing for seasonal fluctuations. This is an ideal range for beer spoilers to work, patiently nibbling residual nutrients and those that arise from ongoing processes. The differences associated with sour fermentation in wood are multiple: the specific microorganisms—the "zoo"—involved in the business of fermentation, the time needed to allow them to do their collective work, the places in the wood in which they hide—wood-grain, crack, or wherever—and the interplay of oxygen in the process. Let's take them individually in a bit more detail.

- **Zoo:** This, of course, is the unique blend of yeasts and other microorganisms that will systematically reduce the fermenting and aging beer to create the flavors of multifarious synthesis. You can lead it by pitching specific cultures and consciously inoculating your barrels, or it can be thrown at you by the environment in which you work, or the barrel you've inherited. Much will be said later about these creatures, and the processes in which they participate, as well as the relationships between them.

- **Time:** More time is typically required—months to years—for aging beers on wood, whether they are sour or not. In its initial processes, primary fermentation in wood is essentially like any other fermentation. With sour beers, the formation of acids is a slow process, with lactic acid dominant, the result of activity by *Lactobacillus*, including *Pediococcus*. In wood, incremental oxygenation over time will also bring about the formation of acetic acid—at levels to be carefully monitored, to be sure—a factor not as readily to be engaged in impermeable stainless steel. Perhaps the loveliest effect of time is the formation of esters. Esters are enzymatic combinations of acids and alcohols that often tend to have low flavor thresholds. Esters based on ethanol—naturally the alcohol of greatest presence—as well as the acids coming into evidence will wreak a fundamental change in aromatic perception of the beer. Ethyl lactate and ethyl acetate will probably be the dominant esters. Actually, *Saccharomyces* yeast, having consumed all the sugars available to it, will go dormant, slowly diminish and autolyze, and be consumed over time, and the resultant autolytic products will manifest as fatty acids with aromas of wet goat and general mustiness and funk, as well as nutrients for sequential processes.

- **Hiding:** Due to its nature, wood will never really be sterile. We can always work on tempering this, but within the wood, insulation from heat, protection from chemicals in crevices (as discussed in chapter 4), such as along the inward-bulging surfaces of heads and staves, in between staves, and in the pores of the wood, as well as amid the protective pellicle on the surface of a sour fermentation, there is a lot of opportunity for microorganisms to hide. As brewers, we of course have other mitigating tools in bitterness, alcohol, variable levels of Free Amino Nitrogen (or FAN), and dryness or acidity from fermentation that will impact viable organisms. On the other hand, however, you want to build up the micro-diversity of your barrels to create a synergistic blend of souring organisms. And, given the physical realities of wooden vessels, even organisms that have been hampered by a relative lack of nutrients or inhibition by alcohol, pH, or hop bitterness can survive in the twilight zone of wood.

- **Oxygen:** For all he does with microorganisms, blending, and the like, no less an authority than Gert Christiaens of the Oud Beersel lambic brewery states that his main purpose in aging in wood is for micro-oxygenation. Similarly, Teo Musso of the Baladin brewery in Piozzo, Italy, imprinted by the winemaking traditions of his family and region, concentrates above all else on the oxygenation effects on his barrel-aged barley wine, Xyauyu. We've addressed in various places already the different variables that will affect the rate of oxygenation in the barrel. Though the wood is a substantive barrier between the beer and the external atmosphere, factors both exterior and interior play a part in this uptake of oxygen. This slow ingress of oxygen creates an environment where facultative aerobic and anaerobic organisms can thrive, particularly such organisms as *Gluconobacter* (formally called *Acetomonas*). Allowing headspace to expand through evaporation can lead to substantial risk of over-acetic development, and so should be monitored and mitigated with topping up. Cellars are rife with ill-topped barrels producing mainly vinegar. *Brettanomyces* can choose to take either an oxidative or non-oxidative path. A simple trick for homebrewers who may have trouble finding barrels sized for their experiments in wood, and, hence, might feel they are missing this essential element of barrel souring, is to grow cultures in a glass growler with a stopper that allows some ingress of oxygen without giving air free passage, and later to similarly stopper aging beer. Such a stopper could be of porous wood, such as the soft spile used for equilibrating cask beer, or of semi-permeable plastic. This can allow more controlled access to oxygen, allowing it to influence contents without ruining them by excessive acetic acid formation. If this method seems farfetched, know that at one point Rodenbach experimented with speeding the souring process in larger tanks by attempting to spur micro-oxygenation as well as synergistic interaction by ultrasonic means. Happily for purists of procedure, it didn't work. One variable perhaps not sufficiently addressed previously is the bunghole or the head space of the barrel. Studies have shown (Alamo-Sanza 2014) that amounts of absorbed oxygen are lower as you go deeper into the liquid within the barrel or foeder. The pellicle that can form on the liquid surface at the top of the barrel/foeder is a collection of filamentous yeast and bacteria that take advantage of the nutrients in the beer and the higher oxygen content in the headspace. The formation of this pellicle is deemed a positive presence for protecting the beer underneath from direct oxygen impact. You should disturb it as little as possible in order to avoid excessive acetic acid formation (see suggestions for less invasive sampling in the section on wood maintenance). In addition, through careful topping, as little oxygen as possible should be introduced as the size of the exposed surface is reduced by filling. Perhaps the best way to achieve this is through a flushed or otherwise oxygen-free tube introducing new liquid below surface level.

Among those in the United States relatively new to this centuries-old game, New Belgium's program for sour beer in wood is something of a benchmark. Not only do they have an impressive forest of foeders, displayed each year to festive advantage at their "Lost in the Woods" release parties, they have faced nearly every challenge imaginable over the years as they have reinvented in their own ways the culture of aging beer in wood. This has involved moving and fundamentally repairing foeders dried and otherwise compromised by the semi-arid Colorado environment into which they've been transplanted, mainly from France and California. It has required a great deal of trial and error and patience. It has also involved careful record keeping, a procedural lesson learned by all of us as we first try to repeat our earliest successful results

Figure 6.1—A page from Lauren Salazar's personal foeder-cellar log.

as brewers. While duplication of sour beers is a goal a touch more elusive than hitting the right level of bitterness in a basic pale ale, it's impossible even to learn from the process unless scrupulous procedural, sensory, chemical, and microbiological notes are taken—in the case of New Belgium, mainly by Lauren Salazar in her little book. Chronicling frequent tastes of each of several dozen foeders, it is an ongoing and living document of the state of the New Belgium wood program throughout (at this point) its many years of continuance. She and her co-worker (and ex-husband) Eric Salazar, and others, have shepherded a program that has inspired the rest of us, also providing advice and instruction along the way. It, too, had its beginnings.

Intermezzo: Naming the Animals

When we started at New Belgium in 1996 we didn't really have access to the right microbiology. Now you can buy it from your regular yeast providers, but we had to build it up from scratch. We started by buying it from American Type Culture Collection (ATCC) and some Belgian university sources. We focused on different Brettanomyces, *some specific* Lactobacillus, *and a few pediococci. We initially let them do their thing in growlers, and measured and tasted them way too frequently. In 1998 we got some barrels and started inoculating specific barrels with specific stuff. We named them, of course, according to what they were, and what we wanted them to show. pH1 and pH2, OCAa and OCAb were some of those barrels. The first two were adjusted, obviously, for pH, the second two were experiments using our Old Cherry Ale. Again we tasted way too frequently, often on Thursday nights, influencing our volleyball skills. We kept on adding stuff to specific barrels as we found it—some lambic, some beer claimed from keg complaints that came back sour without diacetyl, and so on. This really became the New Belgium souring culture: a mixture of found and purchased microflora, some of it in the barrels and later in the foeders we bought. If you want to be authentic, I think, you could repeat this on your own, or you could buy some organisms or maybe get them from a friend. Anyway, you will have to work toward your own zoo, based on what you like.*

—Excerpt from Peter's journals

Of course, some research has been done on the subject, and, not surprisingly, mainly in Belgium. Professor Verachtert at Katholieke University of

Leuven (KUL) has done work with lambic beers, as have others, and there is scholarship on both the spontaneous and non-spontaneous fermentation of sour beers. Professor Charles Bamforth at University of California–Davis has also worked on spontaneous fermentation from an American point of view, and in Berlin Professors Methner and Annemuller have researched sour beer mainly with an eye to *Berliner Weisse*. Of course, this is not in itself a wood-aged sour—nor, as sometimes regarded, was it ever a kettle-soured beer—but it does hark back to a more microbiologically adventurous time when unboiled wort carried ambient microflora into fermentation.

Much has been discussed and written about the wort matrix needed for making sour beer, and it makes sense to consider the balance of microflora—Peter's "zoo"—intended for long residence in barrels full of beer. Traditional lambic brewers conducted long mashes to deplete nitrogen and carry over dextrines to the kettle, followed by long boils to enhance oxygen reduction (redox), also using wheat and lots of old hops for polyphenols, again for redox potential. Another Belgian variation is to conduct a traditional long mash using some adjunct with a short boil with hops. Rodenbach, for example, uses corn grits and used to add whole flower hops prior to boil.

Like many other European brewers, the Belgians can be cagey about their processes, often gauging what it is their listener already knows, wants to hear, and will politely accept. The impish smile and shrug, combined with a few disarming and vague words, urge experimentation without providing specific guidance. Naturally, there are gratifying exceptions, and it must be recognized that the brewing industries of all countries face challenges of the market and commerce unique to each of them. Common themes from the above presentation would seem to be low levels of hopping or nitrogen depletion (little or no FAN) after fermentation, with nutrient complexity high in dextrines and low in protein. Nothing is hard and fast, however.

Introducing unfermented wort to wood barrels can set up challenges controlling eventual results. Even a lambic wort is a rich source of nutrients, and when it is further subjected to an overnight ambient inoculation in a coolship, more "zoo" than desired can not only influence fermentation and its flavors, but take up more persistent residence in the wood. This is especially true in warm weather. *Enterobacters*, for example, should absolutely be banished from fermentation—or any food production. Lambic brewers are acutely aware of the development of *enterobacters*, and have, over time, developed awareness and sought to raise consciousness differentiating a potentially dangerous product such as cheese from an alcoholic one in which pathogens cannot meaningfully survive. Was that a regulatory-related version of a shrug and a grin?

One key to successful spontaneous fermentation without adding yeast is avoiding a long lag phase before naturally occurring yeasts take hold and really start to make things happen. Of course, this is a bit of a catch-22. Older literature mentions lag times as long as 40 days, which is worrisome even to contemplate. Potential off-aromas developed during an extended fermentation lag can include cellar, mold, iron-like, mushroom, and smoke. A pre-inoculation wort pH of less than 4.5 is desirable, reducing buffer capacity via low FAN and allowing acidification. A couple of wild yeasts deemed desirable at this early stage are *Kloeckera apiculata* and *Klebsiella aerogenes*. The main fermentation is typically conducted by *Saccharomyces* yeasts (sometimes *S. bayanus*). It is during the main fermentation, of course, that most of the ethanol, higher alcohols, and esters are formed. Barrels used for primary fermentation will inevitably foam over unless temperatures and fill levels are modulated, and should be subsequently topped up with wort in order to mitigate an oxidative effect, which could invite *acetobacters*, both by exposure to air and the flies such activity can attract.

Most brewers will conduct fermentation elsewhere—in a nice, safe, stainless steel tank, for example—and then introduce beer into barrels. At this point, the main decision is whether to remove or leave in yeast. *Saccharomyces* left in long residence in a relatively warm barrel can lead to autolysis, as yeast is consumed by subsequent organisms, generating aromas of wet goat, wet wool, or wet dog. This in turn can be mitigated by time and patience. Either way works, and each can have a unique positive effect, but leaving yeast in the beer will make it stay stinky longer, and extend the necessary maturation time.

Clearly, we've embarked on a disquisition on the production of sour beers of various types, but as it constitutes necessary background for fermentation and conditioning in wood we'll continue with a rundown of some of the most common specific organisms that can arise within barrels, whether the result of spontaneous fermentation, introduction, or development. Their balance and relationship over time can also strongly affect the development of flavors in wood.

In the course of general brewing production, *Lactobacillus*, or lactic acid bacteria, strikes fear into the hearts of brewers, as they are associated with unclean or uncontrolled practice and have a tendency to do much of what is to be conventionally avoided. In visual terms they can form haze and other precipitate. Some, such as *Pediococcus* (which we will treat later in this chapter), can produce diacetyl, and of course what they are best known for is creating an effect of undesired sourness, mainly in the form of lactic acid. They can also crop up later under generally dirty conditions, such as when beer is poured through unclean draft lines or from improperly cleaned kegs. Lactobacilli are generally hop-sensitive—no doubt one of the reasons hops came into general use in preference to more easily spoilable gruit beers. This sensitivity decreases markedly with increase in pH, possibly as much as 50% when pH is raised by only 0.2. Despite association with lower, more acidic pH, *Lactobacillus* actually has a higher internal cell pH than the healthy yeast in beer. An active transporter known as Hor-A is required to pump hop-derived iso-α-acid out of the cell to keep internal cell pH high, since its presence would otherwise lower it. As there are other forms of hop resistance in lactic acid this is still a matter for research, but the genetic code for Hor-A can be stored on a plasmid, a DNA molecule sometimes occurring within cells separate from chromosomal DNA, which interestingly can also transfer between species.

Does this sound like Flemish to you? What this means is that this plasmid-encoded *Lactobacillus*-derived DNA can transfer between species within your brewery. The trail can be further obscured by the facts that *Lactobacillus* kept in a lab on non-hopped medium will grow but can lose the plasmid, and that organisms isolated from sour beer can also lose their souring capacity when grown on non-hopped medium. One uncomplicated lesson to be learned from all this is to keep things as clean as possible, to ensure that any *Lactobacillus*-related souring is enacted on purpose.

A list of common—and not so common—Lactobacilli follows:

- Homofermentative *Lactobacillus* is so named since it produces lactic acid from sugars. It can cause diacetyl and make mainly lactic acid around an optimal temperature of 30°C (*L. casei, coryniformis*).
- *L. casei*: produces diacetyl.
- Heterofermentative *Lactobacillus* (*L. brevis, buchneri*) can produce alcohols in addition to lactic acid. Produces mainly lactic acid, but also CO_2, acetic acid (from pentoses), ethanol, glycerol, and manitol. Optimal temperature 20–25°C.
- *L. brevis*: the most frequently found beer spoiler. Grows optimally at 30°C and pH 4–6, and can superattenuate by fermenting dextrins and starch. Obligate heterofermentative and generally hop-resistant.
- *L. buchneri*: resembles *L. brevis* but ferments melizitose. Requires ribo-flavin for growth.
- *L. plantarum* is a facultative heterofermentative (can live in the presence of some oxygen and can make ethanol from lactic acid).

- *L. lindneri*: highly hop resistant, optimal growth at 19–23°C, but survives higher thermal treatments than other *Lactobacillus*. All strains are beer spoilers. Grows slow on media but fast in beer!
- The Japanese brewer Asahi reports a new *Lactobacillus* species, *Lactobacillus paracollinoides,* as a potential beer spoiler.

Microbiology, relative cell count, and species will deviate according to process, and these days we see widely varying results based on factors ranging from spontaneous fermentation to clean culture transfer from stainless to wood with or without *Lactobacillus*. In addition, transformations within the ferment can occur. Modern brewers accustomed to kettle souring are familiar with the notion that *Lactobacillus* is fond of warm environments with little or no hops or oxygen present, and once comfortable will multiply quickly and acidify wort with lactic acid. In the mixed fermentations Peter saw at Rodenbach, lactic acid bacteria concentrations could rise from 0.1 to 1 million cells per mL in the late stages of stainless fermentations at 20°C.

When more conventional yeasts were settled by chilling to 15°C, *Lactobacillus* would happily remain in suspension for transfer to other steel tanks for five to six weeks of additional activity. It was not until after this period that the beer was transferred to foeders for a further two years, at the end of which time lactic acid bacteria concentrations would have fallen to 10,000 cells per mL (Martens 1996). In addition, presence of *Lactobacillus* was noted to have resolved into 100% *Pediococcus* after less than a year. Where initially *L. delbrueckii* delbrueckii and *L. delbrueckii* bulgaris were primarily noted, a general giving way to *Pediococcus parvulus* had occurred toward the end of this tertiary fermentation. As it happens, parenthetically yet with some resonance, Peter did his military service in Delbrueck. Further, it was noted at Rodenbach that *Pediococcus damnosus* and conventional yeast coflocculated, the former seeming always to be nominally present in yeast slurry, an illustration, given the undoubted success of the fine sour beers of Rodenbach, that complete eradication of perceived undesirables by pure and single strain dominance might sometimes be doing the job too well. Even within the pharmaceutical industry such symbioses are tolerated, and even encouraged (Peng 2001).

Pediococcus, first called beer sarcina, is a gram-positive *Lactobacillus*, meaning that the substantial thickness of cell walls result in the retention of dye in a gram stain test. This is common to other lactobacilli, as well. It is comfortable during summer months and about four months after lambic brewing and inoculation. With other *Lactobacillus* it will consume leftover, autolyzed *Saccharomyces*, and can generate lactic acid to 5000 ppm and possibly diacetyl and acetoine, the summer flavor of lambic, without CO_2 formation. In conjunction, pH will fall below 4 and attenuation will slowly increase. *Saccharomyces* will then flocculate out due to lack of nutrients, and acidification and consumption by these other microorganisms will begin. Typical lambic flavors will develop, such as caproic, caprylic and capric acid, ethyl caprylate (C8-ethyl or total of C10)—with withflavor descriptors such as fatty, fruity, earthy, and dairy—and and ethyl caprate (C10-ethyl or C12 total). Remnants of malolactic fermentation in wood (or anywhere) can also be consumed by *Lactobacillus*.

As a result of activities of *Pediococcus*, ropiness can occur. This is a viscous mass resulting from a dextrinous secretion from microorganisms such as *P. damnosus* in lambic beers and *P. parvulus* in Flemish sour red beer such as Rodenbach, and is not to be confused with the so-called silky turbidity associated with more specific lactobacilli. It can be removed with the enzyme cellulase, and will disappear with time, especially in conjunction with *Brettanomyces*, the activity of which is debated but seems evident with experience. In older literature this mass is sometimes called "two shine," since it refracts light like a crystal. When it is in evidence, sour beers in process are sometimes referred to as "sick." With patience, they can later become well.

Intermezzo: Ropiness

I was going to take a sample from a foeder for taste panel. I opened the sample cock and nothing came out. We sometimes had issues keeping track of our 294 foeders at Rodenbach with our handwritten system, so my first reaction was to bang on the foeder with my fist to check if it was full. Something should come out if it is full. It sounded heavy and mute as a full foeder would, but no liquid would come out of the sample cock. Sheer pressure due to the foeder's height and relatively low solids load after a week of fermentation and five to six weeks at 15°C typically does not lead to stuff clogging up the sample cock. Oh, wait, a viscous drop started to come out, slowly stretching for 5 cm before I grabbed some and tasted it. It tasted fine, except for the texture. I should come back again next week to sample this one for taste panel!

—Excerpt from Peter's journals

Brettanomyces was first introduced in 1904 at a meeting of the Institute of Brewing by Hjelte Claussen, Laboratory Director of the New Carlsberg Brewery in Copenhagen. He proved that English stock beer (a strong aged beer akin to Barleywine) underwent a slow secondary fermentation with a non-*Saccharomyces*, torula-like asporogeneous (non-spore-forming) yeast. With its strongest associations these days lying with Belgian brewing culture, it's somewhat curious to recognize that the Brettano part of the name refers to British brewing. Myces, of course, comes from fungus. The term *Dekkera* is also sometimes used to alternatively classify *Brettanomyces*. Old English porters, newsworthily rescued from watery graves, have shown evidence of *Brettanomyces*, and the stock ale influence is evidenced here and there in modern British brewing, such as in George Gale Prize Old Ale from Portsmouth, Hampshire. Claussen went so far as to patent the process of *Brettanomyces* introduction to secondary fermentation to produce such beers, but as the alcohol content of British beer in general declined around that time due mainly to a strength-based tax structure, hefty styles including stock ale virtually disappeared.

Clusters (1940) did the first systematic study on 17 different *Brettanomyces* yeasts, mainly isolated from beer. Common characteristics were ogival (pointed, arch-shaped) cells, asporogeneous, short-lived, delayed growth on malt extract and agar, and production of large amounts of acetic acid under aerobic conditions. Claussens also identified two additional species beyond *B. lambicus* and *B. bruxellensis* (the most commonly used by brewers): *B. clausseni* and *B. intermedius*. Current taxonomy recognizes five different species as Dekkera since the formation of acrospores was observed in them: *D. bruxellensis, D. anomalus, D. custersianus, D. naardenensis,* and *D. nanus.*

As specified above, *Brettanomyces* will convert glucose to acetic acid under aerobic conditions, and is super-attenuating, meaning that by normal reckoning apparent extract can be represented by a negative number due to consumption by *Brettanomyces* of sugars left by conventional *Saccharomyces* activity. The potentially resultant lack of glycerol formation can also account for the lack of body of most *Brett* beers. In coenzymatic terms *Brettanomyces* continuously drains its oxidizing NAD+ (Nocitinamide adenine dinucleotide) by making acetic acid from acetaldehyde and does not have the means to recuperate the resultant reducing agent NADH. When small amounts of oxygen are present alcohol and glucose can form acetic acid in different amounts depending on the strain. As complicated as all this may seem, it should at least serve as a caution to minimize oxygen introduction into barrels filled with beer—and especially if they contain *Brettanomyces*—by keeping them topped up as their contents may diminish with aging, evaporation, and even perhaps sampling. *B. intermedius* and *B. custersii* are also capable of metabolizing the sugar present in wood (like cellobiose), which in turn is resultant of toasting or charring. You knew there had to be something there about wood.

Touching once more on the body of *Brett*-aged beers, dextrines with an atomic mass above 20,000 Dalton will drop precipitously with time—to 81% of original measurement in one year; 73% in two years—measured as the total amount of carbohydrates in the beer. During this time the proportional representation of larger dextrines rises relative to smaller ones, even as overall reduction is occurring, with a general effect of lessening body. This dextrine consumption, together with the reductive effect of beta-glucanase on the wood of the barrel, can lead to some alcohol increase.

Brettanomyces also reacts with esters already formed through fermentation, such as isoamyl acetate (usually identified with banana), hydrolising it by cell-bound esterase and producing other esters such as ethyl lactate and ethyl acetate (mild butteriness and nail polish remover, respectively) after about nine months of fermentation. The formation of these esters is also enhanced by pH below 3.3 and at around 20°C, but still falls short of levels in finished lambic beer. This can also produce isobutyric acid (which smells like rancid butter), which occurs naturally in vanilla and carob. It is generally desirable to have higher levels of *B. bruxellenisis* than *B. lambicus* at the beginning of aging, as the former will develop the horse-blanket flavors familiar in even young Orval beer and the latter the flavor of old lambic. After around 10 months, total cell counts drop, with DMS (dimethyl sulfide) and diacetyl down to 100 and 80 ppb. Higher summer temperatures can encourage formation of acetic acid, so once again precautions should be taken to keep barrels full and the temperature down. When storing both *Brettanomyces* and *Pediococcus* for later inoculation in barrels and tanks, $CaCO_3$ should be added to buffer in order to avoid eradication by exposure to locally forming acids.

Here's a brief rundown of the sensory effects of various *Brettanomyces* strains, with some commercial designations:

- *B. intermedius* (now called *anomala*): Circus peanuts (candy) Center for Brewing Science CBS 73
- *B. bruxellensis*: Metallic, earthy, horse blanket, Orval, Center for Brewing Science CBS 74
- *B. lambicus*: Circus peanuts, ethyl acetate and acetic, pineapple in fermentation Center for Brewing Science CBS 75
- *B. anomalus*: More subtle pineapple in fermentation American Type

Culture Collection ATCC 10559, Center for Brewing Science CBS 77

- *B. claussenii*: More subtle than *lambicus* and *bruxellensis* White Labs WL 645
- *B. nanus* (from East Coast yeast): Slow fermenter, iron-like aroma that could be interesting in Saison

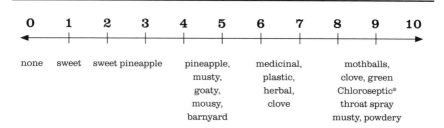

Figure 6.2—*Brettanomyces* flavor scale as used at New Belgium, describing the range of aromas in young to more seasoned beers aged with *Brettanomyces*, fruity to more developed, and even over-mature.

Interesting aromas as well arise from *Brettanomyces*, by itself and in conjunction with other organisms such as *Lactobacillus*. They can appear as 4-vinyl guaiacol, the clove of South German wheat beers, or as medicinal or "band-aidy" 4-vinyl-fenol. The enzymes that produce these compounds are inhibited, to an extent, by dark malts, which could open an interesting product pathway. Together with *Lactobacillus* a "mousy" aroma can be evident from 2-acetyltetrahydropyradine and its derivatives, ethanol and lysine, also described as nutty, corny, or crackers.

Various enzymes present in *Brettanomyces* can also contribute to unique alteration:

- Esterase will break down isoamyl-acetate to a certain equilibrium, but can also break down other esters if its concentration is high. Viable cells of *Brettanomyces* will excrete esterases, whereas *Saccharomyces*—and mainly ale yeasts—will do this only in autolysis. In normally fermented wort *B. bruxellensis* will increase lactate and ethyl acetate, but lower 3-methyl-butyl acetate and 2-phenyl ethyl acetate.
- Amyloglucosidase in *Brettanomyces* degrades dextrines further— around 9.0 g/L in 30 days on fermenting wort and around 25 g/L after a year, but quite variable depending on the strain.
- ß-glucosidase: *B. intermedius,* and *B. custersii* (but not *B. lambicus* or *B. bruxellensis*) are potentially capable of metabolizing the sugar

present in wood cellobiose. This split may be key in differentiations of interpretation. Cellobiose is a disaccharide product of aging, toasting, and charring of wood. Gilliland (1961) called them *B. claussenii* and *B. anomalus*, noting them as able to ferment lactose and cellobiose.

- Alcohol dehydrogenase is present in *Brettanomyces* to a lesser extent than *Saccharomyces cerevisiae*.
- Aldehyde dehydrogenase leads to potential growth on ethanol.
- Vinyl fenol reductase is unique for *Brettanomyces* and also forms 4-ethyl fenol and 4-vinyl guaiacol.

Voodoo Magic—Inoculation, Re-inoculation, and Keeping It All Going

We've gone into pretty deep discussion of the microbiological elements of what we may as well call resident fermentation and aging—their occurrence and presence, their developments and degradations, and also the relationships between them and the time involved in allowing them to gradually weave together, creating overall flavor and character in beer. But we haven't gotten all that much into how it all starts, and, once established, how it continues. All brewing amounts to controlling as much as possible and setting processes in motion that will achieve predictable results, and over the centuries, of course, as more has come to be understood, more of that control is possible. Cultures can be pitched to take the guesswork out of what goes into sour fermentation in general—in wood as elsewhere—but when fermentations are spontaneous or barrels are received from hither and yon, having themselves undergone processes that have imbued them with microbiological uncertainty, absolute knowledge and predictability are, shall we say, *compromised*. Even pitching those sour cultures requires an awareness of when they are needed and how they will interact over time, but with all the possible pathways of what can go on, there's a more than usual spirit of "wait and see." We think we speak for all of us when we say we wouldn't have it any other way.

Nathan Zeender at Right Proper Brewing in Washington, DC, captures a great deal of this spirit when he refers to his outfit as "more of a yeast cult than a brewery." He tends to inoculate his barrels with one or more of his house cultures in order to minimize some of the guesswork that is making sour beer in wood, and recommends having a slew of barrels going at once for effective blending, and with as many mitigating options as possible.

Brouwerij DeBrabandere, outside Kortrijk, Belgium, is a place of many stories, from the development of Petrus in the 1980s intended to take advantage of a local shortage of Rodenbach, to the nudges administered by beer writer Michael Jackson to favor a particular blending stream for that same beer, eventually resulting in Petrus Aged Pale. The brewery was founded in 1894, and according to brewmaster Yves Benoit in its early days mainly used the 37.5 hL oak foeders it possessed as a place to put beer that had gone wrong in fermentation. Over the years cultures were collected from these vessels, blends were done, and a variegated slurry eventually came to be used for making beers in their own right—sour beers such as Petrus. This story reminds us of the discovery of a tasty—if perhaps more for the time (the early 1990s) than for the ages—sour culture in a carboy of beer at brewer Kinney Baughman's Cottonwood Café in North Carolina, subsequently used for a couple of sour—and GABF award-winning—raspberry beers. To our knowledge the beers were not barrel-aged, but they offer further historical testimony to the clear-eyed acceptance of happenstance.

Spurred by the success and demand for the Petrus beers, DeBrabandere has taken to adding foeders to their setup rather than decommissioning them, as was the case when the small ones began giving inconsistent result. Their method of inoculation involves filling new foeders with warm water to below the manway to see if they hold liquid. Once assured of this the foeder is emptied and then refilled with the oldest sour *foederbier* they have, allowing six months for inoculation. They now have over 50 foeders of varying size, the most recently acquired built by Foudrerie Francois in Brive-la-Gaillarde, France.

These days, of course, rather than trusting to fingers-crossed blends of fermentations gone awry, many breweries maintain their sour cultures for reasonably consistent reuse, even if merely producing a barrel here and there of sour beer is the extent of their commercial aim. A larger enterprise demands this, of course, such as the wood program at New Belgium, which requires sufficient quantities of beer for the blending and yearly general release of La Folie sour brown, and other beers such as Eric's Ale, an eponymous sour peach ale by blender Eric Salazar. Even this is small compared with the output of Rodenbach. Much of the administration of these cultures amounts to the methods described by DeBrabandere, taking beer from one sour vessel and using it to inoculate another. This is also the method employed at Two Brothers Brewing in Warrenville, Illinois, where new foeders are inoculated with sour Domaine DuPage.

Places as well as vessels are often considered inoculation-worthy, and steps are sometimes taken that may seem almost to amount to superstition. Still, the reasoning is sound, for if naturally-occurring microflora is what sets fermentations in motion when wort is left for an inoculating period in a coolship, it can also be expected to settle everywhere else in the area, and to maintain a living landscape of the very stuff that makes beer crafted in that particular locale distinctive and delicious—or so it is hoped. Dick remembers years ago, on what was perhaps his first visit to the Cantillon lambic brewery in Brussels, having his attention directed to a half-painted wall on the brewery's top floor, 30 or so feet from its coolship. Only half the room had been recently repainted, it was explained to him by a guide of indeterminate qualification, so that the resident microflora would not be entirely eradicated in the process. The following year, perhaps, the rest of the room would be repainted, by which time this year's fresh paint would be minutely covered over with attendant microorganisms. This particular story may be apocryphal, but it is true that when the Lindeman's lambic brewery moved into new premises they took wooden pieces of the old coolship along in order to import the precise microflora having been resident in their old brewery.

Figure 6.3—Lindeman's lambic brewery took wooden pieces of the old coolship along when they moved into new premises in order to import the precise microflora having been resident in their old brewery. Note the recovered wood in the corners of the new coolship room.

Intermezzo: Mopping the Floor

"Millstone started with wood as a way of bringing cider back to its rustic American roots. The goal was to recreate cider in the way that it was produced in old America, back when almost every farmer had some apples and many people in the community made cider, and they were all using wood barrels. In that tradition, we do all of our fermentation and aging in oak barrels. We bring the juice in as is and do not sulfite, filter, or pasteurize our juice at any point in the process, allowing for a heavily native yeast and bacteria influence on the flavor profile of the cider we are producing. This means we have a multitude of yeast/bacteria in our microflora, which is heavily enhanced by the wood, allowing certain microbes to take up residence there. Further, we only retire our barrels when they begin to leak or have a serious contamination/off odor. This allows us to reintroduce some of the same culture year after year to the next season's batch of cider, which will hopefully help us reach our end game, homogenization of our base cider flavor, so that no matter the style, people can always tell they are drinking a rustic cider from Millstone.

"With this idea in mind, when we outgrew the mill we moved a large portion of our barrels to a warehouse about 15 minutes down the road. Our primary concern with the growth was that we would be getting new barrels in to house not only our ciders but our yeast/bacteria culture, as well. We wanted to re-create the same microflora that already existed in our cidery, so we started collecting the lees from the barrels of our cider after racking in carboys. Once we had about six carboys full to the brim with lees we headed down to the new barrelhouse, carboys in tow, along with several buckets and a mop. Our cellar master set about mopping the entire floor space with our lees while I set up open buckets around the facility dumping in around a gallon of lees per bucket along with sugar to get an active fermentation to spew our cultures into the surrounding space. How effective this method was is debatable, but we've been making stellar cider with that same Millstone character from day one in our new barrelhouse."

—from recollections of Kyle Sherrer of Millstone Cellars in Monkton, Maryland
(We defy any among you to claim that the processes and concerns
of cidermakers have nothing to do with brewing.)

The Elgood's brewery in Wisbech, Cambridgeshire, in the last few years embarked on a program of spontaneous fermentation making use of an old coolship—they call it a cooling tray—in their historic brewhouse, which for many years had served only as a museum piece. In their brewery, in fact, a more modern system of cooling the wort is dependent on a pump that brings in water from the nearby tidal river Nene. Having successfully—and deliciously—generated a few batches of sour, spontaneously fermented beer, they made use of some broad planks taken from a 300-year-old oak felled on the brewery grounds, hanging them horizontally above the coolship in the hope that proximity to newly run hot wort would aid in future inoculation. Though perhaps not as apocalyptic a treatment as that performed with buckets and mops at the cidery in Maryland, it does provide a pretty and historically grounded touch—even if not particularly English—to the efforts of a modern brewer to harness the age-old forces that sour beer. Irresistibly, there is a brewery, Libertine, with locations in Morrow Bay and San Luis Obispo, California, which has hung wooden panels in treatment similar to that at Elgood's and which has never actually pitched yeast, taking every element and occurrence of fermentation from the surrounding coastal California environment. In addition, like the Millstone cidery, they sprayed these panels with bottles of their own beer.

There's a fun kind of counter-intuition at work in the many processes and microorganisms enlisted in the production of wood-aged beers. First, there's the overcoming of strait-laced procedure where cleaning is concerned, and at the same time that recognition of risk is maintained. Tolerance to perversity is here and there required as we cast our spells with mop and bucket, scavenged wood patinaed with age and other residue, even to open-eyed ignorance in the cases of residual ingredients and the processes of spontaneous inoculation. It's lucky we don't produce mustard gas or hulking hungry masses out of some old horror movie. Sometimes we are fascinated at the same time we are disgusted. Yet we can't wait to tell each other what each of us individually has discovered, or perhaps merely synthesized by similar process, itself acted upon by geography and circumstance. Add wood to the traditions and discoveries of sour beer and it can truly be as unique as the brewer, or the very tree that contributed to its production.

7

Blending
and Culture

Among the esoteric arts associated with brewing's processes, blending is perhaps the most subjective and idiosyncratic. Brewers often fall silent when asked advice on blending, not so much because they aren't willing to share ideas, but because it's so difficult to get started. Proportions, relative flavor thresholds and their balance, personal taste versus what the market might embrace (or pay for, as Todd Ashman of FiftyFifty Brewing in Truckee, California, wryly observes), changes wrought by time once the deed is done and the blend in question sets sail—these are things that vary endlessly, and from brewer to brewer. Not all blenders are brewers, of course. It's well-known that some lambic producers purchase wort from one or more outside sources to be fermented, aged, tended, and eventually blended according to the methods and preferences of the producer, who then places his or her own label on the bottle or other vessel in question. This is an established and respected practice, and why not? It's what some distillers do, purchasing wash for ferementation and eventual distillation. It's what a lot of winemakers do, as well, purchasing grapes from an endlessly variable sequence of plots and each year producing a consciously combined amalgam of what they feel to have been that season's best.

Blending in the brewery often carries a negative connotation. Blending, to this way of thinking, is something that happens when things go wrong. The simplest and most benign of examples might take a couple of batches of the same beer straddling ideal specification in some way—one too strong and one too weak, or under- and over-carbonated—putting them together in mathematically-verified proportion to yield the ideal and unripplingly saleable usual recipe. That's the best case. Then there are flawed beers, beers which may carry the sins of diacetyl, DMS, or acetaldehyde—or worse—which it is felt will duck sufficiently under-cover if spread among healthier batches. This, it must be said, is generally a bad idea. Bad beer is bad beer, and should simply go away. Blending bad beer with good beer will usually simply make more bad beer.

Then there is wood beer. Even if you've started your program with only one barrel, the option exists to blend the result with other beer, whether of the same type or not, in order to soften the intensity of wood or microbiological character, introduce carbonation, or simply to see how far you can stretch things to yield more sufficiently affected beer. Once you've amassed a wallfull, however, you'll no doubt pick up on the inconsistent effect of your barrels on the beer inside them. This isn't necessarily a bad thing. If the result were always the same, you wouldn't like that, either, would you? Then there's the effect of blending beers of different ages to come up with something altogether new, even if the beers in question once conformed within production specification, that aside from the factor of time they might be considered the same beer.

Lambic blends are probably among the hardest to pull off. To produce Boon *Oude Geuze*, for example, multiple three- and one-year-old lambics are tasted and blended, with the one-year-old providing young character and live-liness, as well as the nutrients to bottle-condition an entirely flat older beer to a high level of carbonation. The blender therefore needs to project outward in time, anticipating the flavor change that will be wrought by the introduction of carbonic gas, as well as how the balance of acidity and microorganisms will lead to eventual stability.

Armand Debelder of Drie Fonteinen in Beersel is a legend in lambic circles. At times he's had a brewery and at others he hasn't, but his blended geuze (Flemish, French would be gueuze) and *kriek*, as well as many other projects, are prized by beer drinkers throughout the world. Drie Fonteinen has a couple of times been touched by catastrophe: once in the 1990s when fire destroyed the brewery and sent Armand exclusively back to his blending roots; and again in 2009 when a faulty thermostat led to the ruin of some 85,000 bottles of aging beer. The bottles that didn't explode were salvaged for production of *eau de vie*. Amid all of this Armand's stature continued to grow, but even he sat at the feet of his father, so to speak, as he learned the art of blending. As recently as 1994 Gaston Debelder was in charge of the blending at Drie Fonteinen, and it was at about that time that he finally put Armand in charge of his own blends.

So where does that leave the rest of us? In each other's company, for the most part, given that US brewing tradition was effectively snuffed out before we all decided to try to make our own beer. It must be recognized that, with all due respect to the few brewers that survived the 1970s and the fact that solid educational opportunities for us exist, we are an industry of collective autodidacts. Hardly a week passes that we don't ask the advice of some other brewer for something or other that we've decided to take on. Like blending. Like fermenting and aging beer in wood. Like everything. It therefore makes sense to us to turn things over to many of you, the people who have invented, reinvented, and tended a tradition. This all may have started elsewhere—and it certainly flourishes in its territories of origin—but where wood and beer are concerned, you're definitely not just in Kansas—er, Belgium—anymore.

Before we get to the approaches of some of our industry adepts, a few observations should be made on the task at hand. First, there's the simple fact that blending can have many different objectives. There's blending for consistency and spec, and there's blending for one-off transcendence. There's blending for a new beer, and there's blending for something that comes back year after year, with or without seasonal idiosyncrasy in mind. There's blending to tone down a particularly strong flavor, and there's blending that makes the whole greater than the sum of its parts, such as the Gestalt approach referenced by Jeffers Richardson at Firestone Walker's Barrelworks in Buellton, California. And then there are different procedural styles of blending. Probably most common and graspable is the approach of straight percentages—blends, for example, of 10, 15, 20, 25, and so on percent of a particular beer combined with its style compatriot to produce a barrel-influenced version of itself. It's surprising at times how un-linear a process this can be. Kyle Sherrer at his Millstone cidery no doubt practices a varia-tion on this theme, fermenting single apple varieties and then combining them in different blends. Scott Christoffel at Natty Greene's in Greensboro,

North Carolina, blends in the barrel as it is aging, topping up a number of times to tinker with flavors as they develop. Less explainable to those who haven't done it is the spirit quest approach of total immersion and intuitive tightrope-walking, where one's intimate knowledge of each individual beer and barrel is the only tool one takes into the process, naked. Once you've done that, as they say, you never come down.

Since he opened Jolly Pumpkin in 2004, Ron Jeffries has never come down. All his beer is aged in wood, and his flagship beer is a bottle-conditioned golden farmhouse ale called Bam, a sour version of which, Bambic, is a blend of the original beer and a spontaneously fermented wort, inoculated from the air in Dexter, Michigan, or as Ron puts it, by Lambicus Dexterius. He follows pretty much every approach when blending beer.

Blending? Well, I guess I could go on about that for a while. We do all sorts, for all sorts of reasons. So how to gel it down to a salient point or two? Hard.

Blends of a single release such as a seasonal: Most of our seasonals are pre-order beers, but within that we usually try to put in a bit of fudge factor for order add-ons, or barrels that don't make the cut. Foeders are all different sizes, as you know, so what we call 100 bbls varies from 2800 to 3168 gallons. So, when it's all said and done, for a seasonal release we may have beer in 100 bbl foeders, 60, 50, 20, 10 bbl and a handful of regular barrel-sized barrels. Our BTs are 60 bbls, so I taste them all and create blends of similar flavor for each bottling run.

Blends of a single beer of different ages: Generally for beers like our Oro and Roja. A bunch of samples are pulled, and I blend away until I get the flavor profile I'm looking for.

Blending a new beer from other beers: Kind of the same, only I don't know exactly what I'm looking for. A bunch of samples are pulled. I may have an idea of where I want to go, so will direct the sampling. Then I blend until that crazy synergy of flavors that create new flavors not found in any of the original beers is born, and I'm like Heck yeah, that's it.

For all these, except La Roja, which is usually from barrels of the same size, I keep track of the relative percentages of each of the component beers. We have an electromagnetic flow meter (well, three), so the cellar folk can recreate my blends pretty accurately. This part is important. Especially when using a really dark, flavorful—or just plain flavorful—beer. A little bit one way or the other can throw the whole blend off. Maybe not ruin it, but also maybe not get that magical synergistic balance, either.

Basically, you have to taste, and think, imagine, blend, taste, think, blend again. Wash, rinse, repeat. I usually create several blends serially at the same time, just swapping out one element for another, or leaving something out, or adding something new, so I can taste them all against each other at the same time. When you get lucky and it works, it's like Heck yeah, I got this. *Other times it's* Holy *#%!, all these beers/blends suck, what the heck am I going to do now?

I usually need to blend after everyone leaves the brewery—fortunately, about 4:00 p.m. most days. I'm not sure what I'll do when we add a second shift....

Y'all got that? That's why blending is hard to explain. Ron himself goes on to say that as far as actual execution is concerned, he hasn't yet found anyone else who can blend to his personal satisfaction. No slight to his crew, whom he trusts to enact the determined blends, but even for approval of individual batches of bottle-conditioned beer for release, he is a one-man band. There's a lot of that in our industry, Gaston Debelder's trust in his son notwithstanding. For those of us trying to glean tips on actual practice in Ron's narrative, there's a lot of skipping ahead. He's telling you what he does as plainly as he can put it, and he'd like for you to understand exactly what he tastes and smells and feels—and then come work for him, so that he and his wife can go back to Hawaii one day. Kidding momentarily aside, this is where inspiration lies. You can be told how one person does it, and another, and another still, but you can't necessarily be told how to do it yourself. (Cue nudging and winking European.)

Lauren Salazar has lately expanded her role at New Belgium to education, but until relatively recently she ran the brewery's sensory evaluation department in addition to shepherding its continually expanding wood cellar with her ex-husband, Eric. Her little book is legendary, in which she frequently and repeatedly notes the progress of the beer in each of 64 (as of this writing) foeders, as well as various piddling barrel side projects. Over the years she and Eric have conducted numerous blending workshops, at which lucky attendees are allowed to combine any of several beers brought along for the purpose, tasting and discussing among themselves as well as with the masters, eventually creating a growlerful that they are then allowed to take away.

New Belgium's approach to blending and the creation of new beers is unique in the industry. Rather than creating myriad sour beers standing figuratively on their own two feet, they keep two sour base beers going, Felix and Oscar, light and dark, named for the roommates in Neil Simon's "The Odd Couple." Lauren, it must be observed, is great with names. Felix and Oscar may once have been built on a couple of well-known New Belgium beers, Biere de Mars and 1554, respectively, but they have been gradually altered to be very much their own beers. Both are lagers. In their purest forms they can probably most closely be identified with the beers Le Terroir and La Folie, but aside from regular, generally yearly production of those two stalwarts, they are more often combined with other beers to yield an unending array of releases, blended to give what is deemed the right touch of sourness and other character derived from the time spent in wood, along with other ingredients to create much-sought-after and unique offerings. Some of these beers have reached the market as Eric's Ale, a sour peach beer; Transatlantique Kriek, a cherry beer blended over the years with kriek produced at the Boon Brewery in Lembeek and this past year from Oud Beersel; and Pumpkick, a sour pumpkin ale with cranberry.

Lauren has a great deal to say in connection with the sour beers she has had a hand in creating, and about the processes that brought them about. At the risk of taking up some space here, we include the entirety of her musings on her own quest. Every word is worth reading.

> *My two favorite things in the world are being with the barrels and blending.*
>
> *Walking through Cache la Foeder when no one is around and just being with the barrels, taking little sips here and there and jotting down notes to myself in a book I've had since 2000 (I made the first La Folie blend in 2001), I'll thumb back and forth through the pages and see how a barrel was doing the last time I tasted it right after I write today's notes, to get a read on what was, what is, and what will be. I've found that if I haven't tasted through all 64 ladies and gents for a while, I start to feel edgy—like when you leave a sandwich on the counter and go to work—what will Sabbath (our black lab) do? Maybe nothing, maybe eat it, maybe shred it in a million tiny pieces— you just don't know, but you know you'd better circle back and investigate. They're like dogs or like kids (I'm told): sure, they're good, but turn your back for more time than you should—oh boy. Upon completion of a solid week's worth of foeder tasting, I am cool again, totally in control. It's a great feeling.*
>
> *After tasting, I'll sit down and look over the notes—what do they tell me? Sensory evaluation is an incredibly powerful tool—with one look, a*

sniff, and a few sips you can completely diagnose your beer/barrel. What's right and if there's anything out of ordinary. If you have the sensory skills to ID what is the anomaly (assign a cause) then you can correct the action. Diacetyl= SPD (sick phase diacetyl) or just a normal stage of pediococcus lactic fermentation that tells me "Wait one month and taste again." Our foeders are not that complicated—we are not fermenting (well, not ethanol fermentation); we are acidifying in oak. That means that I don't have to wonder if the beer production went well—it did—we checked that on flavor panel before transferring to wood. Instead, I am basically there to see if the barrels need anything—if they are too hot, too cold, hungry, or full and happily making lactic acid. If a barrel is becoming too sour too quick, it might be the temp is too high; if it's sluggish it might be too cold, or there aren't enough bugs in the liquid. I can fix both of those things. It's when the barrel is sour— on time, as planned—then you have another fun project—BLENDING!!!

You must realize, a sour barrel is a hungry barrel. In our case, beer is food. In order to feed the barrel, or more literally, the bugs (wild yeast and souring bacteria within), you must take some or all of the liquid out of the foeder (luxury of a large foeder with a way to fill from the bottom) and replace it with beer (sugar/food). This starts the souring process all over again. Fed and happy, they'll get back to work. The real fun is how much of which barrel to take out to create a beer from your blend. Pierre from Tilquin told me that he thinks blenders who wax poetic about romantical notions of blending are silly to him. I never told him that was me. I get him: He has one Cantillon barrel, three Boon barrels, four Drie Fonteinen barrels, two Girardin = 10, and that's how much he makes. Welp, yeah, that's pretty straightforward and unbelievably delicious every time. And I used to have that same type of "formula" for blending when New Belgium had 20-ish small barrels. It was something like five malty sweet and sour, five big lactic, five interesting, and five lactic/some acetic-ok = blend. Wow, those were the olden days! Acetic?! No, thanks. Really goes to show how little I knew in 2001. But as we grew our foeder cellar, as there were hundreds, then thousands of hectoliters of sour (ready, hungry) beer, that's when it got interesting.

My blending method is pretty straightforward still. I am always thinking of a date range when I want to release the beer and as that date gets closer an amount of beer I think is feasible to produce. As the months go by I taste through the barrels. About six months prior to the blend I start thinking about it. Then three months before I get a little more serious, a little more dialed. Two months, then one month, I all but nail the exact foeder numbers (or names in our case) and the amounts we'll pull from them. My tasting procedure goes a little like this: I taste only one base beer at a time, either Felix (pale sour, in the case of a Le Terroir) or Oscar (dark sour, in the case of a La Folie blend); I get samples, write the foeder name/# on the glass, and cap it with a petri dish (damn fruit flies!). Once I have all the samples—32 of each—I do a real high-level drive-by. One sniff, one sip. I jot down one of three letters. W= waiter. W means the beer is not ready, not sour, wait. B= blender. There's some nice sour in there and still some interesting other attributes left; this can bring complexity to the blend. U= user. Sour, hungry, that's about it—no food left means pretty much no other flavor, too. I also make one other notation—☺, ☺, or ☹. When put next to a B or U it's super helpful for the second pass. If I have 10 B/blenders, but only 5 of them with a ☺, why not just let the ☺ ride and why in the world use an ☹ over a ☺? Yep, that's 14 years of running a sensory science lab boiled down to two characters that only mean something to me and the wood cellar guys—silly, but it works. Second pass, I push all the Ws and Bs with ☺ and ☹ to the back. I pull all the U☺ and taste one more time—are they really that ☺? If so, I calculate how much volume all the U☺ are in total. That's the core of my blend, the sour middle. Now, I've had some great sour beers that came out of one barrel, but they were just that, sour. When I blend all the sour U☺ the mix is great, stellar, but not complex. It's the blend that makes the magic.

When I think about blending, I think about drawing a flower ✿. There's the sour middle, then I take all those B☺ and start placing the petals. Those B/blenders have fun flavors of malt, esters, phenols, and other crazy bretta notes. They're sweeter and have super interesting noses—fun. But which to choose? I also think about my foeders like crayons. I always have but it's become more vivid as the years go by. First there were four; I had trouble blending—not enough. Then there were 10; I thought about when my mom first gave me a box of eight Crayolas. I had all the primary colors; I could create ANYTHING! I could put the blue and red together and make purple, then add white—wow, what else could I ever need? Then the box of 16—yep, we then had 16 foeders. I could blend in delicate notes—cool! Then the box of 32—what? Brick Red—love it. When wood cellar one was complete we had 32 foeders. I got it. I started getting sneaky, layering notes, adding hints. We of course now have 64 foeders; cellar two is complete.

How crazy am I about crayons? Well, I once named a dog Periwinkle and constantly traded with other kids for this color as I had a nasty sharpener habit and was always to the nub of this color—that's Foeder #1 to me. Sure Thing is her name and I use her in EVERY La Folie blend. All she wants to do is make delicious sour beer—who could deny her? The funny thing about the blend also came to me when considering that box of 64: Just because you have 64 doesn't mean you should use all 64 each time you create. We've all done it—add this color on top of that color and eventually... You've. Got. BROWN. Too much. So, back to the flower. You blend all the U☺ and create that sour middle, then you add a few to several petals and that's it, you're done. You keep the main thing the main thing (as they say) and then you add on complexity that becomes secondary attributes. Then you blend it again. Is it the same? Are you on to something? Crayons down, you're done. Buy it, drink it, taste blender's intention.

A moment of silence may be in order. You've got it now, though, right? The whole thing, it turns out, is simple. In order to make beer like Ron Jeffries or Lauren Salazar, you have to *be* Ron Jeffries or Lauren Salazar. Or Armand Debelder, or Patrick Rue, or Vinnie Cilurzo, Todd Ashman, Scott Christophel, Ron Gansberg, Tomme Arthur, Will Meyers, or you. It's worth noting the trust expressed by both Lauren and Ron in the processes that comes both before and after they get into the act of blending, in the work done by brewhouse and sensory staff and those charged with executing the blends.

Lauren isn't the only one among us who names her tanks and barrels, of course. Metropolitan Brewing in Chicago has tagged just about everything—brewhouse vessels, fermenters, and bright tanks, practically even filters and hose ends—with names of fairly obscure characters from Star Trek's various iterations. More to our purpose here, New Holland Brewing in Holland, Michigan, has six handsome horizontal foeders inoculated with bugs and acidifying away in various stages named after funk stars: Chaka Khan, Bootsy Collins, Rick James, and others you could probably guess. No Bernie Worrell quite yet.

While the controlled blending of batches and barrelsful of beer is one of the most ephemeral, rewarding, and subjective of the brewer's arts, the avoidance of unintentional blending in the brewery is a more fundamental subject. It's what any of us making sour beers of any type should be most mindful of when taking on that challenge. For that matter, it's what anyone using more than one yeast has on his or her mind when allowing such things to occupy contiguous space, or when using common equipment for doing so. To some extent it's basic sanitation, but when stakes rise to accommodate large batches of beer and multi-head kegging and packaging lines, specific cleaning and separation protocols should be built into any sour program, and especially when wood is involved.

One basic piece of advice specifically tendered by both Jason Ebel of Two Brothers Brewing in Warrenville, Illinois, and Vinnie Cilurzo of Russian River Brewing in Santa Rosa, California, is to keep separate hoses and equipment, including pumps and fittings, for processes involving sour and more conventional beers. These can be color-coded—Vinnie uses a red band about all hoses to be used for sour beers and red buckets for storage of sour fittings. Physical isolation of barrels and other sour-determined vessels from the brewhouse and from grain-handling areas is an obvious—and these days often grandly more common—step to take when trying to avoid cross-contamination (including the exhaust zones from these areas), but some brewers take this separation to the ultimate step of having completely different breweries for the production of regular beers and for sour beers. This was a relatively easy step for Upland Brewing in Bloomington, Indiana; when they opened a second location, they simply dedicated one of them, their first, exclusively to Belgian and American sour production (though both breweries produce beer aged in wood). Ron Jeffries at Jolly Pumpkin in Dexter, Michigan, produces wort for two breweries in a central brewhouse and diverts it, according to plan, either to the fermenters and barrels of Jolly Pumpkin itself or beyond a separating wall to the fermentation area of the allied North Peak brewery taking up correspondent space in the same building. Separate kegging and bottling equipment is also maintained, as well as separate air handling systems, and workers crossing between the two facilities pass through a sort of airlock, in which boots and gloves must be exchanged before even stepping into the other space. At Wicked Weed in Asheville, North Carolina, brothers Walt and Luke Dickinson each keep themselves dedicated to one side or the other of the process. Walt is in charge of the sour wood program, while Luke keeps his distance and heads up regular beer production.

Given the neither-really-clean-nor-actually-dirty aspect inherent in the use of wood vessels, and especially barrels, it isn't surprising that ranges of opinion and procedure are wide when it comes to what brewers do to their barrels and tanks between fills. No less venerable a brewer than those at Greene King, in Bury-St.-Edmunds, Suffolk, in business since 1799, subjects the wooden tuns in which their 5X Strong Ale ages for two years at a time to no more than a hosing-out with hot water between fills, sulfiting only if leaks have developed. The boys at Upland in Indiana used to rinse their foeders with hot water and scrub them from inside by hand, but now they call it good with a cold water rinse. Gert Christiaens cleans and disinfects the foeders and barrels at Oud Beersel each time they are emptied, choosing to limit spontaneous occurrence to inoculation rather than in the wood, and Khristopher Johnson at Green Bench Brewing in St. Petersburg, Florida, pitched a French saison yeast into his 25 hL Okanagan Barrelworks foeder two years ago and hasn't cleaned it since. Dick can identify with this, having maintained a pet educational project at one of the small breweries he used to operate in Seattle similarly uncleaned for more than 12 years. Admittedly, it was only a three-barrel tank, so stakes were low, but those among us even passingly familiar with fantasy literature might at this point observe that there are as many different kinds of sorcery as there are sorcerers. It's tempting to get into a comparison of wands—steam wands, that is—in treatment of barrels, but rather than further freight a silly metaphor let's hope all that is covered in chapter 4.

Patrick Rue and his crew at the Bruery in Placentia, California, are well-known for crafting a vast range of idiosyncratic and inventive beers, many of which are aged in wood. As we all should, Patrick has taken detailed note of the progress of the Bruery's education where producing barrel-aged beers is concerned. He's broken it down into phases, each of which can be marked off from the others by challenges received and met. Rather than paraphrase, we'll let him tell it.

We've gone through many phases in how we age beer in barrels as we've learned more about barrel aging and sanitation in general. It's important to remember barrels cannot be fully sterilized— there's always risk involved. We've always felt the flavor, when done well, is worth the risk. The phases we've been through:

Phase 1 (1–3 years into barrel aging): Put it in a barrel and see what happens. We ordered freshly dumped bourbon barrels, removed the bung, removed any excess liquid from the barrel, purged the barrel with CO_2, filled the barrel with a bulldog-style racking wand, put the bung back on, and waited to see what happens. Taste every barrel individually prior to racking. We have a modest lab to be able to plate beer to find common beer spoilers. During this phase, we had a pretty high success rate. Call it beginners luck!

Phase 2 (4 years into barrel aging): We have some bourbon barrel aged beers turning inadvertently sour, and as we build up our lab, especially micro, we start plating each individual barrel a few weeks after racking beer into it (as well as pH), and again a few weeks before racking the beer out of the barrel. This helped us to isolate some barrels, but not every barrel with a micro issue will necessarily have growth on plates.

Phase 3 (5 years into barrel aging): Infection issues rear their ugly head, so we changed the way we treated barrels. We buy a steamer, and steam barrels prior to filling as an additional safeguard. We lease separate facilities for our clean barrel aging from sour barrel aging. All other aspects are the same as Phase 2.

Phase 4 (6 years into barrel aging): We see a moderate improvement, although we're still not where we should be as far as micro stability. We test the air when we fill barrels. We were filling right next to our brewhouse, which is the area where we mill grain, remove spent grain, and which stays at a balmy 90 degrees most of the year at high humidity. We find a high level of lactobacillus in the air, so we fill in another cellar which has much cleaner air quality. Barrel aging warehouse is humidified, which can increase microbial stability (yet can also introduce mold problems if excessively humidified). All other aspects are the same as Phase 3.

Phase 5 (7 years into barrel aging): We improve our risk avoidance, but find barrels with micro issues are getting past our testing, especially beers below 15% ABV. With larger, 120 BBL packaging runs of some of these beers, we find it extremely concerning to have one bad barrel make its way through to the brite tank. A flash pasteurizer is procured to use on the occasion we do have unintentional anaerobic bacterial or wild yeast presence. We plan on using it only when our testing indicates a sufficient growth of a beer spoiler to impact the quality in package. While we haven't yet received the flash pasteurizer, our research shows with big, bold bourbon barrel aged beers, triangle testing indicates no discernable difference between non-pasteurized and pasteurized. We're crossing our fingers. All other aspects are the same as Phase 4.

Seven years isn't just the extent of the Bruery's relationship with barrel-aged beers, at this writing it's as long as they've been in business. So there you have it, an entire history of discovery—and recovery—by a brewery well-known and respected in the use of wood for aging beers. Patrick mentions the concern of a single compromised barrel of beer making it past safeguards to affect an entire tankful destined for packaging and distribution, a fear and experience shared by Pete Batule at Upland. Nor is he the only producer of sour and other wood-aged beers to implement some kind of pasteurization. Both New Belgium and Odell Brewing Co. in Fort Collins, Colorado, pasteurize for stability, and who can blame them? The size of their operations demands safeguards against contamination for all the other beers they make. Cleaning protocols for full-fledged packaging lines are as exacting as the French Constitution. We are all here, of course, to give consideration to various programs of beer in wood, but few of us exclusively make our livings from these products. In addition, whether through bottle-conditioning, rigorous laboratory testing, or indeed pasteurization, it's in all of our best interest to have the beers we produce, sour, wood-aged, or whatever these days passes for ordinary, show up in the marketplace in their best possible condition.

Peter recalls the lesson offered by Antoon Lietaer, brewmaster at the Anglo-Belge brewery in Zulte, Belgium, where he served his apprenticeship. In the middle of a packaging run he trotted off to check a problematical filter, and observed on the way that in order to be a good brewer you have to forget the past from time to time. On his return route after the problem was resolved, Peter asked him what he meant. His point was to build safeguards into the process, making sure that the rest of your wort cannot carry over into the next step, should something be amiss. Some of these safeguards can be simple, such as ensuring that all wort is boiled, even what might sit in a standpipe, fill line, or other dead end. It can also extend to deciding to filter or pasteurize in order to eliminate microbiological uncertainty that could lead to exploding bottles in the marketplace. This may have more relevance in Belgium, where post-brewery warm storage of beer is commonplace, but we have our own issues here, as well. The point is that we all weigh possible risk, and especially with sour and bottle-conditioned beer. With a single degree Plato of residual extract left at bottling, an additional full volume or 2 g/L of CO_2 can be generated in the case of unstable beer. The chances we take involve not only our own reputations but that of all craft beer.

Implicit in all this admission is that beer has been dumped. In fact, if there is a single universal truth to barrel-aging of beer it is that not all of it turns out.

Every Jason out there—Perkins at Allagash, Ebel at Two Brothers, Spaulding at Brewery Vivant, and Yester at Trinity—cautions that to get involved in barrel-aging, and especially sour beer production, is to get involved with sending some beer down the drain. Others not named Jason agree with this, by the way, including Jay Goodwin from the Rare Barrel in Berkeley, California. Part of this can be pressed on one. Like a well-trained animal, a foully acetic barrelful can almost find its own way to the drain (or perhaps the cruet), so obvious is its destiny. But sometimes things just don't shape up. Even a nice tangy aroma can belie a flavorless beer. Our friend Tomme Arthur of Pizza Port and Lost Abbey (both in the San Diego area) related that after a knockout first batch of Lost Abbey's Angel's Share, aged in brandy barrels, a second batch run through those same tasty barrels yielded a ho-hum beer. He, too, learned something through that experience, and has since only used repurposed spirits barrels once for the production of that wonderful beer. Along these lines is the observation made by Brent Cordle from Odell Brewing Co. in Fort Collins, Colorado, that the same blends from the same barrels at different times will not yield the same beer. Not all beers, Jason Ebel observes, do all that well in oak, whether because their own flavors are at odds with wood or microorganism or that something about them ungratefully deadens the effect of such loving treatment. None of us, it must once more be observed, need feel compelled to drink uninteresting beer.

Many of us begin wood programs by introducing our regular beers to barrels and checking the variant result. Bourbon-influenced versions of already existing stouts and porters were some of the first barrel-aged beers most of us had, and which inspired us to try it ourselves. Tomme Arthur's first wood beer, Blackball Imperial Stout, was based on his Santa's Little Helper and produced at the Pizza Port Solana Beach location, aged in a Jack Daniel's barrel given to him by Chris Mueller at White Labs and named for the caution flag indicating a no-surf zone. A lot of history there in one sprawling sentence.

Will Meyers of Cambridge Brewing in Massachusetts credits a dream he had—seriously—with resolving an impasse he felt in his career as a brewer back in 1998, which through further introspection and discussion with his boss, Phil Bannatyne, sent him off on what at the time seemed something of a fool's errand: the most expensive project ever attempted at the brewery, with no assurance of eventual success and the necessity for at least three years of barrel aging before anything would even be saleable. The beer was to be called Benevolence. Its process shows a little bit of everything, with a lot of groping and an eventually happy result.

We procured a set of five used barrels from our friends at Sam Adams, bourbon barrels which were former homes for Triple Bock, and the forthcoming Utopias and Millenium, and brewed a strong (25*P) wort featuring Special B and puréed raisins. After primary in stainless with our house ale and Belgian strains the beer was divided into the five barrels which were laid in a mostly junk-filled, dirt-floored section of the basement in our 120-year-old building. Each barrel was gifted a different additional fermentable—honey, date sugar, cherries, raspberries, raisins—and inoculated with a culture of "bugs" I'd been feeding the collective sediment of a considerable assortment of lambic beers. As time progressed we limited ourselves to tasting the beer quarterly, noting that the beer over time dried out considerably and increased dramatically in acidity. Very little, if any, Brettanomyces flavors developed despite a very healthy pellicle in this concoction which over three years was never topped up. The beer became vinous, with extremely complex caramel notes and hints of sherry-like nuttiness, was pleasantly tart, and intense with oak and char and vanillin and subtle spirit. It was extraordinary but still lacking. It was time to make the fresh beer to blend with the barrel-aged.

We brewed a strong Belgian blonde ale of 18°P, unspiced, with invert sugar as adjunct. Upon completion of fermentation in unitank the beer was fabulous. But when we blended it with the dark barrel-aged beer, everything was wrong. It became a hot, phenolic mess. Spicy, sweet upfront but sour and tannic in the finish. Amazingly unbalanced and disjointed no matter how we titrated the blend. In a panic now, we tried the beer in a blend with every other beer we had—Kolsch, Amber, Pale, Porter, Hefeweizen, Tripel, and more—and all failed to do the job. After calming down and attempting to be more focused, we came to the realization that all the beers that at least tasted good in a blend were diluting the complexity of the barrel-aged beer. Those fermented with more assertive yeast strains—high phenol and ester producers—accentuated the high alcohol and odd flavors. What we needed was a clean strong beer with high residual sweetness to add body without diluting the beer's intense character. One and a half kegs of CBC Blunderbuss Barleywine (aging in our cold box) later (at an 8% blend) and we had a winner. Quite literally, as having taken the local beer world by storm we entered it in the Experimental Beer category at GABF one year later, in 2004. It took home a silver medal in that category, a close second to gold medal-winning

Sam Adams Millenium, which was apropos as our beer was aged in the same barrels which previously held theirs. Our beer was polarizing, to be certain. Many was the beer festival-goer who tasted the beer and looked like we had offended their mother and kicked their dog. It was, after all, sour, vinous, raisiny, oaky, wicked strong, oxidative, and spirituous and the average "Microbrew fan" was unprepared. There were others, however, who "got it" and it was with each of these small victories that we felt compelled to continue our pursuits.

More traditionally common is the single base beer brewed for later variation by the addition of fruit, barrel-to-barrel blending, or the construction of Grand Cru versions. This is mainly what is practiced in Belgium to this day, among brewers of lambic and other sour wood beer producers such as De Brabandere, Verhaeghe, and Rodenbach. The variable outcome of different barrels or foeders can in fact be used for different products, or can even turn out to be a key attribute for certain end products. Some ethyl acetate is easy to mask with cherries, for example, and will even enhance the fresh cherry aroma. Possibilities along these lines could be considered endless, with breweries such as Upland using pawpaws and persimmons and grapes. Some breweries borrow from this tradition by producing a base beer used for inoculation. This is the method used at Jester King, outside Austin, Texas, which stores this concoction ready to go in 50-liter kegs, and at Wicked Weed in Asheville, North Carolina, which has a name for this beer, Cassette, and keeps it going in oak barrels for introduction to beers that are otherwise conceived individually.

Most American brewers of beers destined to be aged in wood (including those mentioned above) agree that beers and their recipes should be conceived individually with the influence of wood and its residents in mind, and not simply tinkered with later for differentiation. This plays, no doubt, on the penchant these days among American craft brewers for vast portfolios of beers, in contrast with the traditional European approach to leaner offerings. Naturally, there are exceptions to this analysis. Cantillon, for example, can be counted upon to present new versions of things each time one manages to visit, but even so, they are generally painted from essentially the same palette. New Belgium keeps two sour base beers, Oscar and Felix—dark and light, respectively—but blends them in such endless combination with other beers and myriad treatments that to do otherwise would surely boggle the mind, especially at the scale on which they manage to operate such a program.

Vinnie Cilurzo of Russian River Brewing takes the one-recipe/one-beer approach while recognizing that there is more than one honorable way:

> *Just like a non-wood-aged beer you start with your ingredients and the recipe. To me this is no different when making a funky wood-aged beer. I'm going to create the recipe using the malt and hops that I think will best fit the final beer. The only difference is that there are several more steps to consider downstream. For example, if you know you are making a sour beer you probably want to hold back on bittering hops, as a bitter beer, mixed with a good amount of acidity along with some carbonic acid from the CO_2, is going to make a beer that is not pleasant on the palate. I know there are breweries out there that take one of their production beers and move some of it to a barrel to create something new. There is certainly nothing wrong with this practice, and for some small breweries this is the only way they can achieve making a wood-aged beer, but if possible I think it is very important to create a wood-aged beer's own recipe that was built on the premise that this beer will go into wood, and in the case of all of our wood-aged beers at Russian River will get some degree of Brettanomyces and bacteria.*

This is the first of five ways Vinnie breaks down the construction and execution of a wood-aged sour beer, which also include the addition of secondary fermentables, including fruit, the barrels to be used for aging, any secondary yeasts and bacteria introduced for later aging and finishing, and the overall process enacted along the way. His words continue below.

> *After the recipe is created I look at any potential secondary sugars, which includes any fruit that might be written into the recipe. I learned early on from a very wise brewer that adding unique sources of secondary sugar (which can be a fruit) to a wood-aged beer can lend an even greater aroma and flavor with more personality than without. Of course, there is something simple and beautiful in putting a beer in wood and letting it age with some Brett and bacteria and eventually bottling it. This is the case with our Chardonnay barrel-aged beer, Temptation. But, to achieve some great complexity, a secondary sugar added to the barrel can change a beer.*
>
> *Of course, the barrel itself is one of the key ingredients when talking wood-aged beers. This is a book on wood-aging beer, so I don't need to go into much detail here. But what I will say is your barrel source is critical.*

Of course, being that I am in the middle of wine country, I am in the best position to pick up wine barrels from wineries directly. This allows me to go inspect each barrel if need be, or at least inspect the winery before getting the barrels. Purchasing barrels sight unseen can be problematic but can unfortunately be part of a brewery's barrel program if they are not in close proximity to the source. For Russian River, I'd say one of our critical successes has been the ability to create direct relationships with the wineries and their crews. A little bit of beer doesn't hurt, either—after all, it takes a lot of great beer to make great wine!

Another key component for me when designing a wood-aged beer is the secondary yeast and bacteria that will go into the beer. Not only is the specific type of yeast and bacteria being used important but I also make an exact pitch rate of Brettanomyces when adding Brett to the barrel. But for the bacteria I do this all by taste. The specific quantity of bacteria that will go into the barrel will be based not only on how acidic the bacteria going in is, but also how many times the barrel has been used previously. That is because the wood will retain some bacteria, even if we've done an intensive cleaning, so this residual bacteria still impregnated in the wood will contribute to the next beer going into the barrel. Wood-aged beer is very process driven and thus process becomes a very important component. This is one of the things I like most about these beers. In many cases you'll be using equipment and techniques more associated and used by winemakers than by brewers. Your process decisions can start in the brewhouse and cellar with normal day-to-day brewing decisions such as mash temperature, pitch rate, and fermentation temperature. Beyond that you will need to figure out how to add fruit to the barrel, how you will actually fill the barrels, sample the barrels, empty the barrels, and clean the barrels. How you clean the barrels will directly affect the next batch that goes into the barrel. Between filling and emptying the barrels you'll have more decisions to make such as what type of barrel bung will be used, will you top the barrels to prevent too much oxidation, what temperature will your barrel room be kept at, and, finally, can and will you control humidity.

It would be easy to glance over Vinnie's mention of barrel bungs, but the point is made by a number of brewers that the pressure-relieving bungs, used by winemakers for more deliberate and protracted release of CO_2 from wine as it is settling down in barrels, are not necessarily suitable for a beverage producing larger and more quickly generated volumes of gas. Nor are the blip-blipping carboy airlocks with which those of us who began as homebrewers are well-acquainted, as Tomme found out early on after an addition of fruit triggered a secondary fermentation and blew the bung—and a lot of fruit and beer—all over the ceiling of his cellar. You hear all sorts of stories about holding a bung in place, from billiard balls placed on the bung, allowing gas to release, to ropes, such as at Cinderblock Brewing in Kansas City (they used a rope around the barrel and over the bung to hold it in place). But such breather bungs mentioned above are liable to blow when called upon to pass frothy ferment, reliably enough to constitute a sort of mental sight gag when reading account after account of such mishaps.

Somewhat related is the story Jason Yester tells of the day Trinity Brewing in Colorado Springs was bottling Brain of the Turtle Petite Cerise, a beer made from coffee, cherry skins, almonds, *Lactobacillus,* and *Brettanomyces.* Most of the barrels being bottled were fitted with breather bungs in order to equalize pressure before their removal, but one still bore its non-porous wooden bung. When removed, the barrel pretty much emptied, right into the eye of the guy doing the removal. A likeness of him with a black eye now adorns the label for the beer.

Vinnie's mention of the importance of barrel sourcing echoes the sentiments of other brewers fortunate enough to live and work in areas that generate an abundance of barrels, such as other winemaking seats and in bourbon country. Unless, like the fellows at Country Boy brewing in Lexington, Kentucky, or Jesus Brisino in Guadalajara, Mexico, you live in one of these areas, or are committed enough to your barrel program to travel for inspection at a cooperage or barrel broker, you're pretty much at the mercy of what's available, sight unseen. Tomme has also noticed a general lack of reliability where both the structural quality and microbiological baggage of used rum and tequila barrels are concerned—no doubt having something to do with their relatively exotic and tropical points of origin. With most beginning life as bourbon barrels, perhaps the single-use-conceived method of original construction comes into play, but he also speculates that they are often left lying around, bunged, unbunged, rained on, and otherwise ignored, until sold and shipped to brewers eager for their use—a shame, since the flavor effects of such previous use can be really interesting. At the very least some maintenance and repair might be in order. With their pretty much yearly acquisition of a single tree kept on the brewery premises and pared away as needed for replacement foeder staves, Rodenbach has this angle all figured out. Not surprisingly, they can trace the provenance of their foeders back to their points of manufactured origin in the 1960s, '50s, and '30s. The foederie that once made their tanks sat right where their brewhouse is now.

As with many good things, barrels eventually reach the end of their productive lives. People have different methods and tolerances where such things are concerned, and different levels of daring related to refurbishment and general risk-taking. Where one brewer might see fit to break down, scrape, and even re-toast a barrel, another might skip straight to the bonfire. At his Millstone cidery in Maryland, Kyle Sherrer only gives up on a barrel when it simply won't hold liquid anymore (ditto Gert Christiaens at Oud Beersel), or if it has developed an off-aroma that he doesn't like. Pete Batule and Caleb Staton at Upland in Indiana also use their noses to decide whether a barrel needs a rigorous sprayball cleaning, and if after such treatment it still smells off, they'll reject it for good. Jason Perkins and his crew at Allagash will also get rid of a barrel if it has simply given up the ghost and contributes no flavor at all to the process.

The Fifth Element

After traveling to Belgium in 2004 with my brewing friends, I became incredibly inspired and thirsty to create a barrel-aged sour beer. To create my first sour I knew I needed more than pure inspiration; I needed help from my friends and beer community. There was so much that I had to figure out to lay a beer down for a year in oak and have it taste the way I wanted. Over the course of the next year I called nearly everyone I knew and respected to ask beer questions. I talked to Garrett about bottle conditioning, Dick about Saisons, Mallett about calculations, and I can't even mention how many times I talked to Vinnie about Brettanomyces, tradition, and more. But that's not all. Brynildsen was kind enough to send me used barrels to age in. I needed four because my goal was 100 cases. I traveled to New Belgium and tasted all the foeders in their oak cellar, and Lauren sent me a growler of my favorite to inoculate my barrels. Of course we named a barrel "Lauren."

I read and re-read Phil Markowski's book, Farmhouse Ales, *and Jeff Sparrow's book,* Wild Brews. *And every day I would call Dan Burick from Utah Brewers Cooperative, my mentor, friend, and fellow brewer whom I respect immensely, to discuss how all this information might come together in the end. What I realized is that there are not just four ingredients in beer, there are five. The fifth element is our brewing community that we share all our knowledge and passion with to help us create great beer for our local communities. So, thank you to everyone who helped me along the way. I hope you like the beer we made.*

Cheers,

Jennifer Talley

Jenny wrote this a number of years ago, sent to those she felt had helped her in creating a beer that, like many mentioned in this book, have won some very nice medals at the Great American Beer Festival. It captures the spirit of much of what we've tried to convey. Along these lines, we're hoping that the metaphor is obvious, in this chapter ostensibly on blending, but really about so much more, that the ideas of many in our industry and movement have come together to combine experience and technique in the interest of instructing ourselves, and each other, in the arts of using wood to make beer. Indeed, the statements of many take time out to make this observation of cumulative culture, and to credit European brewing and international winemaking traditions, as well as individual people whom they feel have been particularly giving in the sharing of information. It might be tempting to compare us to Lauren's crayons in all this contribution and overlayering, but together we never seem to reach the point at which everything turns brown, that too much nuance has accumulated for clarity and increased understanding. It's as though our spectrum is endlessly accommodating, broadening as needed to admit the new amid the accomplishments of those longer established. This bears responsibility on both sides, and amounts to a general respect for old ways and new, these ideas combining in a sturdy and living whole, accruing over time—forgive us—like the rings on a tree.

Appendix A:

Techniques for Wood- and Barrel-Aging for Homebrewers

The information and advice offered in the various narratives of this book are intended to be useful to brewers of a variety of stripes, including those who brew at home. In their cases some interpretive latitude is no doubt necessary, as they are far less likely to have on hand the equipment and mere volumetric resources available as a matter of course to most professional brewers. Still, brewers are collectively an ingenious lot, and given that so many of us made the leap at some point from homebrewing to professional brewing, the ingenuity that served us then continues to serve us as we solve problems and develop new ideas in the brewing workplace. And that information and ideation can flow back in the opposite direction. It therefore seems a good idea to assemble a few points here specific to the small-scale production of wood-aged and -influenced beers in the home and club brewery.

The small batch size generally enacted when brewing at home requires an even hand when introducing the bold flavors of wood and attempting to synthesize productions often associated with racks of dozens—even thousands—of barrels, to say nothing of wood-beer-producing breweries possessing rows of oaken foeders. Actual barrels may not even come into play, given the standard sizes most commonly available; no doubt more commonly used are powders and chips, spirals, staves, and chair legs, generally (though not necessarily) of oak and left in contact with typically sized batches of 5–15 US gallons for varying lengths of time.

Chris P. Frey (a.k.a. Crispy) of the Ann Arbor Brewers Guild, American Homebrewers Association®, and Brewers Association Board of Directors counsels literally working in tablespoons when influencing the flavors of small batch beer. He often soaks his chips in bourbon, coconut rum, or other spirits and generally begins by adding a couple of heaping spoonfuls into end-fermented beer. He'll start tasting within a couple of weeks, and adding as he sees fit, to the point at which he is satisfied and ready to rack, either to another conditioning carboy or straight to bottling. This apparently hasty process would seem to contravene the practice of those such as Founders' Jason Heystek, who will leave barrels entirely undisturbed for at least three months before even tasting, but given the scale and resultant need for nimbleness where the manipulations of such strong flavors are involved, as well as the insatiable curiosity of the average homebrewer, it's no doubt forgivable to so worry the contents of a carboy so much more closely staring one in the face, each precious drop of which was personally created on one's own stove. Not that Crispy is the average homebrewer. Much of his insights and research inform this analysis of method.

The vagaries of domestic settings more generally attuned to the comfort of human beings than the aging of long-term fermentation projects come perhaps even more quickly and directly to bear on beer stored in barrels than carboys strategically placed on porches and in basement corners for merely thermal attemperation. Much of domestic comfort, after all, has to do with regulation of humidity, and neither the dry air of Midwestern winter or high-country elevation nor the humidity of summer and the American South provides ideal conditions for barrel aging. Barrels are far more liable to give up liquid either aqueous or alcoholic, and with greater rapidity. Acetic influence is also a far likelier event than in the average professional cellar, either through the structural compromise threatened by dryness or the fruit flies encouraged by excess humidity. Such things as misters and wet towels can come into play, the latter periodically laid across individual barrels to moisten and plump up the grain of the outer wood. It's doubtful that whole-sale humidification of a household greater than one would be undertaken for the sake of a barrel or two of aging beer, but perhaps the persuasive powers of the devoted hobbyist are not to be underestimated.

Relationships, in fact, come into play when the establishment and mainte-nance of barrel programs are discussed. Convincing one's domestic partner, for example, that a barrel, or two, or perhaps more, left unmoved for a matter of years might prove a difficult sell, no matter the eventual appreciation for the finished beer. And that for a single turn. Barrels can be placed on carts and casters, of course, at less risk to a potential pellicle than simply slugging them around in case of needing to be moved, but even then weights in excess of 500 pounds are involved.

Many clubs own cooperative or communal barrels. Some of the lucky ones, referencing the above concern of household space, are able to store them at professional breweries, making a sort of pro-am event of emptying and filling. New Belgium has been known to extend this courtesy to local homebrewers. But, in fact, when filling a 55- or 60-gallon barrel with freshly brewed beer, the cooperation of a reliable team is something next to essential for the project to succeed. Several to a dozen brewers able to provide adequate wort to fill a barrel all at once is the best scenario; less likely to succeed is a few people brewing multiple times and filling the barrel incrementally and over an extended period, leaving inevitable headspace and exposing contents repeatedly to possible outside influence.

As in a professional setting, barrels will inevitably need to be topped up over time. For this extra wort or end-fermented base beer should be reserved, stored in a tight container such as a Cornelius-type soda keg, for periodic introduction into the barrel as it surrenders contents to its wood and envi-rons. And just as with any other barrel-aged beer involving sourness, effort should be made to avoid disturbing or piercing the pellicle. Some consider this concern answered by sticking a tube or racking cane sufficiently below the level of the liquid in the barrel to avoid roiling this top layer, but probably safer and less invasive would be to fit the barrel in advance with some kind of lower port, both for sampling and introduction of topping-up beer. Probably better than piercing the pellicle with a cane at all would be simply to (gently) introduce beer through the bung, to make its way around and through with-out compromising the protective layer. It's also to be observed that given the greater degree of generally being messed with, as well as domestic conditions placing the barrel and its contents at ambient risk, spontaneous occurrence of microorganism is likely to be far less felicitous than if conscious choices are made and designated microflora are introduced to begin with.

To the thinking of many, the real fun doesn't begin until barrel-aged beer is ready for blending. This might seem to exclude homebrewers and their likely more spare containers of possibility, but these days 5-, 8.5-, and 10-gallon barrels are available for readier individual use. In addition, the possibility exists, through the use of inserts such as chips and spirals and the like, to have a number of alternative small-batch versions of the same (or related, or totally different) beer aged on different combinations of things to expand possibilities for blending and mitigation of intensity. And if priming uncarbonated beer—and especially uncarbonated sour beer—for bottling or in-keg conditioning, it would likely be advisable to use less sugar source given the ongoing reductive ambitions of souring and otherwise tempering microorganisms, *Brettanomyces* in particular.

Standard homebrewing equipment may not prove to be of a scale to safely, cleanly, and expeditiously transfer the contents of barrels. Racking canes, for example, may need to be lengthened or fashioned anew, and simply for the sake of time spent, some kind of "bulldog" could be adapted or devised for moving contents faster than by gravity and simple siphoning. This involves the introduction of a couple of pounds of CO_2 pressure through a gas nipple fixed into the same bung penetrated by the racking tube.

When cleaning barrels on a home or club scale, processes are mainly just adapted from professional use, but recognizing that barrels are cumbersome, home floor drains are not as suitable as those in most real breweries, but since you've likely only got a barrel or two to clean at any given time, it's something simply to be muddled through. Crispy recommends a triple rinse of 15 gallons or so of pre-boiled 170°F water. As in a professional setting, barrels can be sterilized with a sulfur wick for storage, taking professional care to ventilate well. And it must be said once more: Newly procured barrels carrying residual or liquid spirits should never be examined or sterilized with open flame.

For experimenting homebrewers, the horizon can be as broad as for professionals where wood- and barrel-aging of beer is concerned, setting aside for a time the advantages of scale commanded by larger and better-financed practitioners. And there are lessons to be learned at every level. Crispy outlines his solution for the philosopher's-stone-type mystery of the stuck fermentation, borrowing from the mysteries of sour barrel-aging.

Sour Barrels (and Their Dregs):
A Cautionary Tale by Christopher "Crispy" Frey

It is said that homebrewers do lots of goofy things and explore the boundaries, occasionally creating something so awesome that they get picked up. Not on this occasion.

I had a Belgian Strong Ale that suffered the dreaded "stuck fermentation." This puppy starts about 1.110 (SG) and the last batch I brewed a few years ago got stuck around 1.060. I tried all sorts of tricks, asked club members for advice, warmed it, roused it, added another round of high tolerant Belgian Ale yeasts, only to get it down to 1.050 or so.

Around the time of the annual Flanders Red F.O.R.D. barrel dump and fill I got the thought to add some of the dregs from the barrel into the Belgian beer. I did it, and a couple months later it was at 1.010! Success!

Until I tried a sip (after bottling, mostly in champagne bottles). For those with an adventurous spirit, I have a few bottles of this hellish swill/awkward fermentable. A Belgian Quad with a Flanders Red finish just isn't what the public is clamoring for.

Appendix B: Wood Primer for Homebrewers

There are as many ways to use wood in homebrewing or small batch brewing as there are brewers. This primer should get you started. If you are new to using wood, follow the advice of many quoted in this book and taste often, especially when the wood you are using is "new" wood—it doesn't take long for wood flavor to overpower your beer if left in too long. While it can't literally be "undone," it can be aged to allow some of the tannins to dissipate. And of course there is always blending after the fact. Aging with wood takes some experimentation to recognize what values and intensities the wood contributes so you can adjust it to your taste.

Things to remember:

- Make sure to use untreated wood if cutting, toasting, or preparing your own wood. This means there so should be no finish or chemical treatments. Woods commonly used for smoking foods can be a good choice since they are approved for contact with consumables. They should still be sanitized, however.

- Most woods used in barrel making and for use in aging are hardwoods— oak, cherry, chestnut, etc. Be sure to research a wood if it's unknown to you in conjunction with food/beverage use, in order to rule out any possibility of toxicity.
- Don't use chemicals to sanitize your wood. Steam or steep in spirits.
- Wood makes a great home for microbes of all kinds: *Brettanomyces, Pedioccocus,* and *Lactobacillus* for starters. Great for sour beer, not so great if you are shooting for a clean beer. If you pull your wood from a sour beer and want to keep your "zoo" for the next batch, dry the cubes completely on all sides and store in an airtight container in the freezer.
- Keeping a batch of spirit, wine, port, or sherry-soaked cubes around isn't a bad idea. If diminished by second or third use, some of the soaking spirits can be added to the finished beer, or the batch could be split for blending.
- To get an idea of the flavors that a particular wood might impart, you can make a wood tea by steeping a small amount (1/2 tsp or one cube) in a cup of hot water, or do a cold steep. Taste and evaluate what flavor components can be noticed in the aroma and with a small sip. Different lengths of steeping and interaction with the beer will also affect flavor, but this can give you a starting point when designing your recipes. The tea can also be added directly to finished beer, both for testing and as a flavoring technique in itself. This will give an idea of what the wood itself will taste like, but perhaps the best method is to try it out in beer. The presence of alcohol aids in extraction, and you can get an early feel for effect by agitation. This can be as simple as adding a measured amount in a bottle of beer, recapping and shaking it, and getting a quick idea of effect.
- You can reuse cubes, spirals, etc., but keep in mind if you are making clean beer that wood is a great home for microbes. You can try sanitizing them and re-using them, recognizing the reduction in tannins and other active flavors over time. Steam, soak, and re-use as needed until satisfied with flavors and aromas.

Preparation:

Soaking cubes: Toss cubes into a small pot of hot water for about five minutes or steam them (covered) in a microwave, allowing a few minutes of standing time before removal. Drain and rinse in a colander. Add cubes to a mason jar and proceed with soaking.

Spirits: Add spirits just until covered. Soak for one day to two weeks to infuse the cubes with flavor.

Wine: Add wine to fill the container to prevent enough head space that acetobacters take hold and turn it to vinegar. Soak for one to six months depending on preference. The longer you soak, the deeper the flavor will penetrate.

Two-stage soak: Put new cubes into a mason jar, cover with spirits, and allow to soak for a week or so. Discard spirits (it will have leached out some of the harsher flavors) and cover again with fresh spirits of your choice. Age for four to six weeks before adding to your secondary fermentation vessel (buckets are easier than carboys for introduction and removal).

Wine: This technique is primarily used with spirits but can also be used with wine. When charring cubes, you may want to allow three to six months for soaking in wine as it will take the wine longer to penetrate.

Most commonly used wood-aging techniques for homebrewers:

	Preparation	Contact time	Advantages	Caution	Amount
Chips	Rinse, steam, or soak with hot water to reduce harsh flavors; soak in spirits if you choose (1 week for regular toasts and for up to 6 months for charred wood).	From hours to a week. Taste test regularly.	Fast flavor extraction, good for short aging (like IPAs and APAs where you want to retain fresh hop flavor).	Easy to overdo it, one dimensional flavor (but nice base for later wood additions), high surface to beer ratio can lead to high extraction of flavors.	.5 oz for a 5-gallon batch. You can always add more but you can't take the flavor back out easily!

	Preparation	Contact time	Advantages	Caution	Amount
Cubes	Rinse, steam, or soak with hot water to reduce some of the harsher flavors; soak in spirits if you choose (1 week for regular toasts and for up to 6 months for charred wood).	Several months to a year.	Good for long aging processes (think imperial stouts and barley wines).	It takes longer for the beer to get to the heart of the cube but it will add great depth and complexity.	1–2 oz per 5 gallons (depends if first use or if it has been used multiple times). Too little oak for too long will emphasize the tannins.
Spirals	Rinse, steam, or soak with hot water to reduce harsh favors, soak in spirits if desired.	1-3 weeks depending on whether new or well-used.	More surface contact with the beer and easier to remove than chips.	Because there is more surface area, the exposure time should be shorter to avoid over-oaking.	One spiral is adequate for a 5-gallon batch and it can be steamed or soaked and reused.
Staves	Cut or split for use in carboy or bucket secondary fermenters, or in finished beer in a Cornelius keg. Sanitize like other wood or bake in the oven.	Soak up to 6 months if heavily charred—like cubes they can take take a long time for absorption.	Great for long-term aging.	This method can take longer if the stave has had a long history or is heavily charred.	You may be limited by how you are using it. Taste frequently and adjust as needed.
Powders or essence additions	Powdered or granulated oak (most common). No preparation.	Adds flavor instantly. Use sparingly and taste often.	Instant gratification.	Easy to overdo.	Follow instructions generally provided.

Bibliography

Alamo-Sanza, Maria del, et al. 2014. *Recent Advances in the Evaluation of the Oxygen Transfer Rate in Oak Barrels*. J. Agric. Food. Chem. 62, 8892–8899.

Accum, Frederick. 1821. *Treatise on the Art of Brewing*. London: Longman, Hurst, Rees, Orme & Brown.

Ashley, Ryan. 2015. Personal communication (Director, Distillery Operations at Four Roses Distillery, LLC).

Baker, Julian L. 1905. *The Brewing Industry*. London: Methuen & Co.

Baron, Stanley. 1962. *Brewed in America*. Boston: Little, Brown and Company.

Bilger, Burkhard. 2008. "A Better Brew." *The New Yorker*, 11/24/08.

Bird, David. 2010. *Understanding Wine Technology*. Newark, Nottinghamshire, UK: DBQA publishing.

Boulton, Roger B. 1995. *Principles and Practices of Winemaking*. New York: Chapman & Hall.

Brown, Rachel C. et al. 2006. *An odour detection threshold determination of all four possible stereoisomers of oak lactone in white and red wine*. Australian Journal for Grape and Wine research 12, 115–118.

Chantonnet, Pascal. 1999. *Volatile and Odoriferous Compounds in Barrel-Aged Wines: Impact of Cooperage Techniques and Aging Conditions*. ACS Symposium Series 714, American Chemical Society, Washington, DC.

Collin, Thomas. 2012. *The Impact of Variability in the Toasting Process at a Commercial Cooperage on the Volatile Composition of Oak Barrels and Barrel Aged Wines*. Doctoral Dissertation. UC–Davis.

Comoy, Jean-Baptiste. 2007. *Manual for the Use and Maintenance of Large Containers*. Seguin-Moreau, Cognac, France.

Cope, Kenneth L. 2003. *American Cooperage Machinery and Tools*. Mendham, NJ: Astragal Press.

Cornell, Martyn. "Pontos in America." *Zythophile* blog, 12/24/09.

Coyne, Franklin E. 1940. *The Development of The Cooperage Industry in the United States, 1620–1940*. Chicago: Lumber Buyers Publishing Co.

Dewers, Robert S. 1948. *A Problem in the Tight Cooperage Industry*. Fort Collins, CO: Colorado A&M College.

Dick, Gary. 2014. Personal communication.

Doorman, G. 1955. *De Middeleeuwse Brouwerij en de Gruit*. Gravenhave, Martinus Nijhof, Netherlands.

Elkington, George. 1933. *The Coopers: Company and Craft*. London: Sampson Low, Marston & Co.

Foster, William. 1944. *A Short History of the Worshipful Company of the Coopers of London*. Cambridge,UK: Cambridge University Press.

Gaab, Jeffrey S. 2006. *Munich Hofbräuhaus and History*. New York: Peter Lang.

Hankerson, Fred Putnam. 1947. *The Cooperage Handbook*. New York: The Chemical Publishing Co.

Hornsey, Ian. 2007. *Chemistry and Biology of Wine Making*. Cambridge: The Royal Society of Chemistry.

Humprey, John W. 2009. *Greek and Roman Technology: A Source Book*. London, UK, Taylor & Francis e-Library.

Independent Stave Co. 1998. International Barrel Symposium. Lebanon, MO: Independent Stave Co.

Independent Stave Co. 2001. Fourth International Barrel Symposium. Lebanon, MO: Independent Stave Co.

Independent Stave Co. 2008. International Barrel Symposium. Lebanon, MO: Independent Stave Co.

Jackisch, Philip. 1985. *Modern Winemaking*. Ithaca, NY: Cornell University Press.

Jackson, Michael. *Food and Drink: The Magic that Gives Marston's Its Pedigree*. The Independent, 9/5/92.

Jeffs, Julian. 1992. *Sherry*. London-Boston: Faber and Faber.

Kallai, Sonny. 2014. Personal communication.

Kilby, Kenneth. 1971. *The Cooper and His Trade*. Fresno, CA: Linden Publishing Co.

Kilby, Kenneth. 1977. *The Village Cooper*. Aylesbury, UK: Shire Publication Ltd.

Kilby, Kenneth. 2004. *Coopers and Coopering*. Buckinghamshire, UK: Shire Publication Ltd.

Kleinmann, Christine R. 1998. *Microwave Treatment of Oak Wood for Barrel Manufacturing*. Fort Collins, CO: Colorado State University.

Koob, J., et al. 2014. *PCR-Analysen Bierschädlicher Bakterien 2012 und 2013*. Brauwelt, 10 2014 154, 288–290, Nuremberg, Germany: Fachverlag Hans Carl.

Kraup, G. ~1960. *Literaturdocumentation Prof. Dr.-Ing. Kraup G.* Berlin: Versuchs- und Lehranstalt für Brauerei .

Kugel, Seth. 2008. *Alure of Cachaça Spreads to U.S. from Brazil*. New York Times, April 9. New York.

Lacambre, G. 1851. *Treaté Complet de la Fabrication des Bières et*, Bruxelles, Belgium.

Lane, R. D. 1964. "Cooperage Logs and Bolts: Production and consumption in the central states 1962." Columbus, OH: US Forest Service.

Lane, R. D. 1965. "Consumption of cooperage logs in the central states 1964." Columbus, OH: US Forest Service.

Lange, August. 1894. *Die Kunst des Böttchers oder Küfers in der Werkstatt wie im keller*. Weimar, Germany: Berhard Friedrich Boigt. .

Leberbe, Hans. 1926. "Die Bierbrauerei." Stuttgart, Germany: Verlag von Ferdinand Enke.

Lewenau, Jos. Arnold. 1818. *Anleitung zu Beträchtlichen Holzsparungen bei den Brauhäusern*. Wein, Austria: J. G. Ritter von Mösle.

Lewis, Matthew. 2009. *Non-targeted Small-molecule Profiling of Beer by Ultra-performance Liquid Chromatography-Mass Spectrometry*. 72nd ASBC meeting, Tucson, AZ.

Leyser, E. 1910. *Die Malz und Bierbereitung, ein Lehr und Nachschlagebuch*. Stuttgart, Germany: Verlag von Max Waag.

Lintner, Carl. 1878. *Lehrbuch der Bierbrauerei*. Braunschweig, Germany: Druck und Verlag von Friedrich Bieweg.

Little, Elbert L. 1999. *Atlas of United States Trees*. Washington: United States Department of Agriculture.

Logan, Bryant. 2006. *Oak the Frame of Civilization*. New York: W.W. Norton and Company, Inc.

Maga, Joseph. 1989. *Formation and Extraction of cis and trans-β-methyl-ϒ-octalactone from Quercus alba*. Distilled Beverage Flavor: Recent Developments. Ellis Horwood Ltd. Chichester, UK, 171–176.

Mahajan, Ishita. 2008. *Flavour of Wine Treated with Toasted New Zealand Woods*. Auckland, New Zealand: Auckland University of Technology.

Margalit, Yair. 1990. *Concepts in Wine Chemistry*. San Francisco: The Wine Appreciation Guild.

Martens, Hilde. 1996. *Microbiology and Biochemistry of the Acid Ales of Roeselare*. PhD #294 Faculteit Landbouwkundige en Toegepaste Biologische Wetenschappen, Katholieke Universiteit Leuven, Belgium.

Masson, Gilles, et al. 1997. *The β-methyl-ϒ-octalactone Stereoisomer Contents of European and American Oak*. Journal des Sciences et techniques de la Tonnellerie: Marillac Vigne et Vin Publications International, 1997 3 9–15.

Meier, Dirk. 2006. *Seafarers, Merchants and Pirates in the Middle Ages*. Woodridge, UK: The Boydell Press.

M. G. 1886. *Die Wirkung von Spähnen auf die Gährung.* Berlin: Versuchs-und Lehranstalt für Brauerei.Wochenschrift für Brauerei 46: 703.

Monckton, H. A. 1981. *The Story of the Brewers Cooper.* Sheffield, UK: Publishing and Literary Services Limited.

Newton and Aiken, et al. 1997. *A Study on the Effect of Heating Oak Wood.* Lebanon, MO: Independent Stave Co.

Newton and Thomas, et al. 1997. *A Model Predicting the Oak Species Used for Producing Chardonnay Wine by the Sur Lie Method.* Lebanon, MO: Independent Stave Co.

Newton and Sayre, et al. 1997. *A Comparison Between Chardonnays Aged in American Oak Barrels of Water Bend or Dry Heat Bent Staves.* Lebanon, MO: Independent Stave Co.

Newton and Spinelli, et al. 1997. *A Comparison of Chardonnay Wine Made in Autotoast and Conventionally Toasted Barrels.* Lebanon, MO: Independent Stave Co.

No name, April 25, 2013. "Gourmet-biere mittels Holzfassreifung." Nurnberg: Hans Carl Verlag. Brauwelt, 153(17): 500–503.

Nordland, Odd. 1969. *Brewing and Beer Traditions in Norway: The Social Anthropological Background of the Brewing Industry.* Oslo: Universitetsforlaget.

Paupie, Franz Andreas. 1794. *Die Kunst des Bierbrauen.* Prague, Czech Republic.

Peng, X., et al. 2001. *Flocculation and Coflocculation of Bacteria and Yeast Applied Microbiology and Biotechnology.* 55 (6): 777–781.

Phillips, Rod. 2002. *A Short History of Wine.* New York: Harper Collins.

Pinchot, Gifford. 1907 (123). "Production of Slack Cooperage Stock in 1906." Washington, DC: US Forest Service.

Pinchot, Gifford. 1907 (125). "Production of Tight Cooperage Stock in 1906." Washington, DC: US Forest Service.

Pollnitz, Alan P., et al. 1999. *Determination of Oak Lactones in Barrel-aged Wines and in Oak Extracts by Stable Isotope Dilution Analysis.* Journal of Chromatography 11/1999 857(1-2): 239–46. University of Adelaide, Tarndarnya, Australia.

Prida, Andrei, et al. 2006. *Effect of Species and Ecological Conditions on Ellagitannins Content of Oak Wood from an Even-Aged and Mixed Stand of Quercus robur L. and Quercus petreae L.* Annals of Forest Science (63): 414–425. INRA, France.

Prida and Puech. 2006. *Influence of Geographical Origin and Botanical Species on the Content of Extractives in American, French, and East European Oak Woods.* Journal of Agricultural and Food Chemistry. Washington, DC: American Chemical Society. 54: 8115–8126.

Prida, Andrei. 2015. Personal communication.

Robinson, Jancis. 2006. *The Oxford Companion to Wine.* Oxford, UK: Oxford University Press.

Rous, C., et al. 1983. *Phenolic Extraction Curves for White Wine Aged in French and American Oak Barrels.* American Journal of Enology and Viticulture. Davis, CA: American Society of Enologists. 34: 211–215.

Schahinger, G., et al. 1992. *Cooperage for Winemakers: A Manual on the Construction, Maintenance and Use of Oak Barrels.* Adelaide, Australia: Ryan Publication.

Schrenk, Hermann von. 1908. *Cypress for White Oak in Wine Barrels.* Cleveland, Ohio: Wood Craft, April 1908.

Singleton, Vernon L. 2000. *Barrels for wine, usage and significant variables.* Journal des Sciences et techniques de la Tonnellerie: Marillac Vigne et Vin Publications International. 2000, 6, 15–25.

Southby, E. R. 1889. *Systematic Handbook of Practical Brewing.* Westminster, UK: Brewing Trade Review.

Sterckx, Femke L., et al. 2012. *Wood Aging Part I: Influence on Beer Flavor and Monophenol Concentrations.* Journal of the American Society of Brewing Chemists. St. Paul, MN: American Society of Brewing Chemists. 70(1): 55–61.

Sterckx, Femke L., et al. 2012. *Wood Aging Part II: Influence of Wood Aging Parameters on Monophenol Concentrations.* Journal of the American Society of Brewing Chemists. St. Paul, MN: American Society of Brewing Chemists. 70(1): 62–69.

Swan, J. S., et al. 1997. *Oak's Effect on Chardonnay.* Wines and Vines, June. San Francisco: Hiaring Co.

Tierney-Jones, Adrian. 2006. *Can Beer Be Good Finishers?* Beers of the World, Feb/March 2006, (4): 48–50.

Townsend, Raymond R. 1963. *The Cooper in Virginia: Interpretive Notes.* Williamsburg, VA: Colonial Williamsburg Foundation Library.

Townsend, Raymond R. 1963. *Coopers.* Williamsburg, VA: Colonial Williamsburg Foundation Library.

Unger, Richard W. 2004. *Beer in the Middle Ages and the Renaissance.* Philadelphia: University of Pennsylvania Press.

Vandewalle, André. 2013. *Brugse Bierhistories.* Hamerken, Brugge, Belgium.

Vivas, Nicolas. 1997. *The duration effect of natural seasoning of Quercus Petraea Liebl. and Quercus robur L. on the diversity of existing fungi flora and some aspects of its ecology* Journal des Sciences et techniques de la Tonnellerie: Marillac Vigne et Vin Publications International. 3: 27–35.

Waelput, Erik. 2004. *Eer het vat in duigen valt.* Antwerpen, Belgium: Garant.

Wagner, Joseph Bernard. 1910. *Cooperage: A Treatise on Modern Shop Practice and Methods, from the Tree to the Finished Article*. New York: J.B. Wagner.

Wägner, Ladislaus Ritter von. 1884. *Handbuch der Bierbrauerei*, Ersten Band. Weimar, Germany: Bernhard Friedrich Boigt.

Wahl, Robert, et al. 1901. *Brewing, Malting and Auxiliary Trade*. Chicago: Wahl & Henius.

Western Brewer. 1903. *One Hundred Years of Brewing*. Chicago: H.S. Rich & Co.

Wilder, Douglas Santiago, et al. 2014. *Ethyl Carbamate in the Production and Aging of Cachaça in Oak and Amburana Barrels*. Journal of the Institute of Brewing. London: Harrison & Sons. 2014, 120: 507–511.

Wilding, Geoffrey and Carolyn Case. 1966. *Coopering*. Staffordshire, UK: County Council County Museum.

Work, Henry H. 2014. *Wood, Whiskey and Wine: A History of Barrels*. London: Reaktion Books.

Wright, Herbert Edwards. 1897. *Handy Book for Brewers*. London: Crosby Lockwood and Son.

Index

Entries in **boldface** refer to photos and illustrations.